Michigan's West Coast
Explore the Shore Guide

A Journey to 500 Public Parks and Points of Access Along the Lake Michigan Shoreline

Brian Hutchins

Abri-Press
Roscommon, MI
abri-LLC.com

Michigan's West Coast

Explore the Shore Guide

A Journey to 500 Public Parks and Points of Access Along the Lake Michigan Shoreline

Abri-Press
Abri-LLC
Abri-LLC.com
10815 Oakwood Rd.
Roscommon, MI 48653
© 2005 by Brian Hutchins

The author and publisher have made every effort to ensure the accuracy and completeness of information contained in this book. The author and publisher cannot exclude the possibility of errors, omissions or changes in conditions, property ownership or legal rights of access to the places depicted and as such assume no responsibility for any that occur. The user should be aware that private inholdings of land may be found within the general boundaries of public parks and forests. Respect the rights of private landowners. Adhere to posted signs and regulations. The maps provided are for general depiction of the locations described in the book. Maps and the provided latitude and longitude coordinates should not be used for marine navigation.

ISBN 0-9760754-9-0
LCCN 2004115331

First Printing 2005.
Printed and bound in the United States of America.

Contents

Preface

My wife Mary and I have long had a love of the shores. We have tramped, paddled or explored coastlines along the Atlantic and Pacific Oceans and each of the Great Lakes. Every stretch of beach soothes the soul in its own way; the lapping of the waves, the quiet of morning fog or the voices of children playing in the surf.

Lake Michigan, particularly the western shore of Michigan's Lower Peninsula, holds an especially strong attraction to us. Mary was born and raised in Petoskey and much of her family still resides in that area. Even though we visit often, we never tire of the Emmet County coastline. My parents built our family cottage next to the since established Sleeping Bear Dunes National Lakeshore and have lived there permanently for a couple of decades. I have seen the shore's biggest park form during the last thirty-some years and attended the first of its public planning meetings. I remember boating to and camping on South Manitou Island's beach before the national park when, during a hike, you still "bumped" into cattle from the ranch.

Twenty years ago, while traveling to Los Angeles for business, two California friends, Paul and Beverly Hill, told me of the *California Coastal Access Guide*. Published by the California Coastal Commission, the book listed every public access point to the state's shore. I bought a copy and used it on a drive to their home on the central coast. Its usefulness impressed me. Through the years the book flew from Michigan to California and back many times, was borrowed by friends for their vacations and it never failed its purpose. Those familiar with it will find much similarity with this book and that is no accident.

This guide is written from my point of view and it might be useful to know what that is. I like to hike, bike, ski and paddle. If it takes a little effort to get to a place, that's fine. Hence, when I look at a beach, I like to see how far I can walk it. Skiing up and down snow-covered dunes is fun and the farther the better. A short portage of the canoe from parking lot to the water is part of the pleasure. Don't worry that I have left out the easy places of access, but rather that I included the hard to reach venues as well.

A number of listed sites are not on the shore proper. You will find museums and educational stops plus places that offer great recreation along the rivers and inland lakes adjacent to Lake Michigan. On each page, I have tried to offer a full day of activities for that local area. In some places, too little public coast exists to ensure this, so I have added nearby sites to fill the void.

Several friends have asked why I would want to write a book that might encourage more use of these places. I must say that I have wondered that myself. While there are times when special coastal places are crowded, you can conclude that the more users who enjoy our coastlines, the greater the support for its preservation. Recently, many shoreline property owners have sought to restrict the public's access to the Great Lakes, making it more important than ever to highlight this wonderful resource. If the shore is important enough to you that you shelled out money for this book, then I am willing to believe that you support wise use and safeguarding of our shores.

Lastly, public places on the coast are changing as you read these words. Several governmental programs contribute to recreational development in Michigan and shoreline projects enjoy a high priority for funding. Facility upgrades, particularly with local parks, have been common. Conservancy groups actively seek coastal lands. During my research, I witnessed a new park pop up within a few weeks of a previous visit. The information contained within will slowly age. Let's hope it ages in a good way with more opportunities for the public to enjoy the earth's most unique resource.

Brian Hutchins, Roscommon

Acknowledgements

A number of organizations and individuals contributed directly to this publication.

From the Michigan Department of Natural Resources and its dedicated employees, past and present, I absorbed years of information that unwittingly would end up in this book. Michael Moore, friend and retired Director of the Michigan Department of Natural Resources, forwarded me a copy of the *Let's Fish Lake Michigan*; a book provided to him by Jack Bails of the Great Lakes Fisheries Trust. Michael McDonald, friend and longtime recreation grant specialist for the Michigan Department of Natural Resources, offered details about many of the parks along the coast. He also accompanied me on a trip to his native Berrien County to visit a number of these places. Harry and Sue Hutchins reviewed drafts and helped with the Beaver Island information. Their children, Tyler and Holly accompany them in several photos. Ben Carr of the Michigan Snowshoe Center provided numerous insights as well as contact information. The staff at the Clarke Historical Library, Central Michigan University, Mt. Pleasant Michigan, helped me find documents to verify information. My parents, Mary and Alan Hutchins, often provided accommodations as well as encouragement.

Special thanks go to my wife, Mary and son, Jeff, who hiked many beaches and trails with me during this effort. Mary edited drafts, Jeff critiqued graphics and each supported me during the two years it took to complete this book.

Si Quaeris Peninsulam Amoenam Circumspice

"If you seek a pleasant peninsula, look about you."
Michigan state motto

Introduction

What's in Store for You?

Dunes and sandy beaches make the eastern coast of Lake Michigan special. Many people vacation here summer after summer at the parks, the resorts or their summer homes. Small towns cater to the tourist with unique shops and attractions. Spectacular sunsets greet each day's end. Tributary streams, filled with spawning trout and salmon, attract fishing enthusiasts every spring and fall. Islands and bays provide unique environments for both wildlife and visitor. Hike, bike, bird-watch, swim, sunbathe, build sandcastles, fly a kite, fish, float or boat your way along its coast. The shore lover will find many recreational opportunities. This guide lists virtually every public access point to Lake Michigan along Michigan's Lower Peninsula coast. Meander along and have fun!

The Character of the Coast

Prevailing westerly winds buffet the eastern coast of Lake Michigan with air and water. Wind blows the sand and the scant vegetation catches it, forming sand dunes along much of this freshwater, inland sea. Where glacial cliffs (moraines) parallel the shore, sand is often blown to the top forming perched dunes hundreds of feet above the water level. Waves form the sandbars that challenge the outflow of each stream emptying into the lake. Man has fought back by building channels and breakwaters at the major outlets along the lake, artificially keeping them open for commerce. Towns sit alongside most of these harbors.

Dunes and bluffs contribute greatly to the coast's character. They once made it difficult and unprofitable to develop the shore. In the past, shifting sand swallowed towns daring to encroach on the beach. Many shoreline ghost towns, unprotected from the brunt of gales, survived during years of profitable shipping but succumbed to the elements when the economy failed to provide enough to fortify the beachhead. The shoreline sands lack fertility for farming, but inland, orchards thrive. Lake Michigan's cool spring temperature keeps plants from early budding, defending them from damaging frost. By autumn, the lake has warmed and the warmth reduces the chance of an early fall frost. Apples, grapes, peaches and cherries are four prominent fruit crops.

Imagine splitting the coast in two with Manistee as the middle. The shore to the south is sand with virtually no stone or rock. The coastline is a near vertical north-to-south. Cities, towns and man-made harbors dot the way. In between are vacation homes, power plants, dunes and parkland. Much of the south end lies close to large cities such as Chicago and Grand Rapids. The proximity to population makes for busy summers.

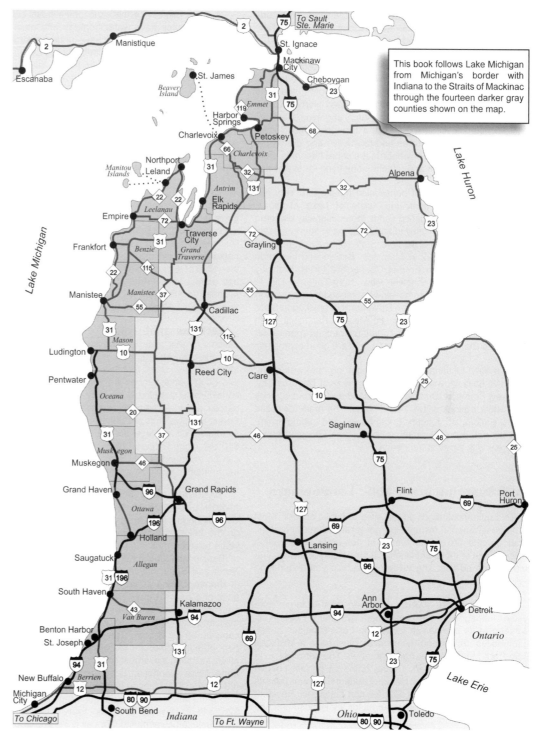

This book follows Lake Michigan from Michigan's border with Indiana to the Straits of Mackinac through the fourteen darker gray counties shown on the map.

The coast starts to change north of Manistee. Rock and stone begin to show in some areas. Many come to hunt the Petoskey Stone, a fossilized coral made of limestone. Other flat, rounded stones are good for stone skipping, an activity that addicts both child and adult. Still, sand predominates along much of the north coast. The tall perched dunes of the Sleeping Bear, near Empire, being the most noted sand pile. Natural bays, such as the Platte, Good Harbor, Grand Traverse and Little Traverse, form a curvy shoreline. Northern Lake Michigan is sprinkled with the islands of the Beaver Island Archipelago. The cities and towns live and die on the tourist economy. As you drive north, the shore becomes more diverse, changing often and offering something for everyone.

The preponderance of dunes also means that very few highways provide a continuous vista of Lake Michigan. Shoreline erosion and shifting sands forced highway planners to place major roads slightly inland. Still, many short pleasant drives exist within sight of the lake. State Highways M-63 north of Benton Harbor, M-22 in Manistee, Benzie and Leelanau counties and M-119 in Emmet County are three. Highway US-31 has many nice coastline views from Traverse City to Petoskey. Additionally, some slower, secondary roads skirt the shore in places. Lakeshore Drive north of Muskegon State Park, Peninsula Drive on the Old Mission Peninsula north of Traverse City and several county-maintained roads near Wilderness State Park in Emmet County are good examples.

At a few locations, cities sit right on the waterfront. Protective bays allowed the downtown areas of Traverse City, Petoskey, Frankfort, Suttons Bay, Leland and Harbor Springs to lie within a block or two of the water. The main townsites of New Buffalo, St. Joseph, South Haven and Ludington are close as well. Here you can combine some shopping and a bite to eat with a day at the beach.

Park Systems and Public Landowners

This guidebook leads you to sites of public access. Most are in governmental ownership from local to state to federal. Other parcels are in the hands of non-profit conservation groups. Each of these entities has a philosophy and rules that guide their land use. The following will help you understand their systems.

MICHIGAN STATE PARKS: Michigan has a large park system managed by the Department of Natural Resources. Eighteen of its premier parks dot the Lake Michigan coast. Automobiles, trucks and motorcycles must have a Michigan State Park Motor Vehicle Permit to enter. The permit is good at any Michigan State Park. During 2004, day permits cost $6 for state residents and $8 for non-residents. Annual permits cost $24 for residents and $29 for non-residents. Resident seniors (65 or older) can get a permit for $6. Pedestrians and bicyclists enter for free.

A large number of the state parks have campgrounds. Some campsites have water frontage and others require a modest hike to the shore. Most have modern restroom facilities that include showers, plus electricity at the campsite. Usually there are sanitation facilities for trailers and motorhomes. Water and sewer hook-ups at the site are available at Holland State Park. Several parks have primitive facilities with vault toilets. Most sites have campfire pits and picnic tables. Costs vary with the type of facilities offered ranging from $9 to $23 per night. Campgrounds will be full many days during the summer and on holiday weekends. Check in advance or make reservations by calling (800) 44PARKS. Information is available on the web at www.michigan.gov/dnr.

MACKINAC STATE HISTORIC PARKS: Colonial Michilimackinac and Mackinac Island State Park are two of three historic parks located on the Mackinac Straits where Lake Michigan and Lake Huron join. Old Mill Creek State Park lies nearby and just outside the scope of this book. These parks feature exhibits and reenactments of area life during the 1770's. Open from early May to mid-October. Single day admission: $9 Adult, $5.75 Youth (6-17), Children free. Multiple day tickets also available. Information available at www.MackinacParks.com or (231) 436-4100.

MICHIGAN STATE FOREST SYSTEM: Michigan has the nation's largest state forest system. Most of the forest land near the Lake Michigan coast are located north of Manistee. Much of the state forest shoreline has been absorbed into other parks through the years. Beaver Island still has considerable state forest along or near its shore. Many other parcels provide recreation and camping near Lake Michigan. Forest campgrounds are primitive with vault toilets. Normally a campfire pit and table are at the site. Self-registration costs $10 per night. Disperse camping, away from campgrounds, can be arranged at no charge. There is no fee for day use. Information is available on the web at www.michigan.gov/dnr.

NATIONAL PARK SERVICE, SLEEPING BEAR DUNES NATIONAL LAKESHORE: In the 1970's, the National Park Service began land acquisition for the largest, single park on the Lake Michigan coast. Acquisition continues, but 30 years later the park is nearly whole. It consists of large parts of Benzie and Leelanau counties including the islands of North and South Manitou. An information center is located in Empire. During 2004, the park fee was $10 for a 7-day pass or $20 for a one-year period. Seniors and other NPS passholders have a different cost. The park has two major mainland campgrounds as well as hike-in and wilderness camping on the islands. The perched dunes, from which the park gets its name, are the major draw. The park has much more, including the largest collection of public shore along this route. More information is available at www.nps.gov/slbe or (231) 326-5134. Manitou Island Transport sails to the islands during the summer season. A round trip to either island costs $25, $14 if 12-years or under. Ferry information found at www.leelanau.com/manitou/ or call (231) 256-9061.

UNITED STATES FOREST SERVICE, HURON-MANISTEE NATIONAL FOREST: Parts of the Huron-Manistee National Forest are located in the coastal counties of Muskegon, Oceana, Mason and Manistee. The National Forest has a number of campgrounds and recreational opportunities. The only USFS Lake Michigan shoreline properties are in northern Mason County. This includes the unique Nordhouse Dunes Wilderness as well as the Lake Michigan Recreation Area. The Forest Service charges user fees for access into some areas as well as for camping. Self-registration with pay envelopes is common. Carry some dollar bills with you to avoid problems making change at remote registration stations. Daily entrance fee - $3, annual fee - $20.

THE NATURE CONSERVANCY: This organization, through its local chapters, has preserved many unique places along the coast. Often their preserves are available for some types of public use, usually without fee. Some will have posted use policies to protect the land and its wildlife. Please read and follow the rules. Their efforts benefit us all.

LOCAL GOVERNMENT PARKS: Local governments manage a number of parks. They range from full-service municipal beaches to undeveloped lands used for access only. Many have had major upgrades in recent years through state and federal grant initiatives. Most developed county parks have entrance fees in the summer. Many of the city or township owned parks are free. A few have camping. There are exceptions to these generalizations. Refer to the individual listings for a clearer representation.

ROAD END ACCESS: In many locations, a county road ends at the Lake Michigan shore. The county owns the right-of-way, usually 66 feet wide, at the road end. The public normally has access at these points. Most do not have a good beach and those that do have limited space. Parking is usually limited as well. Some have no parking at or near the road end. A few of the roads end atop bluffs that require steep descents down primitive paths to reach the beach. Facilities of any kind are rare.

So, why include these in the listings? Some of these places have a boat ramp, although at most it will be difficult to launch large boats. Canoe or kayak launching is normally quite easy. Bicyclists riding the shoreline will find these nice stopping points and any parking restrictions will not affect bikes. Public access in some areas along the coast is limited. A road end may be the only access for several miles and sunsets will be just as spectacular as at the larger parks!

Public and Private Property Rights

In past times, the public walked the sandy beaches of Lake Michigan without much thought about the homes or resorts that sat on the waterfront. In many places, the tradition remains. In recent years, however, some property owners along the Great Lakes coastline have actively sought greater restriction of the public to the shore in front of their property. More signs, such as "Private Beach," appear each year in an attempt to keep the lake to themselves. Much of this change derives from increased development, more visitors and the pressure that puts on the waterfront.

The legal rights of the owners, the public and the State of Michigan are contained in a patchwork of old state and federal laws, court and Attorney General decisions. Interpretations can change with time but it appears safe to characterize the current situation as follows.

- Several defining points exist along the shore. The "bottomland" is that which the lake covers. The "high water mark" is a legally defined line that roughly matches where the vegetation starts to grow. The beach or shore between the high water mark and the water line is land that becomes bottomland during periods of high lake levels.
- The property owner has complete property rights upland of the high water mark.
- The State owns the bottomland and you may walk, boat or make other passage if in or on the water along Michigan's Great Lakes shore.
- The property owner has control over the area in between except they may not install permanent structures, dredge or fill without permit from the State. This has been a contentious point in recent years. The low lake level that exists now means that a large amount of beach is exposed and vegetation has grown. Owners and the State have had differences as to what activities require a permit. The situation has renewed debate about the legal rights along the coast.

In 2004, The Michigan Court of Appeals reversed a pro-public shore use decision regarding Lake Huron by saying that the public may not enter the dry shore in front of private Lake Huron property. This has been interpreted by many shoreowners to affect Lake Michigan. The case is being appealed to the State's Supreme Court for reversal back in the public favor. The higher court's action may well clarify shore rights in Michigan forever.

Do not construe this treatise as perfect interpretation of lakeshore law but rather as an acquaintance to the subject. As in most endeavors involving people and their property, good judgment should prevail. If you don't think you should be there, check for a nearby listing in this book. There is probably a fine public park which will avoid a conflict.

Fishing Licenses and Regulations

For those 17-years or older, a fishing license is required to fish the Michigan waters of the Great Lakes or any of the State's inland lakes and streams. Licenses are sold at many stores, especially those which carry bait and tackle. You can also purchase them online at www.michigan.gov/dnr. Creel limits, fish size, allowable bait and seasonal restrictions vary and you should check the fishing rules for the current information. License sales agents have rule booklets. Several license types are available. One-year licenses are valid from March 1 to March 31 of the following year. Senior and military personnel discounts may apply. License costs in 2004 were;

- Resident Annual All Species - $27
- Non-Resident Annual All Species - $41
- Resident Annual Restricted (no trout or salmon) - $14
- Non-Resident Annual Restricted (no trout or salmon) - $30
- 24-Hour (one-day, all species) - $7

Harbors, Marinas and Boat Ramps

The Michigan Waterways Commission sponsors a number of public marinas along the coast. Generally, a portion of the slips are available for transient use and some for seasonal mooring. Aside from dock space, facilities generally include shower, restroom, electric hook-up and fuel. Some have launch ramps. Costs and availability vary. Find more information at www.michigan.gov/dnr. Each state-sponsored marina found on this coast is listed in this book.

Public boat ramps are located on most Michigan lakes, rivers and harbors. This book lists the ones which provide convenient access to Lower Peninsula Lake Michigan. Some ramps have fees. The 2004 cost for those with fees were $6 per day or $24 for an annual permit that accesses all Michigan DNR ramps. For a complete list of Michigan boat ramps by county see www.michigan.gov/dnr

Bicycling the Shoreline

The coastal area has a number of bicycle routes that include bicycle lanes along the highway, rail-to-trail developments and low-traffic rural, paved roads. Contact: Michigan Department of Transportation, Bike Maps, P.O. Box 30050, Lansing, MI 48909 or call (517) 373-9815. Maps are available individually or in sets costing from $1 to $38. Find these and additional bicycling resources a www.michigan.gov/mdot.

For $8, The League of Michigan Bicyclists offers a mapped route from Spring Lake (Grand Haven area) to Mackinaw City along Lake Michigan's Shoreline. Contact them at League of Michigan Bicyclists, P.O. Box 16201 Lansing, MI 48901-6201 or call (517) 334-9100. Order online at www.lmb.org.

Families with Small Children

While most of the developed parks have playground equipment, the lakeshore offers unique experiences enjoyed by youngsters. The majority of the shore is sand, so digging and sand building top the list. Bring plastic pails and shovels. Some of the best places are at the small creeks that enter the big lake. Typically, these creeks are shallow. Your child will mix splash time with sand architecture.

Shore safety is discussed on page 30. Most State Park beaches fly color-coded flags alerting you to current conditions. Few beaches have lifeguards anymore. Those that do are usually at well established city park beaches.

Abbreviations

To facilitate your reading, the guide uses abbreviations to shorten governmental titles, directions and some park names.

Governmental agencies and sub-unit abbreviations
DNR : Michigan Department of Natural Resources
MDOT: Michigan Department of Transportation
NPS: United Sates Department of Interior, National Park Service
SBNL: Sleeping Bear Dunes National Lakeshore (NPS)
SP: Michigan State Park
USFS: United States Department of Agriculture, Forest Service

Cardinal directions

N: North	NE: Northeast
S: South	SE: Southeast
E: East	NW: Northwest
W: West	SW: Southwest

Other
CR : County Road
HWY: Highway
M: Michigan highways use an "M" designation such as M-63

Map Legend

Use this key for the maps found in this book.

 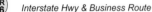 *Interstate Hwy & Business Route*

Federal Hwy & Business Route

 State Hwy

 County Route

 City, Town, Village or Landmark

River, Stream or Creek

Hiking or Bicycle Trail

 Limited Access Highway

33 *Interchange & Exit Number*

Federal or State Highway

Primary County Highway

Other Paved Secondary Road

Gravel Road

Poor Dirt Road

 Park Area

Wilderness or Special Designation Area

Chart Legend

Each site grouping features a chart that summarizes the environment and types of facilities offered there. The following defines the chart titles.

ENTRANCE FEE. A fee is charged for the site's primary use. "Park Systems and Public Landowners" on page 8 describes entrance fee requirements.

PARKING. Denotes that a parking lot or adequate space for several cars to park exists within or next to the site.

MODERN RESTROOMS. Facility has access to flush-type toilets and sinks. Most park toilet buildings close during the off-season from fall to early spring.

VAULT OR PORTABLE TOILET. Primitive-type toilet such as campground-style outhouse or chemical, construction-site-style portable toilet is available. Often, portable-type toilets are removed during winter season.

STAIR OR PATH TO SHORE. These locations require the user to climb stairs or walk a distance from the parking lot to access the beach. The site description describes long or arduous hikes or climbs to help the user judge the difficulty.

SWIMMING. Denoted if good to excellent swimming is available. This does not mean that a designated swimming area is marked or that lifeguards are available. Very few beaches have guards anymore. Final judgement of the swimming conditions is yours.

PICNIC AREA. Picnic tables and usually barbecue grills available at the site. The site description tells if the park has a pavilion. At some parks, pavilions can be reserved and might not be available for casual use during peak periods.

DRINKING WATER. Potable drinking water is available during the summer season.

CAMPGROUND. Camping is available at the area, usually for a fee. Site description details the facilities offered.

TRAILERED BOAT LAUNCH. Site has a ramp for launching most trailer-type boats. A fee is charged for some ramps. Lake Michigan water level rises up or down with the drought cycles. The lake level has been very low recently making some ramps unusable by larger craft. The site description provides information about the quality of the ramp.

KAYAK / CANOE. Reasonable access exists at the site for putting in these hand-carried craft. In some cases, a short portage from a parking lot may be needed. Most sites do not have docks or embankments. Launching the craft may require wading. The site description explains the more difficult circumstances. Some of these launch points are on large,

open waters. Recognize your limitations and the weather conditions. Do not take chances.

MARINA. Site has a Michigan Public Harbor Marina with seasonal and transient rental slips. Restrooms and shower facilities are on hand for the boaters. A few of the conveniences are open to the non-boating public at some marinas.

FISHING. Reasonable fishing opportunities available at the location. These may range from access to stream mouth, pier or surfcast fishing. Michigan fishing regulations are discussed on page 9. The Great Lakes Fishery Trust has funded a number of fishing platform projects along the east shore of Lake Michigan. Their website, www.glft.org, lists these and other access points. For a quick reference of pier fishing, see page 14.

HIKING. The access point has trails or significant area for hiking.

BIKING. The site has trails, paths or roadway designated for bicycles.

X-COUNTRY SKIING. Location offers groomed or ungroomed Nordic ski trails. Some ungroomed ski trails began as hiking trails and now have dual use. These can be narrow or have difficult curves making them unsuitable for novice skiers. Scout these carefully.

PLAYGROUND. Play equipment available.

LIGHTHOUSE. Visit or view a historic Great Lakes lighthouse from the location. Some lighthouses are open to the public, some are not. See listing for details.

BEACH STROLLING. A significant length of public beach allows for hiking and beachcombing along the shore.

SANDY BEACH. At least part of the shore has a sandy beach.

STONY OR ROCKY SHORE. At least part of the shore is rocky or has stones.

DUNES. At least part of the area has coastal sand dunes. Usually, the dunes must be traversed to reach the shore.

BLUFF. At least part of the site has a bluff near or at the shoreline. Often these provide spectacular views. In many cases, you must descend the bluff to reach the beach or shore. Some bluffs are either ecologically too fragile or too steep to descend.

WETLAND. Coastal wetland exists. Many of these listings have interpretive plaques or nature centers that describe the unique flora and fauna.

At a Glance

a quick look at facilities and features along the West Michigan shore

State and Federal Parks

Many travelers look for state or federal parks as they often represent the most unique recreational opportunities. These dot the coastline regularly as the map shows at quick glance.

The Michigan Department of Natural Resources maintains 18 State Parks (SP) along the shore. The National Park Service (NPS) hosts the largest coastal recreational area at Sleeping Bear Dunes National Lakeshore. The U.S. Forest Service (USFS) manages two adjoining properties in Mason County. The Mackinac State Historic Parks add two more highlights. Most of these recreational gems have a mile or more of coast. Many provide access to breakwaters, lighthouses, dunes and inland lakes. Camping is available at most.

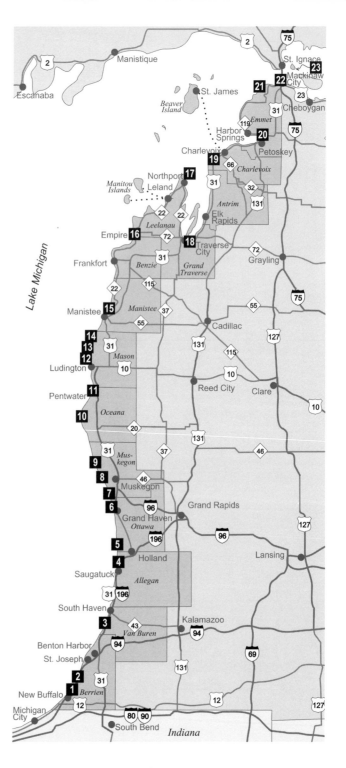

	Park	County	Page
1	Warren Dunes SP	Berrien	23
2	Grand Mere SP	Berrien	25
3	Van Buren SP	Van Buren	33
4	Saugatuck Dunes SP	Allegan	43
5	Holland SP	Ottawa	47
6	Grand Haven SP	Ottawa	51
7	P.J. Hoffmaster SP	Muskegon	55
8	Muskegon SP	Muskegon	59
9	Duck Lake SP	Muskegon	61
10	Silver Lake SP	Oceana	69
11	Charles Mears SP	Manistee	71
12	Ludington SP	Mason	79
13	Nordhouse Dunes (USFS)	Mason	81
14	Lake Michigan Recreation Area (USFS)	Mason	81
15	Orchard Beach SP	Manistee	87
16	Sleeping Bear Dunes National Lakeshore (NPS)	Benzie & Leelanau	101-103, 107-119
17	Leelanau SP	Leelanau	121
18	Traverse City SP	Grand Traverse	135
19	Fisherman's Island SP	Charlevoix	145-147
20	Petoskey SP	Emmet	161
21	Wilderness SP	Emmet	165-167
22	Colonial Michilimackinac State Historic Park	Emmet	171
23	Mackinac Island State Historic Park	Mackinac	173-177

Lighthouses

Lighthouses hold great fascination. Imagine walking the raised catwalks of the St. Joseph, South Haven, Grand Haven or Manistee lights to service them during gales. Think of the solitude at Big or Little Sable Points, South Manitou or Beaver Islands. Enjoy the architecture of Holland, White River, Point Betsie and the Grand Traverse Lighthouses. St. Joseph, Muskegon, Grand Haven and Manistee breakwaters each have two light towers at their harbor entrance.

The Lake Michigan coast has a number of lights. Easy access is available to most but some are private, viewed from outside a fence only. Older lights and lighthouses found along the route of this book are listed below. New-style navigation signals are not listed, nor are lights that require non-scheduled boat transportation. See their individual site write-up for more details.

	Lighthouse	Location	County	Page
1	St. Joseph	N Breakwater	Berrien	29
2	South Haven	S Breakwater	Van Buren	35
3	Kalamazoo River	N of Oval Beach, Saugatuck. (view from distance)	Allegan	41
4	Holland	S Breakwater.	Ottawa	47
5	Grand Haven	S Breakwater.	Ottawa	51
6	Muskegon	S Breakwater	Muskegon	57
7	White River	S Breakwater	Muskegon	61
8	Little Sable Point	Silver Lake State Park	Oceana	69
9	Ludington	N Breakwater	Mason	77
10	Big Sable Point	Ludington State Park	Mason	79
11	Manistee	N Breakwater	Manistee	87
12	Frankfort	N Breakwater	Benzie	99
13	Point Betsie	4 miles N of Frankfort	Benzie	99
14	South Manitou Island	South Manitou Island	Leelanau	117
15	N Manitou Shoal	Manitou Passage (view only)	Leelanau	117
16	Grand Traverse	Leelanau State Park	Leelanau	121
17	Old Mission Point	Old Mission Park	Grand Traverse	131
18	Charlevoix	N Breakwater	Charlevoix	149
19	Beaver Head	S end of Beaver Island	Charlevoix	155
20	St. James Harbor	N entrance to St. James Harbor	Charlevoix	153
21	McGulpin Point	2 miles W of Mackinaw City (view only)	Emmet	169
22	Old Mackinac Point	Mackinaw City	Cheboygan	171

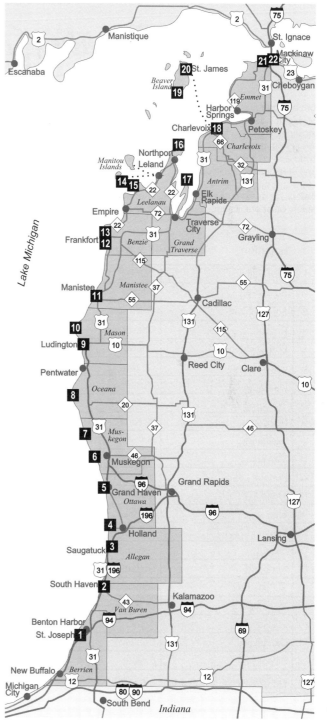

Fishing Piers

Depending on technique and time of year, most of Lake Michigan waters offer productive fishing. Species vary by location but generally expect brown trout and steelhead in the spring, perch, pike, walleye and bass in mid-summer, coho and chinook salmon from late summer to early fall and steelhead again in autumn.

Any of the coastal harbors have charter boats for hire to reach off-shore fishing. Fish a stream mouth, surfcast the shore or cast from a pier for an inexpensive fishing experience. The breakwaters and piers, listed below, provide ready-made opportunities for fishing. The Great Lakes Fishery Trust develops fishing access along the shore. Their booklet, *Let's Fish Lake Michigan* (see "Additional References," p.172) presents details about these sites along with fishing hints, and stocking information.

	Location	County	Page
1	New Buffalo	Berrien	21
2	St. Joseph	Berrien	27, 29
3	South Haven	Van Buren	35, 37
4	Holland	Ottawa	47
5	Port Sheldon	Ottawa	49
6	Grand Haven	Ottawa	51
7	Muskegon	Muskegon	57, 59
8	White Lake	Muskegon	61, 63
9	Pentwater	Oceana	71
10	Ludington	Mason	75, 77
11	Manistee	Manistee	85, 87
12	Portage Lake	Manistee	89
13	Arcadia	Manistee	91
14	Elberta	Benzie	97
15	Frankfort	Benzie	99
16	Leland	Leelanau	115
17	Northport	Leelanau	121
18	Suttons Bay	Leelanau	123
19	Traverse City	Grand Traverse	129
20	Elk Rapids	Antrim	139
21	Charlevoix	Charlevoix	149, 151
22	Petsokey	Emmet	159
23	Mackinaw City	Cheboygan	171

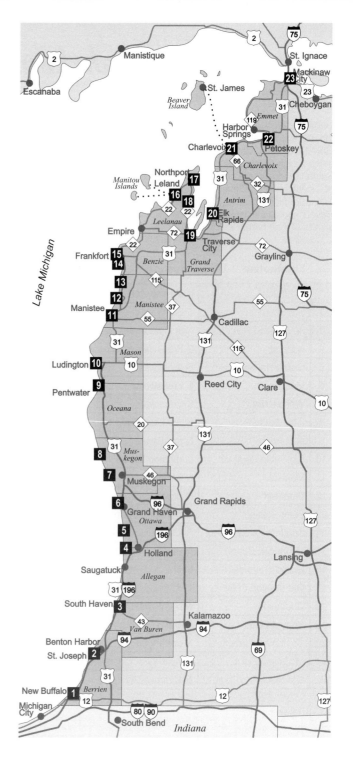

Coastal Campgrounds

A number of parks offer camping on or very near the lakeshore. Some sites require a short walk to the shore. The campground at Silver Lake State Park is on Silver Lake. The Platte River Campground is a mile hike or a slightly longer drive to Lake Michigan. During the summer, the campsites fill quickly. Refer to the site listing for reservation and contact information.

	Park	County	Page
1	Warren Dunes SP	Berrien	23
2	Weko Beach	Berrien	23
3	Covert Township Park	Van Buren	33
4	Van Buren SP	Van Buren	33
5	Holland SP	Ottawa	47
6	Grand Haven SP	Ottawa	51
7	P.J. Hoffmaster SP	Muskegon	55
8	Muskegon SP	Muskegon	59
9	Pioneer County Park	Muskegon	59
10	Meinert County Park	Muskegon	63
11	Claybanks Township Park	Oceana	67
12	Silver Lake SP	Oceana	69
13	Charles Mears SP	Oceana	71
14	Buttersville Park	Mason	75
15	Ludington SP	Mason	79
16	Lake Michigan Recreation Area (USFS)	Mason	81
17	Orchard Beach SP	Manistee	87
18	Arcadian Campground Marina	Manistee	91
19	Platte River Campground (SBNL)	Benzie	101
20	D.H. Day Campground (SBNL)	Leelanau	109
21	South Manitou Island Campgrounds (3) (SBNL)	Leelanau	117
22	Village Campground, N. Manitou Island (SBNL)	Leelanau	119
23	Leelanau SP	Leelanau	121
24	Marion Island Park	Grand Traverse	131
25	Traverse City SP	Grand Traverse	135
26	Barnes County Park	Antrim	143
27	Fisherman's Island SP	Charlevoix	147
28	Beaver Island Campgrounds (2)	Charlevoix	153, 155
29	Magnus Park	Emmet	159
30	Petoskey SP	Emmet	161
31	Wilderness SP	Emmet	167

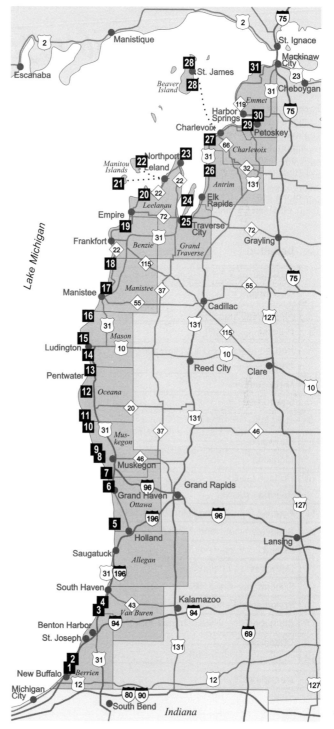

Long, Public Shoreline

Few things compare to a long, slow walk along the beach. The environment changes with each visit. The lake, peaceful and calm one day shows its strength with crashing waves the next. A cooling morning fog gives way to the afternoon searing sun. Flotsam, after traveling many miles, washes ashore and waits to be discovered. Colorful stones gleam in the water. Stroll along any of the beaches below. You won't be disappointed!

	Park	Approx. Shoreline Miles	County	Page
1	Warren Dunes SP & Weko Beach Park	3	Berrien	23
2	Grand Mere SP	2	Berrien	25
3	Saugatuck Dunes SP	2	Allegan	43
4	P.J. Hoffmaster SP	2	Muskegon	55
5	Kruse, Lake Michigan & Pere Marquette City Parks	2	Muskegon	57
6	Muskegon SP	3	Muskegon	59
7	Silver Lake SP	3	Oceana	69
8	Ludington SP, Nordhouse Dunes (USFS) & Lake Michigan Recreation Area (USFS)	12	Mason	79, 81
9	Platte River Point & Platte Bay (SBNL)	11	Benzie & Leelanau	101, 103, 107
10	Sleeping Bear area, Sleeping Bear Point, Sleeping Bear Bay (SBNL)	8	Leelanau	107, 109
11	Pyramid Point & Good Harbor Bay (SBNL)	10	Leelanau	111, 113
12	South Manitou Island (SBNL)	12	Leelanau	117
13	North Manitou Island (SBNL)	20	Leelanau	119
14	Cathead Bay, Leelanau SP	2	Leelanau	121
15	Fisherman's Island SP	3 & 4	Charlevoix	145, 147
16	State Forest Lands, Beaver Island	2	Charlevoix	155
17	Sturgeon Bay, Waugoshance Point & Big Stone Bay, Wilderness SP	15 & 3 plus island shores	Emmet	165, 167
18	Headlands County Park	2	Emmet	169

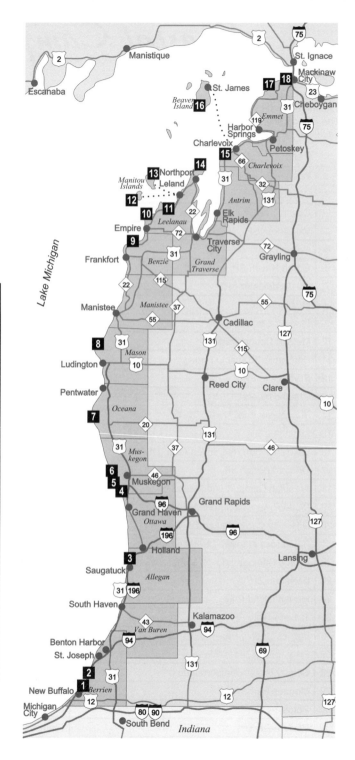

County by County

a road trip of the public Lake Michigan shore from Indiana to the Straits of Mackinac

Lake Michigan

Travel Distances

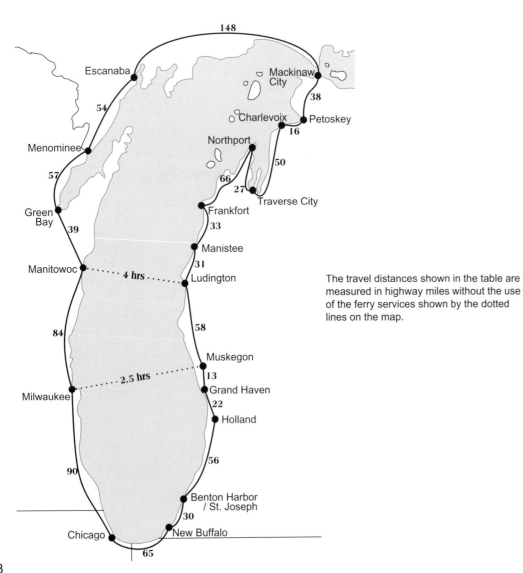

The travel distances shown in the table are measured in highway miles without the use of the ferry services shown by the dotted lines on the map.

Distance in Miles	Benton Harbor	Muskegon	Ludington	Traverse City	Petoskey	Mackinaw City
Benton Harbor, MI	●	90	145	220	266	302
Charlevoix, MI	262	184	142	50	16	52
Chicago, IL	95	186	244	315	358	383
Cleveland, OH	288	329	388	412	419	442
Columbus, OH	310	349	408	432	439	462
Detroit, MI	183	188	241	242	260	281
Duluth, MN	515	634	616	496	459	423
Frankfort, MI	205	118	64	38	105	140
Grand Rapids, MI	83	40	58	139	185	221
Green Bay, WI	300	391	450	373	303	267
Holland, MI	56	35	90	165	212	247
Indianapolis, IN	177	256	317	378	456	479
Lansing, MI	120	104	158	171	202	224
Ludington, MI	145	58	●	92	158	194
Mackinaw City, MI	302	231	194	102	38	●
Madison, WI	224	309	370	437	422	386
Marquette, MI	469	397	361	269	203	167
Milwaukee, WI	185	276	334	405	420	382
Minneapolis, MN	499	584	645	621	551	515
Muskegon, MI	90	●	58	134	195	231
New Buffalo, MI	30	116	170	247	293	328
Northport, MI	247	162	120	27	94	130
Petoskey, MI	266	195	158	67	●	36
Saginaw, MI	190	131	145	146	167	188
Sault Ste. Marie, MI	360	289	252	160	94	58
South Bend, IN	40	130	177	244	289	325
Toledo, OH	187	216	275	299	306	329
Toronto, ON	435	410	469	459	466	489
Traverse City, MI	220	134	92	●	67	102

Berrien County

Most of Berrien County's lakeshore sits below bluffs or dunes. Summer homes and cottages line much of the coast. On clear days, the Chicago skyline appears over the Lake Michigan horizon, yet the county's small towns and orchards lend a rural tint. The twin cites of Benton Harbor and St. Joseph provide some urban flavor as well as a number of well-organized, full-service city beaches. Warren Dunes and Grand Mere State Parks offer long stretches of public shore. Both have large dunes and remote areas where you can get away from big crowds if you are willing to hike.

For the best free park areas, try Lincoln Township Beach and Nature Trail near Stevensville, Lion's Beach in St. Joseph, Rocky Gap County Park near Benton Harbor or Hagar Township Park north of Benton Harbor.

The north breakwater at St. Joseph has two picturesque lighthouses connected to the shore by an upper level catwalk. The catwalk was used by lightkeepers to access the lights during storms when waves would sweep the breakwater. The concrete structure makes a great place to take an evening sunset walk. The breakwater also provides very good fishing especially during spring and fall runs.

For other things to do, visit the vineyards, located a bit inland. Vintners use Lake Michigan's climatic influence to grow grapes. Wine tasting is available in the area. In addition, New Buffalo and St. Joseph have small, downtown shops that cater to the traveler. Both are within walking distance of the beach. Try stopping at the local restaurants in and around these towns during your shopping.

Good roads follow the lake coast. Interstate-94 parallels the shore in the lower two-thirds of the county. This provides a speedy route to access points along the coast. Be cautioned that I-94 carries large volumes of commercial truck traffic between Detroit and Chicago. Driving it rarely results in relaxation. Red Arrow Highway and US-12 form the two-lane highway that pre-dated I-94. Using these roads slows the pace and makes the shore access points easier to find. North of Benton Harbor, M-63 and the Blue Arrow Highway become the shoreline connectors leading to and from Van Buren County.

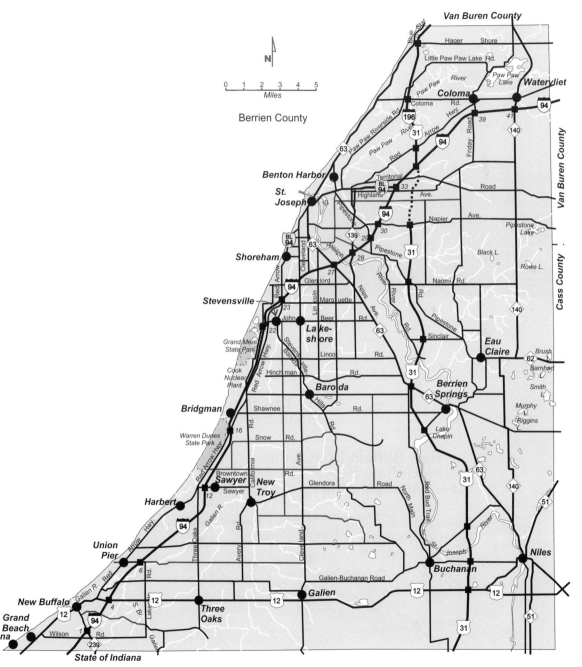

Berrien County

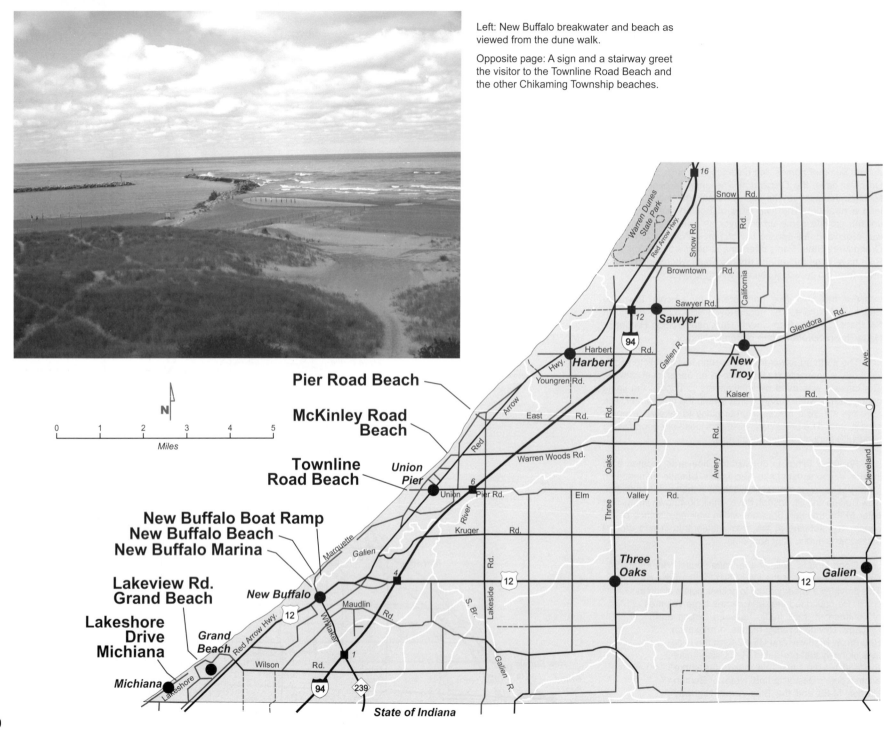

Left: New Buffalo breakwater and beach as viewed from the dune walk.

Opposite page: A sign and a stairway greet the visitor to the Townline Road Beach and the other Chikaming Township beaches.

Pier Road Beach

McKinley Road Beach

Townline Road Beach

New Buffalo Boat Ramp
New Buffalo Beach
New Buffalo Marina

Lakeview Rd.
Grand Beach

Lakeshore Drive Michiana

Union Pier

New Buffalo

Grand Beach

Michiana

Sawyer

Harbert

New Troy

Three Oaks

Galien

State of Indiana

New Buffalo and South Berrien Shore

Name	Location	Entrance Fee	Parking	Modern Restrooms	Vault or Portable Toilet	Stair or Path to Shore	Swimming	Picnic Area	Drinking Water	Campground	Trailered Boat Launch	Kayak / Canoe	Marina	Fishing	Hiking	Biking	X-Country Skiing	Playground	Lighthouse	Beach Strolling	Sandy Beach	Stony or Rocky Shore	Dunes	Bluff	Wetland
Michiana Lakeshore Drive	Michiana. From US Hwy 12, enter via Wilson Rd, 2 miles SW of New Buffalo or via Lakeshore Drive from Michigan City, IN.					●															●			●	
Grand Beach Lakeview Road	Grand Beach. Enter via Wilson Rd, 2 miles SW of New Buffalo.					●															●			●	
New Buffalo Marina	New Buffalo. Whitaker St. 3 blocks W of US-12.	●	●	●					●				●												
New Buffalo Beach	New Buffalo. Marquette Drive at NW end of Whitaker St. 4 blocks NW of US-12.	●	●	●			●	●	●			●		●	●						●		●		
New Buffalo Boat Launch	New Buffalo. Marquette Dr. near NW end of Whitaker.	●	●	●					●		●	●		●											
Townline Road Beach	0.5 W of Union Pier. From I-94 use Exit 6, Union Pier Rd., travel W continuing as the road changes to Townline.		●				●	●													●			●	
McKinley Road End	3 blocks N of Townline Road. Follow Lakeshore Dr. to McKinley Rd.		●				●	●													●			●	
Pier Road End	5.5 miles N of New Buffalo. From Red Arrow Hwy, NW at Pier Rd.		●				●	●													●			●	

Public land is limited in this area near the Indiana border. New Buffalo Beach provides the best access.

MICHIANA LAKESHORE DRIVE: Michiana is an older beach community. It has limited opportunity for access because of the lack of parking. Several beach access points can be found intermittently on the bluff-lined lakeshore. These lie along Lakeshore Drive. Bicycling through the area on its narrow, low-traffic streets would be a pleasant way to reach these points and to visit this unique place. The residential roads can easily give you vertigo, as they wind through the community. Pay attention to where you have been so you can find your way back out.

GRAND BEACH LAKEVIEW ROAD: Grand Beach is a nearly-isolated community of old summer homes. A couple of road ends could provide access to the shore, but there is no parking. Streets are narrow and the old community has a canopy of hardwood trees. This listing is more for the curious driver looking for an interesting glimpse into the lakeshore's past.

Note: Grand Beach is squeezed between Lake Michigan and the busy railroad tracks. Wilson Road provides the only access across the tracks from US HWY 12.
    GPS: 41°46.314'N; 86°48.039'W (Wilson Rd. and US-12)

NEW BUFFALO MARINA: The city harbor and marina are located on the Galien River a short distance from New Buffalo Beach and the mouth of the river.
    Telephone: (616) 469-6887
    GPS: 41°47.883'N; 86°44.833'W (Marina), 41°48.117'N; 86°45.217'W (Channel)

NEW BUFFALO BEACH: The park has a sandy beach and a concession. New Buffalo Beach has some other amenities including a short boardwalk on the dunes and availability of a sand wheelchair for those who have need and wish to be on the beach. Part of the beach frontage lies on Lake Michigan. Another portion sits within the harbor on the mouth of the Galien River.
    GPS: 41°47.992'N; 86°44.867'W

NEW BUFFALO BOAT LAUNCH: This is the site of a quality boat ramp with ample parking along the Galien River a short distance from the mouth at Lake Michigan. Boats capable of clearing the Whitaker Road Bridge can enter the lake through the breakwater opening.

TOWNLINE ROAD BEACH: Townline Road is in a residential area of Chikaming Township which manages this beach. A wooden platform sits up on the bluff at the road end. A tall stairway leads to the sandy beach. Only a couple of parking spots are available on the south side of the street. Most of the small parks in this area are managed for nearby residents. Two others are listed below.
    GPS: 41°49.693'N; 86°42'237'W

MCKINLEY ROAD END: Here is a small, lakeshore park with a sandy beach. A short trail and stairway lead to the beach. Parking is very limited.
    GPS: 41°49.881'N; 86°41.798'W

PIER ROAD END: Used by local residents for the most part, the end of Pier Road has limited parking. A wood platform at the top of the bluff descends to a sandy beach below. No facilities.
    GPS: 41°51.103'N; 86°36.070'W

Left: The modern beachhouse and parking accommodations at Weko Beach.

Opposite page: A dune behind the main swimming beach at Warren Dunes State Park.

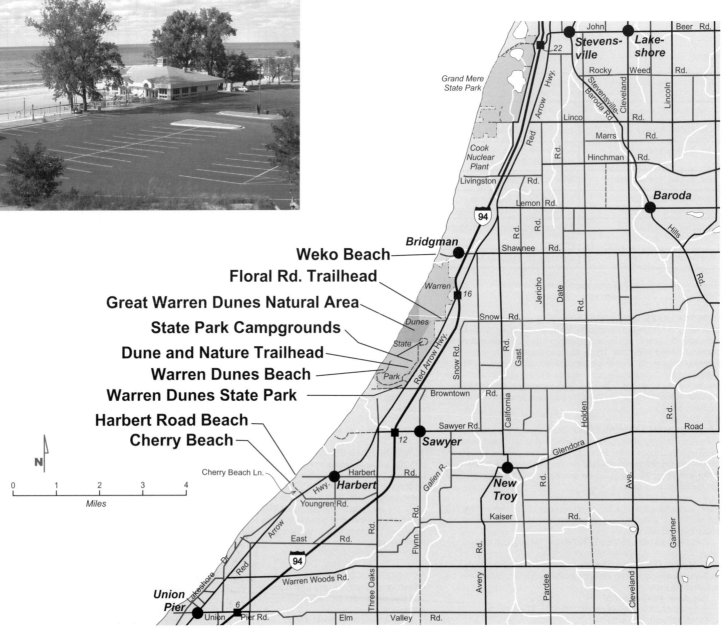

Berrien County

Warren Dunes and Weko Beach Area

Facilities   Environment

Name	Location	Entrance Fee	Parking	Modern Restrooms	Vault or Portable Toilet	Stair or Path to Shore	Swimming	Picnic Area	Drinking Water	Campground	Trailered Boat Launch	Kayak / Canoe	Marina	Fishing	Hiking	Biking	X-Country Skiing	Playground	Lighthouse	Beach Strolling	Sandy Beach	Stony or Rocky Shore	Dunes	Bluff	Wetland
Cherry Beach	1 mi. SW of Harbert. W from Red Arrow Hwy on Cherry Beach Ln.		●		●	●	●																	●	
Harbert Road End Beach	1 mile W of Harbert. W from Red Arrow Hwy on Harbert Rd.		●			●	●														●			●	
Warren Dunes State Park	3 miles S of Bridgman on Red Arrow Hwy. Use I-94 exit 12 or 16.	●	●	●	●		●	●	●	●				●	●		●	●		●	●		●		
Warren Dunes Beach	Warren Dunes State Park.	●	●	●			●	●	●											●	●		●		
Dune and Nature Trails	Warren Dunes State Park.	●	●												●								●		
State Park Campgrounds	Warren Dunes State Park.	●	●	●	●					●					●			●							
Great Warren Dune Natural Area	Warren Dunes State Park.	●	●				●	●							●					●	●		●		
Floral Road Trailhead	Warren Dunes State Park. On Floral Rd. W from Red Arrow Hwy. about 0.5 miles S of I-94 exit 16	●	●		●	●	●		●						●			●		●	●		●		
Weko Beach	Bridgman, 0.7 mi. W of Red Arrow Hwy. on Lake St. (Shawnee)	●	●	●			●	●	●	●	●	●		●	●			●			●		●		

Warren Dunes and Weko Beach combine to provide one of the best public access points at the south end of the lake

CHERRY BEACH: Surrounded by controversy, this 253-foot sandy beach is posted for township resident parking only. Non-residents are allowed to park on non-holiday weekdays or enter by foot any time. Part of the parking lot and park is county road and the road commission supports complete public use. The park lands were given to the township for public use by the Warren family. It is likely that the township will be forced to be more accommodating in the near future.
   GPS: 41°52.170'N: 86°38.909'W

HARBERT ROAD END BEACH: A few parking spots are available at the end of Harbert Road. A stairway leads to a nice, sandy beach.
   GPS: 41°52.273'N: 86°38.717'W

WARREN DUNES STATE PARK: The wonderful features of Warren Dunes and its proximity to Chicago ensure heavy usage during the summer. The greatest asset of the park may be the length of its shore, about 2.5 miles long. At its south end is a large, developed beach. Tower Hill and several other dunes lie on the backside of the beach parking area. The campgrounds are essentially behind Tower Hill and a good hike to the shore. The north end of the park is more serene. You will find woods, more dunes and a designated natural area with several trails. This relatively undeveloped area makes up over half of the park's 1950 acres. If you like it quiet, off-season can be a delight when nearly empty parking lots greet the visitor even on warm, sunny days. Michigan State Park Motor Vehicle Permit required.
   Telephone: (269) 426-4013
   Web: www.michigan.gov/dnr
   GPS: 41°54.103'N; 86°36.070'W

WARREN DUNES BEACH: The developed beach area of Warren Dunes State Park includes three large parking lots, concession and change buildings. The beach is pure sand. Large dunes lie behind the parking areas. Hiking trails start from the north end of the north lot.

DUNE AND NATURE TRAILS: A parking area with picnic shelter and trailhead is located near the modern campground. Turn right at the ranger station shortly after entering the park. Trails lead to the dunes, beach and Great Warren Dunes Natural Area listed below.

STATE PARK CAMPGROUNDS: Warren Dunes has two camping areas with a total of 180 sites. One has electricity at each site and modern restrooms with showers. The other has rustic facilities; vault toilets and no electricity. Reservations can be made by calling 1-800-44PARKS.

GREAT WARREN DUNE NATURAL AREA: Access to this designated area of Warren Dunes State Park is made via the park's foot trail system. The main trailhead is near the campgrounds. As the name implies, the area is kept undeveloped. It includes the Great Warren Dune that rises over 200 feet above lake level affording a spectacular view. Crossing the dune leads to the Lake Michigan shore.

FLORAL ROAD TRAILHEAD: An alternative access to the Warren Dunes State Park trails can be found on Floral Road at the north end of the park. An unpaved parking lot with vault toilet and water pump sits on the north side of the short residential street.
   GPS: 41°55.307'N: 86°34.733'W

WEKO BEACH: Weko Beach has a modern changehouse with restaurant and concession as well as camping and other features. The parking area is next to the beach at lake level. A sidewalk runs parallel to the water making it possible for those in a wheelchair to get close to the action. A series of boardwalks and stairs provide a path up the dunes offering nice vistas. Weko abuts the north end of Warren Dunes State Park making over 3 miles of public-owned, pure sand beach to roam. The boat ramp provides the only launch facility between New Buffalo and St. Joseph. Campsites and cabins available for rent.
   Telephone: (616) 465-3406
   Web: www.bridgman.org/parks.htm
   GPS: 41°56.509'N: 86°34.881'W

Shoreham

Glenlord Beach

Lincoln Twp. Beach & Nature Trails

North Lake Park

Grand Mere Road Beach

Grand Mere State Park

Grand Mere South Access

Livingston Road End

Lake-shore

Stevens-ville

Baroda

Bridgman

Warren Dunes State Park

Cook Nuclear Plant

Grand Mere State Park

Above left: Lake Michigan from the dunes at Grand Mere State Park.

Left: Lincoln Township Beach from the small bluff overlook. A nearby residence pokes into the lake precariously protected only by a stone barrier.

Opposite page: The natural and isolated beach at Grand Mere State Park

24

Berrien County

Stevensville and Grand Mere

Name	Location	Entrance Fee	Parking	Modern Restrooms	Vault or Portable Toilet	Stair or Path to Shore	Swimming	Picnic Area	Drinking Water	Campground	Trailered Boat Launch	Kayak / Canoe	Marina	Fishing	Hiking	Biking	X-Country Skiing	Playground	Lighthouse	Beach Strolling	Sandy Beach	Stony or Rocky Shore	Dunes	Bluff	Wetland
Livingston Road End	2 mi. N of Bridgman, from Red Arrow Hwy W 1 mi. on Livingston Rd.																				●		●	●	
Grand Mere State Park	2 mi SW of Stevensville. Thornton Dr. Use I-94 exit 22.	●	●		●	●	●	●	●						●			●		●	●		●		
Grand Mere South Access	3 mi SW of Stevensville. Thornton Dr. the W on Willow Rd to Wishart Rd.						●	●							●						●		●		
Grand Mere Road Beach	1.5 mi W of Stevensville at end of Grand Mere Rd.		●				●	●													●				
North Lake Park	Stevensville, 1 mi W on Grand Mere Rd.		●	●				●				●		●				●							
Lincoln Township Beach and Nature Trail	Stevensville, 1 mi W on Notre Dame Ave.		●		●		●	●	●						●						●				●
Glenlord Beach	2 mi. N of Stevensville. Glenlord Rd. 1 mi W of Red Arrow Hwy.		●		●			●																●	

Grand Mere State Park's natural setting of dunes, beach and coastal wetland sits near a couple of small township parks.

LIVINGSTON ROAD END: Located just south of the Cook Nuclear Plant, the nearby beach area is highly restricted. There is no parking area at the road end and no parking is allowed on Livingston Road within 1/4 mile of the shore area. You must descend a high bluff to the beach.
GPS: 41°58.199'N; 86°34.125'W

GRAND MERE STATE PARK: The park is largely undeveloped with the exception of the wheelchair-accessible trail around South Grand Mere Lake. Unfortunately, the aging and cracked asphalt trail makes it difficult for wheelchair use. Other trails lead over the dunes to Lake Michigan. Plan on hiking at least one mile to reach the shore. Grand Mere's 985 acres and mile-long shoreline provide much room to roam for those willing to pack it in. If you like some seclusion, try this park.
Telephone: (269) 426-4013
Web: www.michigan.gov/dnr
GPS: 41°59.140'N; 86°33.017'W

GRAND MERE SOUTH ACCESS: Willow Road forms much of the south park boundary. A two-track trail known as Wishart Road heads north from Willow ending within 1/2-mile at a small parking area. Wishart is a dirt road normally passable by cars. A foot trail leads from the end of the road. The shore is about a one-mile walk. Remember that you can easily get disoriented on the open dunes. Make sure you know your way in and out.

GRAND MERE ROAD BEACH: Found at the end of Grand Mere Road, this access is often shown on maps as Lincoln Township Beach. In this listing, the name Grand Mere Road Beach is given to differentiate it from a nearby park with a similar name. Parking is very limited, the area is small and the beach is sandy. Restroom facilities can be found at North Lake Park, a half-mile away.
GPS: 42°00.520'N; 86°32.940'W

NORTH LAKE PARK: A pleasant park north of Grand Mere State Park, the beach area on North Grand Mere Lake is not great for swimming but the park provides a launch point for paddlers wishing an alternative to Lake Michigan. Picnic and restroom facilities are available.
GPS: 42°00.680'N; 86°32.415'W

LINCOLN TOWNSHIP BEACH AND NATURE TRAIL: The 34-acre park provides a variety of activities. Try bird watching at its wetland or hike the trails through the back woods. Swim or sunbathe on the 200-foot sandy beach. Picnic areas and covered shelters can be found in each portion of the park. Development is low key at this park. Playground equipment is limited.
GPS: 42°01.180'N; 86°32.015'W

GLENLORD BEACH: Bluff erosion has taken away the beach access. The viewing platform still exists and is wheelchair-accessible.
GPS: 42°02.606'N; 86°31.576'W

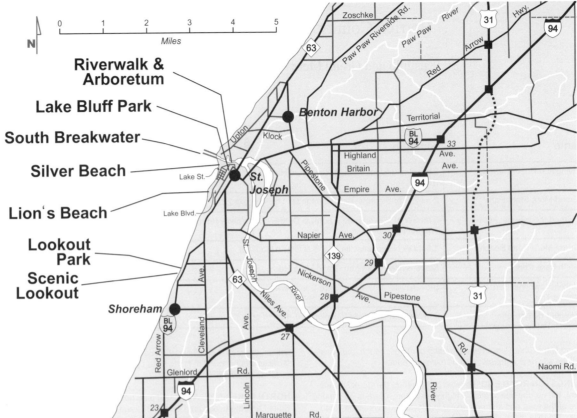

Riverwalk & Arboretum

Lake Bluff Park

South Breakwater

Silver Beach

Lion's Beach

Lookout Park

Scenic Lookout

Shoreham

Benton Harbor

St. Joseph

Top left: Large sculptures dot the landscape at Silver Beach.

Left: Autumn fishing is productive from the breakwater.

Right: Lion's Beach includes plenty of play equipment for the children.

Opposite page: The breakwaters and harbor lighthouses are in view from Silver Beach.

St Joseph South of the River Channel

Name	Location	Entrance Fee	Parking	Modern Restrooms	Vault or Portable Toilet	Stair or Path to Shore	Swimming	Picnic Area	Drinking Water	Campground	Trailered Boat Launch	Kayak / Canoe	Marina	Fishing	Hiking	Biking	X-Country Skiing	Playground	Lighthouse	Beach Strolling	Sandy Beach	Stony or Rocky Shore	Dunes	Bluff	Wetland
Scenic Overlook	3 mi. S of downtown St. Joseph on Red Arrow Hwy (Bus. I-94).		●																					●	
Lookout Park	2.7 mi. S of downtown St. Joseph on Red Arrow Hwy (Bus. I-94).		●					●																●	
Lion's Beach Family Park	St. Joseph. Lion's Park Dr. 4 blocks NW of M-63 from Market St.		●	●			●	●	●			●						●			●				
Silver Beach Park	St. Joseph. Water and Lake Streets.	●	●	●			●	●	●					●				●			●				
South St. Joseph River Channel Breakwater	St. Joseph access from Silver Beach Park. Water and Lake Streets.		●	●					●					●											
South River Walk and Upton Arboretum	St. Joseph. Water at State Street		●						●						●										
Lake Bluff Park	St. Joseph. Lake Blvd. downtown.		●	●		●		●	●															●	

Recent investment in the St. Joseph parks make these, more urban-style locations a pleasure to visit. The primary listings below sit along or near the St. Joseph River Channel and Breakwater.

SCENIC OVERLOOK: Located just north of Hawthorne Ave. on Red Arrow Highway and marked by a highway sign, this overlook has no facilities but has a barrier-free viewing platform.
GPS: 42°04.435'N; 86°30.402'W

LOOKOUT PARK: Here is a view high above the lake and picnic spot located along Red Arrow Highway (Bus. I-94) between High and Hawthorne Streets. It is loosely connected to the overlook listed above. These overlooks mark the site of a 1954 landslide along the shore. The slide took houses and nearly the Red Arrow Highway itself. Development includes a Korean War Memorial, benches and landslide marker.
GPS: 42°04.567'N; 86°30.325'W

LION'S BEACH FAMILY PARK: As the name implies, Lion's Beach orients toward children and families. The 500-foot-long beach is sandy with some small stones. While the beach is the centerpiece, there is plenty of playground equipment. Lion's Beach provides a free, low-key alternative to Silver Beach a few blocks to its north.
GPS: 42°06.044'N; 86°29.502'W

SILVER BEACH PARK: The sand of Silver Beach is a favorite of sun worshippers and swimmers. A concession and changehouse are two of the amenities. Sidewalks lead toward downtown and the Lion's Beach area, each just blocks away. Large sculptures sprinkle the landscape. The south breakwater of the St. Joseph River Channel borders the north edge. See next listing. Vehicle fee.
GPS: 42°06.612'N; 86°29.257'W

SOUTH ST. JOSEPH RIVER CHANNEL BREAKWATER: Access the St. Joseph South Breakwater via Silver Beach Park. Fishing, especially in the late summer and early fall is a favorite activity as are sunset strolls. A view of the two St. Joe lights can be seen across the channel.

SOUTH RIVER WALK AND UPTON ARBORETUM: Located between the downtown area and Silver Beach, the walkway links the two locations. A dozen parking spaces can be found on Port Street at the bottom of the hill. A variety of tree species grow in the linear park. There are a few sculptures as well. Watch the turntable-type railroad bridge rotate open to allow boats through or close for passing trains.

LAKE BLUFF PARK: The downtown area of St. Joseph sits on the bluff a few blocks inland from the lakeshore. Lake Blvd. parallels the bluff's edge and the park lies between. It is an old park with grass, large shade trees and a number of picnic tables. A stairway leads down the bluff towards Silver Beach about two blocks away. Street parking is available.
GPS: 42°06.533'N; 86°29.035'W

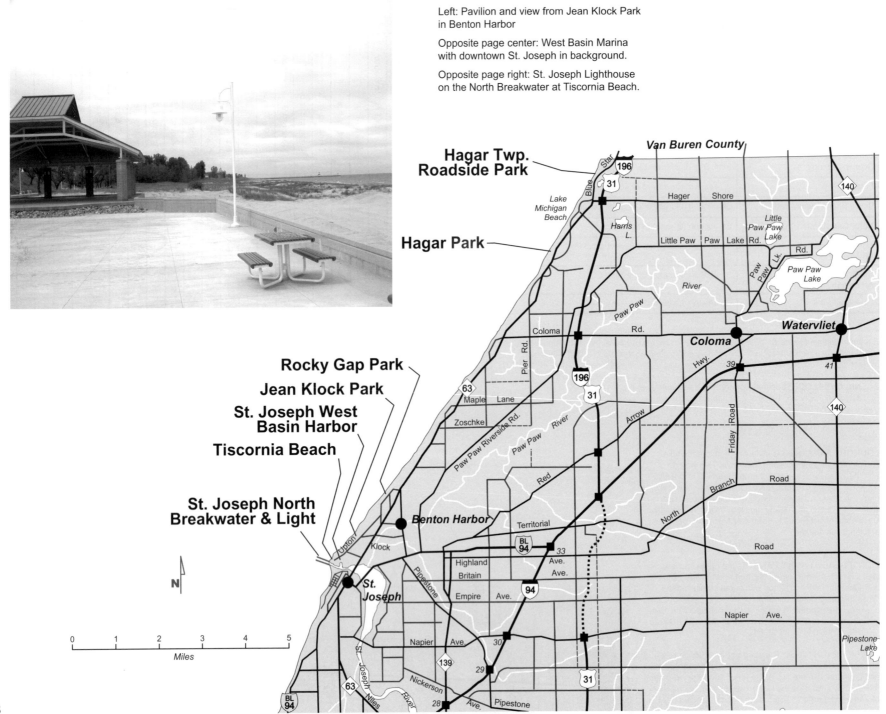

Left: Pavilion and view from Jean Klock Park in Benton Harbor

Opposite page center: West Basin Marina with downtown St. Joseph in background.

Opposite page right: St. Joseph Lighthouse on the North Breakwater at Tiscornia Beach.

Hagar Twp. Roadside Park

Hagar Park

Rocky Gap Park

Jean Klock Park

St. Joseph West Basin Harbor

Tiscornia Beach

St. Joseph North Breakwater & Light

Van Buren County

N

0 1 2 3 4 5

Miles

Name	Location	Facilities																			Environment				
		Entrance Fee	Parking	Modern Restrooms	Vault or Portable Toilet	Stair or Path to Shore	Swimming	Picnic Area	Drinking Water	Campground	Trailered Boat Launch	Kayak / Canoe	Marina	Fishing	Hiking	Biking	X-Country Skiing	Playground	Lighthouse	Beach Strolling	Sandy Beach	Stony or Rocky Shore	Dunes	Bluff	Wetland
North Breakwater and Lighthouse	St. Joseph at Tiscornia Park. From M-63, exit on Klock Blvd., then to Marina Dr. follow signs.	●	●		●	●	●							●					●		●				
Tiscornia Beach	At St. Joseph North Breakwater. St. Joseph. From M-63, exit on Klock Blvd., then to Marina Dr. follow signs.	●	●	●			●	●	●					●				●	●		●				
West Basin Marina	St. Joseph on N side of St. Joseph River. From M-63, exit on Klock Blvd., then to Marina Dr.		●	●					●				●												
Jean Klock Park	Benton Harbor. Exit M-63 at Jean Klock Blvd.	●	●	●			●	●	●									●			●				
Rocky Gap Park	2 miles N of St. Joseph on Rocky Gap Rd W of M-63.		●			●	●	●										●			●			●	
Hagar Park	Blue Star Highway, 8.5 miles NE of Benton Harbor.		●			●	●	●										●			●			●	
Hagar Township Roadside Park	Blue Star Highway. 10 miles NE of Benton Harbor.		●			●	●	●													●		●		

Benton Harbor and St. Joseph each have parks north of the St. Joseph River. Berrien County and Hager Township have facilities north of the cities with numerous cottages and homes in between.

NORTH BREAKWATER AND LIGHTHOUSE: The North St. Joseph River Channel Breakwater has a lighthouse and a tower light. Both are automated now. The superstructure for the elevated catwalks, used by the lightkeeper to access the lights during storms, remains. The breakwater is popular for fishing. Access the breakwater via Tiscornia Park where restrooms and other facilities are available.

TISCORNIA BEACH: The City of St. Joseph operates Tiscornia Park. There is a vehicle entrance fee during the summer. Changehouse and concessions are available. The sandy beach lies north of the St. Joseph North Breakwater. Tiscornia provides access to the breakwater as well.
GPS: 42°06.924'N; 86°29.273'W

WEST BASIN MARINA: The facility primarily serves those with boat slips. Street parking is available. This is a good harbor for viewing a variety of boats.
Telephone: (616) 983-5432
GPS: 42°06.767'N; 86°29.050'W (Marina),
42°06.967'N; 86°29.733'W (channel)

JEAN KLOCK PARK: Klock, Benton Harbor's major park beach, has a changehouse and a covered viewing area of the shore. The large beach is sandy with small dunes. The St. Joseph Breakwater and Lighthouse can be seen a short way down the shore. Much of the development is new, but upkeep lags some. The size and quality of the beach area makes it potentially the best in the county.
GPS: 42°07.546'N; 86°28.245'W

ROCKY GAP COUNTY PARK: Rocky Gap has paved parking for about 25 vehicles on the bluff above the lake. A short staircase leads to the sandy beach.
GPS: 42°08.047'N; 86°27.975'W

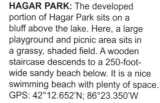

HAGAR PARK: The developed portion of Hagar Park sits on a bluff above the lake. Here, a large playground and picnic area sits in a grassy, shaded field. A wooden staircase descends to a 250-foot-wide sandy beach below. It is a nice swimming beach with plenty of space.
GPS: 42°12.652'N; 86°23.350'W

HAGAR TOWNSHIP ROADSIDE PARK: This small park sits 0.5 miles north of Hagar Shore Road near the county line. Walk a short distance over small dunes to access the beach. It is sandy with a few small stones. Swimming is good. A covered picnic table and grill are located near the parking.
GPS: 42°14.250'N; 86°22.011'W

Shore Safety

Both swimmers and boaters should keep aware of weather conditions. Great Lakes storms can erupt fast and furious. In 1967, I witnessed the tragic result of a fast brewing, unpredicted storm that hit Benzie County during the height of salmon fishing activity. Within hours, a number of fishing boats sank. Nine boaters died. Many fishermen desperately beached their craft to save their lives. The beach was littered with fishing tackle and flotsam. Faces that earlier in the day had smiles, turned long with disbelief. This event brought more focus on pleasure boat safety. Each harbor posts weather conditions at various locations and boaters should heed Coast Guard warnings.

Swimming has its hazards as well. In 2003, 7 lost their lives at three different beaches in Berrien County on one day. Each had been caught in a rip current. To form a rip current, wind pushes waves and water up against the shore. Underwater sandbars may impede the outflow water. As the water piles up, it must find a way to flow back out. It finds the channel of least resistance and a rip current forms where the outbound flow occurs. When the current is strong, a swimmer may be pulled away from the shore on one of these flows. Trying to swim against the flow directly back to shore will tire the swimmer, increasing the chance of drowning. The best procedure is to swim parallel to the shore until free from the current and then proceed toward shore. Generally the rip current will not be very wide. Few Lake Michigan beaches have lifeguards, but many, including all the designated swimming areas of the Michigan State Parks, use a color-coded flag to warn of potentially hazardous swim conditions. Signs explain the system. Remember that Great Lakes water is relatively cold. Water temperature is often less than 70 degrees Fahrenheit even in the summer. Watch for potential hypothermia.

The breakwaters and piers found regularly along the coast provide great fishing, a place to watch the sunset or visit a lighthouse. During storms, however, they can be perilous. Waves have washed people off the breakwaters, usually into deep, cold waters. Stay off the breakwaters during storms or times of large waves. Some of these structures have safety devices such as ladders for climbing back on the pier or life rings for tossing to someone washed over. The breakwaters are a fun place to be but caution is necessary.

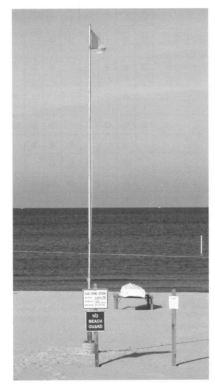

Clockwise from the top right:
- Breakwaters and piers are no place to be during waves like these.
- Frankfort and Elberta breakwaters have rescue devices and an emergency call box.
- State Park designated beach areas use a signal flag system to advise swimmers.
- The flag flies at unguarded beach.

Van Buren County

Van Buren has the shortest coastline of the state's Lake Michigan counties, but it also has a number of public access sites. The shore is sandy with a few shoreside bluffs. Two large recreational areas, Van Buren State Park and Covert Township Park, are to the south. Both have camping and swimming. The Palisades Nuclear Plant takes up much of the space between them, adding a curiosity but not much distraction. The area in and around Covert Park has some good-sized dunes. Van Buren Park has a long, sandy beach, the largest public section between Grand Mere and Saugatuck.

South Haven, the county's singular coastal town, anchors the north. City beaches flank each side of the harbor formed where the Black River empties into Lake Michigan. Each beach area has a wide expanse of sand. The town's breakwaters attract fishermen. A red, cylindrical lighthouse dots the end of the south breakwater. The town's business district lies within a few blocks of the shore. From it, try hiking the walkway along the south side of the river. You will pass the marina area packed with boats during the summer season. The stroll ends at South Beach and the harbor lighthouse. On the north side of the river, the Michigan Maritime Museum tells the story of the lakes, its vessels and people. The entrance fee is modest and a visit rounds out your coastal experience. It is easy to experience a pleasant day in South Haven.

This is the heart of the southwest Michigan fruit belt. Orchards are plentiful. Grapes are grown for wine and juice. South Haven celebrates its blueberry crop with a festival each July. The Lake Michigan weather influence makes this agriculture possible.

An express highway serves the Van Buren coastal area. The dual designated US-31 / I-196 freeway heads north from Benton Harbor in Berrien County on the way to Holland. This main highway is never more than 2 miles from the shore. The old US-31 two-lane route, called Blue Star Memorial Highway, parallels the coast just west of the freeway. It serves as the primary local route. From Blue Star, use North Shore Drive or 76th Street (Monroe Blvd.) to get to South Haven's beach parks.

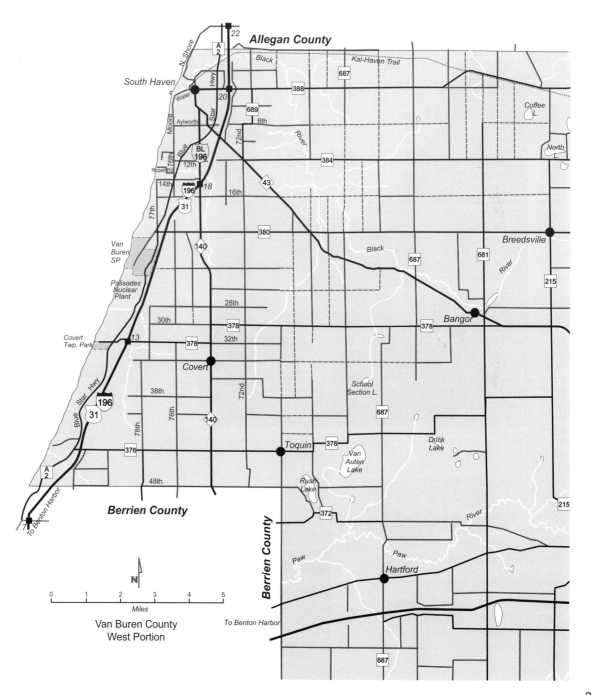

Van Buren County
West Portion

Above: A stairway, up and over dunes, leads from the campground to the beach at Covert Township Park.

Right: South Haven Township Beach is one of the few on the southern lakeshore with stones to find.

Opposite page: The Palisades Nuclear Plant looms at the south end of Van Buren State Park.

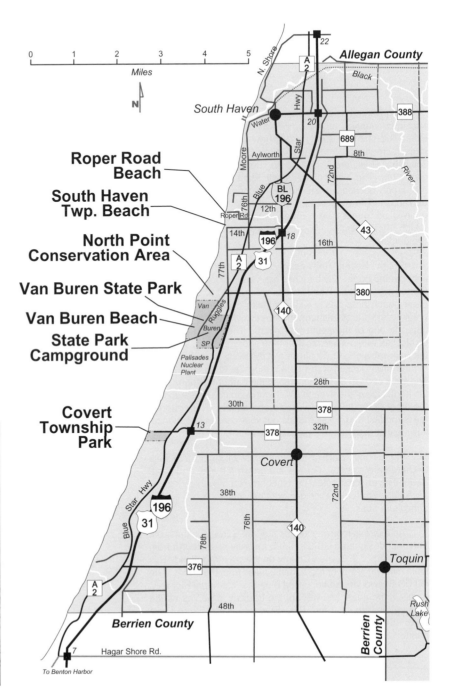

Roper Road Beach

South Haven Twp. Beach

North Point Conservation Area

Van Buren State Park

Van Buren Beach

State Park Campground

Covert Township Park

Facilities   **Environment**

Name	Location	Entrance Fee	Parking	Modern Restrooms	Vault or Portable Toilet	Stair or Path to Shore	Swimming	Picnic Area	Drinking Water	Campground	Trailered Boat Launch	Kayak / Canoe	Marina	Fishing	Hiking	Biking	X-Country Skiing	Playground	Lighthouse	Beach Strolling	Sandy Beach	Stony or Rocky Shore	Dunes	Bluff	Wetland
Covert Township Park	7.5 miles S of South Haven. From I-196 exit 13 go W 1 mile on 32nd Ave.	●	●	●		●	●	●	●	●								●			●		●		
Van Buren State Park	4.5 miles S of South Haven. Blue Star Hwy to Ruggles Rd. From I-196 use exit 13 or 18.	●	●	●		●	●	●	●	●										●	●	●	●		
Van Buren State Park Beach	Van Buren State Park.	●	●	●		●	●	●	●											●	●	●	●		
State Park Campground	Van Buren State Park.	●	●	●		●	●		●	●								●			●	●	●		
North Point Conservation Area	4.5 miles S of South Haven at entrance to Van Buren State Park. Blue Star Hwy to Ruggles Rd. From I-196 use exit 13 or 18.		●			●	●								●					●	●		●	●	
South Haven Township Beach	2.5 miles S of South Haven. Blue Star Highway then W on 14th St. 0.8 miles.		●			●	●													●	●		●		
Roper Road Beach	2.2 miles S of South Haven. From 76th St. (Monroe Blvd.) W on Roper Rd.		●				●					●									●				

The south portion of Van Buren's coast includes two large parks, a nuclear power plant and private cottages.

COVERT TOWNSHIP PARK: Covert Park has 100 campsites located in a tall forest. Wooded dunes separate the camping area from the beach. A lengthy series of wooden stairs and boardwalk lead over the dunes. The beach is sand with intermittently spaced erosion control jetties. Fees charged for entrance and camping.
   Telephone: (269) 764-1421
   GPS: 42°17.965'N; 86°19.560'W

VAN BUREN STATE PARK: Park activity revolves around camping and swimming. At 346 acres, Van Buren is the largest lakeshore park in the county. The shore extends nearly one mile with the Palisades Nuclear Power Plant forming the south boundary. The plant is clearly visible from the beach. Wooded dunes parallel the beach. Michigan State Park Motor Vehicle Permit required.
   Telephone: (269) 637-2788
   Web: www.michigan.gov/dnr

VAN BUREN STATE PARK BEACH: The beach is sand with a few stones and is located several hundred feet from the parking area. Swimming is very good. A new restroom and concession building have been added at the beachfront. Wheelchair access is available to the beach area via a paved sidewalk, but it ends without a wide pad making it difficult to move out of the way of other pedestrians.

STATE PARK CAMPGROUND: The popular campground has over 200 sites. Facilities include showers and electricity at the site. It is located eastward of the beach parking lot. Paths lead to beach (listed above) about a quarter-mile walk. Make reservations at 1-800-44PARKS.

NORTH POINT CONSERVATION AREA:
This is a wooded area located on the north border of Van Buren State Park. A small brown sign near the state park entrance marks the location of the trailhead that leads towards the shore. The curvy trail is unmarked afterwards with several branching trails. Keep track of your course so that you can find your way out. The trails end with a descent of the dunes to the water. A favorite of local residents, there is room to park a few cars along the shoulder on each side of Ruggles Road.

SOUTH HAVEN TOWNSHIP BEACH: The park has a narrow beach located several hundred feet down a steep path. The shore of this small park is mostly sand with some small stone. Set in a quiet residential area, the parking area is small. There are no facilities.
   GPS: 42°22.023'N; 86°17.604'W

ROPER ROAD BEACH: A small stream winding through the woods borders the south portion of this small parcel. The beach is sand with a few small stones. Unfortunately, some unsightly erosion control made of broken concrete slabs and old tires spoils an otherwise pretty site. It is an easy place to launch a kayak.
   GPS: 42°22.344'N; 86°17.567'W

Above left: The marina docks along Riverside Park sit empty awaiting winter.

Above right: The barrier-free Moore Boulevard Platform offers a view of South Beach and the South Haven Lighthouse.

Opposite page: Access the South Haven Lighthouse from South Beach but not when the waves crash like these.

South Haven Marina
Riverside Park
South Breakwater & Lighthouse
South Beach
Moore Blvd. Platform

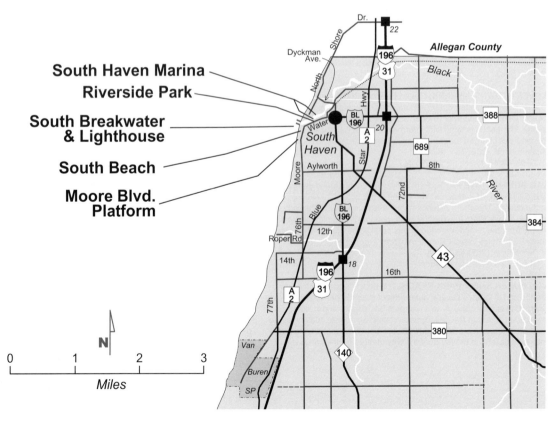

Van Buren County

South Haven South of Black River

Name	Location	Entrance Fee	Parking	Modern Restrooms	Vault or Portable Toilet	Stair or Path to Shore	Swimming	Picnic Area	Drinking Water	Campground	Trailered Boat Launch	Kayak / Canoe	Marina	Fishing	Hiking	Biking	X-Country Skiing	Playground	Lighthouse	Beach Strolling	Sandy Beach	Stony or Rocky Shore	Dunes	Bluff	Wetland
Monroe Blvd. Platform	South Haven. Monroe Blvd near Superior St.		●			●															●			●	
South Beach	South Haven. At end of Water or Erie Streets.	◆	●	●			●	●	●					●	●			●	●	●	●				
Black River Channel, South Breakwater & Lighthouse	South Haven. At South Beach Park.		●	●			●	●	●					●					●		●				
Riverside Park	South Haven. Water St.		●	●		●								●	●										
South Haven Marina	South Haven. Water St. (S river channel) or Black River St. (N river channel)			●					●				●												

◆ *See the note concerning parking below.*

South Beach, the South Breakwater and Riverside Park nicely interconnect with South Haven's downtown business district. The overlook on Monroe Boulevard looks towards the harbor entrance.

MONROE BOULEVARD PLATFORM: Located on the bluff above South Beach is a viewing platform designed for wheelchair and limited-mobility access. A memorial gift for Kristen Thompson, it is one of the best overlooks developed for this purpose on the Lake Michigan shore. Look over the entire South Beach, the South Haven Lighthouse or catch the day's sunset. A stairway leads down to South Beach as well. Parallel parking is available on Monroe Blvd.

SOUTH BEACH: The beach has many features including a concession and skateboard park. It provides access to the South Haven Light at the end of the south breakwater. Adjacent Riverside Park, located up-channel, connects the park to downtown providing a nice hike. Access the lighthouse on the channel breakwater from here.
GPS: 42°24.112'N; 86°16.883'W

◆*Parking fee collected at self-service pay stations during the period of May 1 to Labor Day from 9:00 AM to 6:00 PM. Fee is $5 per day. Metered street parking is located a short distance away on Water Street. Additional, free street parking located closer to downtown a few blocks away.*

BLACK RIVER CHANNEL, SOUTH BREAKWATER AND LIGHTHOUSE: The black lighthouse dome caps the red tower of the South Haven Lighthouse. It is located at the end of the concrete, south breakwater. An elevated, steel catwalk remains, once needed for reaching the lighthouse during storms in pre-automation days. Access the light via the South Beach. Fishing is popular here.

RIVERSIDE PARK: Just upstream from the south side of the Black River's channel to Lake Michigan lies Riverside Park. The park forms a walkway from downtown to the South Beach Park, lighthouse and breakwater. Boat docks of the South Haven Marina line part of the riverbank. Some street parking is available on Water Street. Other parking can be found at either terminus.
GPS: 42°24.112'N; 86°16.883'W

SOUTH HAVEN MARINA: Over 200 boat slips make up the marina. Many are for transient use. It is located on both sides of the Black River near the channel opening to Lake Michigan. Boat viewing is best from Riverside Park along the south side of the channel.
Telephone: (616) 637-3171
GPS: 42°24.250'N; 86°16.617'W

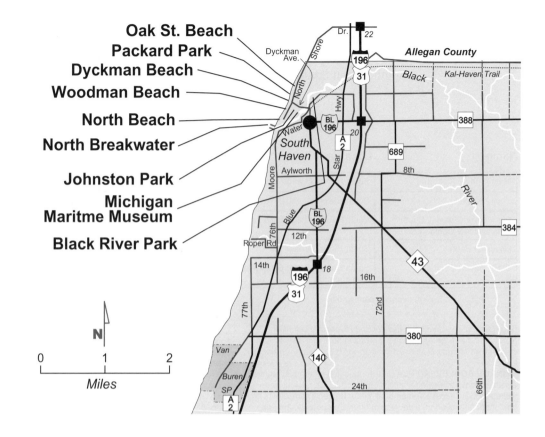

Oak St. Beach
Packard Park
Dyckman Beach
Woodman Beach
North Beach
North Breakwater
Johnston Park
Michigan Maritme Museum
Black River Park

Above: North Beach during a quiet, early morning.

Near right: This sign at Dyckman Beach and similar ones at other north shore parks mark their location.

Far right: A short stairway leads to the sand at Oak Street Beach.

Opposite page: Proof that sand does not stay put, work crews periodically scoop it from the street located behind North Beach and put it back "where it belongs."

Van Buren County

South Haven North of Black River

Name	Location	Entrance Fee	Parking	Modern Restrooms	Vault or Portable Toilet	Stair or Path to Shore	Swimming	Picnic Area	Drinking Water	Campground	Trailered Boat Launch	Kayak / Canoe	Marina	Fishing	Hiking	Biking	X-Country Skiing	Playground	Lighthouse	Beach Strolling	Sandy Beach	Stony or Rocky Shore	Dunes	Bluff	Wetland
																					Facilities → Environment				
Black River Park	South Haven. Take Dunkley Ave. N from Dyckman Ave. at bridge.		●	●				●	●		●	●	●	●											
Michigan Maritime Museum	South Haven. 260 Dyckman Ave.	●	●	●					●																
Johnston Park	South Haven. Dyckman Ave. one block E of North Shore Drive.		●	●				●	●									●							
Black River Channel North Breakwater	South Haven. Lakeshore Drive at North Beach Park.		●				●							●							●				
North Beach	South Haven. From North Shore Drive W on Avery Street to Lakeshore Dr.	◆	●	●			●							●				●		●	●				
Woodman Beach	South Haven. North Shore Drive at Woodman St.	◆	●				●	●													●				
Dyckman Beach	South Haven. North Shore Drive at Dyckman Ave.	◆	●				●	●													●				
Packard Beach	South Haven. North Shore Drive just N of Dyckman Ave.	◆	●	●			●	●	●	●								●			●				
Oak Street Beach	South Haven. North Shore Drive at Oak St.	◆	●				●	●													●				

◆ *See the note concerning parking below.*

Several fine beaches are found on South Haven's north side as well as a boat launch and a maritime museum.

BLACK RIVER PARK: The 11-acre park can be found upstream from the marina, about 1/4-mile north of the Dyckman Avenue Bridge. It has an excellent boat ramp plus restroom and picnic facilities.

MICHIGAN MARITIME MUSEUM: The museum focuses on Michigan's Great Lakes maritime history. Exhibits include lifesaving

vessels and boat building. Open every day from Memorial Day to Labor Day. Closed on Tuesdays at other times of year. Admission cost in 2004 was $2.50 for adults and $1.50 for seniors and age 5-12.
Telephone: (269) 637-8078 or (800) 747-3810
Web: www.michiganmaritimemuseum.org

JOHNSTON PARK: A well-shaded park that sits on a hill above the Black River, Johnston provides a welcome place to escape the sun for a while. The facilities include a playground, basketball courts, tables and grills. Packard, Dyckman, Woodman and North Beaches are within a few blocks. This makes Johnston Park an alternative parking point for those who do not mind the walk. Additionally, the Michigan Maritime Museum is next door.

BLACK RIVER CHANNEL NORTH BREAKWATER: You can view the lighthouse on the south breakwater from here. North Beach's sandy beach with facilities and parking are adjacent. Fishing.

◆*Note: The five beaches listed next are included in the South Haven "Beach Parking Program." The program regulates parking during the period of May 1 to Labor Day from 9:00 AM to 6:00 PM. Self-service pay stations are located at the lots. Fee is $5 per day. Free street parking is available but limited in this area of town. Using these beaches during peak periods may require some walking.*

NORTH BEACH: North Beach is the classic urban-style beach with concessions, restrooms and beach volleyball. North Channel Breakwater access is available from here. Great swimming. Parking falls under the South Haven beach parking program.
GPS: 42°24.311'N; 86°16.771'W

WOODMAN BEACH: A sandy beach similar to and about a block from Dyckman Beach (see next). Parking is limited and falls under the South Haven beach parking program.
GPS: 42°24.390'N ; 86°16.766'W

DYCKMAN BEACH: A 50-foot wide sandy beach. Parking is limited and falls under the South Haven beach parking program. The north breakwater and lighthouse can be seen from Dyckman. A viewing platform above the beach is wheelchair-accessible.
GPS: 42°24.438'N; 86°16.735'W

PACKARD BEACH PARK: Packard Park has a short stairway from the parking area to the beach. A barrier-free viewing platform is located at the top of the stairway. A large, grassy area for picnicking lies between the street and parking area. Play equipment is minimal. Grills and tables are available. The beach is pure sand. Parking is under the South Haven beach parking program.
GPS: 42°24.600'N; 86°16.658'W

OAK STREET BEACH: A 50-foot wide sandy beach. Parking is limited to 12 spaces which are under the South Haven beach parking program.
GPS: 42°24.753'N; 86°16.569'W

Industry on the Lake

The Great Lakes have a long relationship with commerce. They form a natural transportation network used first by native peoples, then later French and English fur traders. Northern lumber was cut and sailed to Chicago and other cites for building. Heavy industry centered in the Midwest states and Ontario Province because of the ease of shipping heavy, raw materials such as iron ore, limestone and coal to mills and factories. Lake freighters provided cheap cargo hauls relative to rail or truck. Ferries crossed Lake Michigan with rail cars, automobiles and passengers.

As you head along the lakeshore, see how commerce weaves its way into the communities. You will find the past remnants of commercial activity at ghost town sites like Pier Cove in Allegan County and Aral in Benzie County. Each became a "temporary" transport hub for the local resources of the area. In the case of Aral, the forest ran dry and the milling of lumber for loading on the waiting schooners was no longer sustainable. The town died and time has left us with dock pilings and foundations that remind us it was there. Fort Michilimackinac (Emmet County) provides a more visible history of past commercial activity side-by-side with a classic example of today's tourist economy. Leland (Leelanau County) still exhibits some of the feel of a commercial fishery port. Ludington (Mason County) hosts commercial car ferry service to Wisconsin. Muskegon's harbor welcomes commercial vessels, large and small, and a sand mine operation is located a bit south of the city's Kruse Park. Walk south on Van Buren State Park's beach and you will see Palisades Nuclear Plant. Use Consumer Energy's walkway along the north breakwater at Port Sheldon (Ottawa County) to get close to industry, as you walk by large intake pipes feeding the coal-fired power plant.

Lake water serves industry directly. A number of nuclear and conventional power plants use the water for steam production and cooling. Because of this, power plants take a prominent place on the shore. Many regard the sight of smokestacks and cooling towers with disgust. Others understand that economic advantage dictated the location.

The Ludington Pumped Storage Facility, midway along the shore, is an electric production plant of a different sort. Turbines pump water from Lake Michigan into a huge, man-made reservoir at night, storing the water as potential energy.

During peak energy demand, the water flows back to the lake through the turbines to produce electricity. The process requires a large body of water to work. Unfortunately, the turbines have gobbled a number fish through the years. Fishing interests and the plant's operators squared off over the fish loss. A court settlement in 1996 formed the Great Lakes Fishery Trust (GLFT) in which the plant operators financially compensate for the fish loss. The money is used to increase fishing opportunities.

The larger cities of the south shore and their surrounding communities often draw their water directly from the lake. This water supply supports all types of economic activity including the water you use in your motel room. Notice that at some parks pumping stations or intake plumbing share the beach with you. Weko Beach (Berrien County) and Van Buren State Park (Van Buren County) are examples of where parks and water facilities co-exist.

The westerly winds of the area help to pile sand at its east shore. Dunes, both large and small, form along this edge. Sand mining still exists in a few locations. Making molds for foundry casting is a primary use. The abundance of iron particles in the sand make it impractical for glass making.

The raw material for cement production is plentiful along the northern shores of Lakes Michigan and Huron. A cement plant sits conspicuously on the shore south of Charlevoix. Developers reconstituted a former cement quarry site near Petoskey into the exclusive resort community of Bay Harbor. The hotel and retail shop portion of Bay Harbor is open to the public.

Whether you consider them to be invaders of the pristine shore or necessities of modern life, the industrial sites are here for the same reason as you; to take advantage of the Lake Michigan resource.

From the top:
 • A cement plant occupies Charlevoix's South Point.
 • A lake freighter enters Muskegon's harbor with a load of coal.
 • Ludington Pumped Storage Plant utilizes Lake Michigan water to store potential energy.
 • The Bay Harbor development rises from a former cement plant and quarry.

Allegan County

For much of Allegan County, public access to the shore is poor. Having said that, a few gems are worth the trip. For the most part, the shore area has a rural flavor. Towns are few. The side-by-side municipalities of Saugatuck and Douglas form the only city area until reaching the influence of Holland at the county's northern edge. The first ten miles of Allegan shore north of Van Buren County, have no significant public land and bluffs line most of the coast here until reaching Saugatuck. At Saugatuck, dunes take over, dominating the shoreline up to Lake Macatawa in Ottawa County.

The Saugatuck-Douglas area draws tourists for both its beaches and its "artsy" flavor. Galleries are plentiful in the several blocks that form the delightful shopping center of Saugatuck. Sculpture and other art forms inhabit the streetscape and parks. The city has a quaint atmosphere void of national business chains. The town harbor, formed by the Kalamazoo River and Kalamazoo Lake, gives a marine flavor as well. Much of the business district sits along the waterfront. During the summer, finding a parking place can be difficult but a visit is worth the effort.

The county's most obvious public parcels are Oval Beach in Saugatuck and Saugatuck Dunes State Park north of town. Each is a wonderland of sand but with different perspectives. Oval Beach features the amenities of changehouses, concessions and close-to-the-shore parking. Mt. Baldhead and its trails lie to its east. Saugatuck Dunes has several miles of natural beach with virtually no development. You must hike a mile through forested dunes to reach the shore. Both have an entrance fee, although you can enter Saugatuck Dunes via Shore Acres Park without paying.

A few lesser known parks provide free access. Try West Side County Park, Douglas Beach or Laketown Township Beach for a nice day at the shore. West Side has a full range of facilities including modern restrooms and play equipment. It is a bit off-the-beaten track. Douglas Beach is small and integrated into its laid-back shore community. Although summer residences are next to Laketown Beach, the beach is still quite isolated. The view from its dunes is spectacular.

The US-31 / I-196 freeway serves as the main artery along this portion of the coast. Blue Star Highway, 70th Street and Lakeshore Drive skirt the shore south of Saugatuck. To the north, 66th Street follows the coast toward Ottawa County. Bluffs, dunes and trees prevent all but a few glimpses of the lake during your drive.

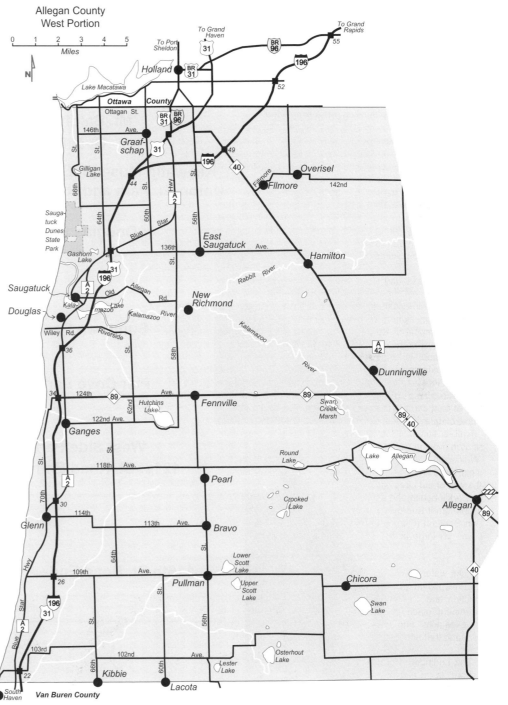

Allegan County West Portion

Below top: Downtown Saugatuck and Kalamazoo Lake from Mt. Baldhead.

Below bottom: Like many road ends, the one at 121st Street offers no amenities just a simple trail to the sand shore.

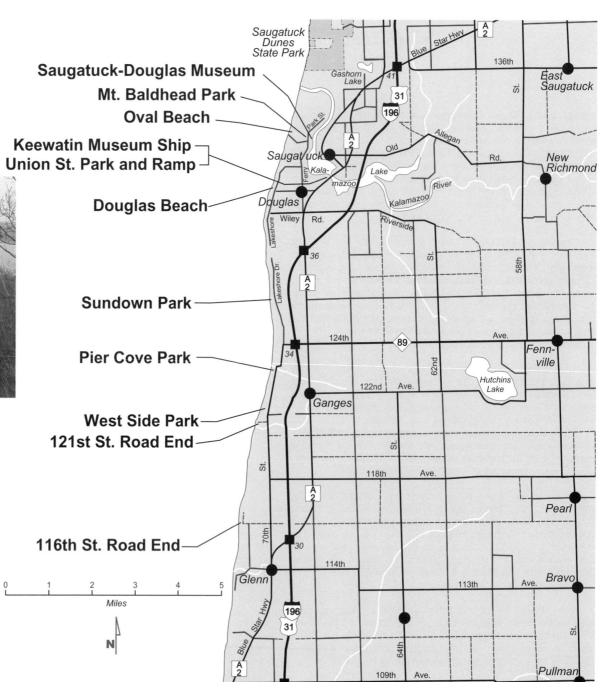

Saugatuck-Douglas Museum
Mt. Baldhead Park
Oval Beach
Keewatin Museum Ship
Union St. Park and Ramp
Douglas Beach
Sundown Park
Pier Cove Park
West Side Park
121st St. Road End
116th St. Road End

Allegan County

Van Buren County Line to Saugatuck

Facilities   **Environment**

Name	Location	Entrance Fee	Parking	Modern Restrooms	Vault or Portable Toilet	Stair or Path to Shore	Swimming	Picnic Area	Drinking Water	Campground	Trailered Boat Launch	Kayak / Canoe	Marina	Fishing	Hiking	Biking	X-Country Skiing	Playground	Lighthouse	Beach Strolling	Sandy Beach	Stony or Rocky Shore	Dunes	Bluff	Wetland
116th Street Road End	1.5 miles N of Glenn. From I-196 exit 30 SW on Blue Star Hwy then N on 70th one mile to 116th.					●	●														●			●	
121st Street Road End	5.5 miles S of Douglas. From I-196 exit 34 W on 124th S on Lakeshore Dr. and 70th Ave.		●			●	●					●									●				
West Side Park	4.5 miles S of Douglas. From I-196 exit 34 W on 124th S on Lakeshore Dr. and 70th Ave.		●	●		●	●	●	●									●			●			●	
Pier Cove Park	70th Ave., 0.5 miles W of I-196 exit 34 on 124th Ave then S on Lakeshore Dr.		●			●	●	●													●				
Sundown Park	1 mile N of I-196 exit 34. W on 124th Ave then N on Lakeshore Dr.		●					●																●	
Douglas Beach	Douglas. Lakeshore Drive.		●	●		●	●	●	●												●			●	
Oval Beach	Saugatuck. Take Ferry St. N then W on Perryman Beach Rd.	●	●	●			●	●	●										●		●		●		
Mt. Baldhead Park	Saugatuck. Take Ferry St. N then straight on Park Rd.		●	●		●		●							●								●		
Saugatuck-Douglas Museum	Saugatuck. Take Ferry St. N then straight on Park Rd.		●	●																					
Union Street Park & Ramp	Douglas. From Blue Arrow Hwy., turn N on Union St.		●		●			●			●	●		●											
Keewatin Museum Ship	Douglas. From Blue Arrow Hwy., turn N on Union St.	●	●		●																				

The south shore of Allegan County is mostly private. West Side Park provides the best access south of the Douglas-Saugatuck area.

116TH STREET ROAD END: A primitive path leads down a steep bluff to the sandy beach. There is room for one car to park.
   GPS: 42°39.855'N; 86°12.913'W

121ST STREET ROAD END: South of West County Park a short distance, the road end at 121st has a nice sandy beach. Parking is primitive and access is down a short, sandy path. The path is flat, so a canoe or kayak carry is reasonable. Plummerville Creek flows into the lake nearby. *Note: This short, gravel section of 121st Avenue is located south of the main portion of 121st Street.*

WEST SIDE PARK: West Side County Park provides one of the few, and certainly the best, public beach access points between Douglas and South Haven. The park is about 11 acres with a large playground, small baseball field and well-shaded picnic grounds on the bluff above the lake. Stairways lead to a 1000-foot-wide sand beach on Lake Michigan. Swimming is excellent. Parking is very good. Facilities are well kept.
   GPS: 42°36.454'N; 86°13.570'W

PIER COVE PARK: Pier Cove once was a thriving town during the lumber boom until the late 1880's. When the timber supply exhausted, the town warehoused and shipped fruit. By the early 1900's, shipping ceased and the town failed. This small beach park sits where the town and pier once stood. Parking consists of ten spaces on 70th Avenue. A stairway leads to the beach below.
   GPS: 42°35.170'N; 86°13.590'W

SUNDOWN PARK: A small park between residences along the dead end section of Lakeshore Drive, Sundown sits on a bluff with a view of the lake below. The steep bluff does not have access to the beach.
   GPS: 42°36.454'N; 86°13.570'W

DOUGLAS BEACH: The Douglas lakeshore sits above the lake on a bluff. Look for the red-brick, red-roofed restroom building which sits along the Lakeshore Drive atop the bluff. A couple of picnic tables and a grill are there as well. A stairway leads down to the 150-foot wide sandy beach. Old summer homes and trees line the streets in this area just the way you would have pictured it forty years earlier.
   GPS: 42°38.625'N; 86°13.559'W

OVAL BEACH: Oval is a full-service beach with concessions, changehouse, big parking lots and plenty of sandy beach. Add to this the dunes behind the lakefront with trails on Mt. Baldhead. Picnic grounds are in the forested area behind the beach. To the north, off park property, sits the reconstructed Kalamazoo River Lighthouse. Trails connect Oval Beach with Mt. Baldhead Park on the Kalamazoo River. Expect crowds on summer days.
   GPS: 42°39.855'N; 86°12.913'W

MT. BALDHEAD PARK: This park is located on the "backside" of Oval Beach near the end of Park Street along the Kalamazoo River. A tall stairway leads to the top of Mt. Baldhead. From the top, look down on Saugatuck across the river. Continue to the east on the trail to reach Oval Beach. A picnic pavilion is located at the parking area. The staircase climb is arduous. Pedestrian access can be made from downtown Saugatuck by crossing the Kalamazoo River via the hand-cranked "chain ferry" and then walking one block north.

SAUGATUCK-DOUGLAS HISTORICAL MUSEUM: The local museum is located along the Kalamazoo River across from the Mt. Baldhead Park. Open in season. The small museum also has outdoor interpretive displays on the riverfront that can be viewed anytime.

UNION STREET PARK & BOAT RAMP: Found along Kalamazoo Lake, the park has an excellent boat ramp. It is the closest launch point to reach Lake Michigan via the Kalamazoo River Channel.

KEEWATIN MUSEUM SHIP: Tours are available during the summer of the docked passenger ship *Keewatin*. The tall and narrow ship plied Lake Huron until the first half of the 20th Century and provides a feel for the days when passenger service was common on the Great Lakes. Located at Union Street Park.
   Telephone: (269) 857-2876
   web: www.kewatinmaritimemuseum.com
   GPS: 42°38.813'N; 86°12.173'W

Above: The stairway descent over the dune to Lakewood Township Beach follows an equally tall ascent from the parking area.

Below: Saugatuck Dunes.

Opposite page: The dock walkway along the Kalamazoo River near Wicks Park, downtown Saugatuck.

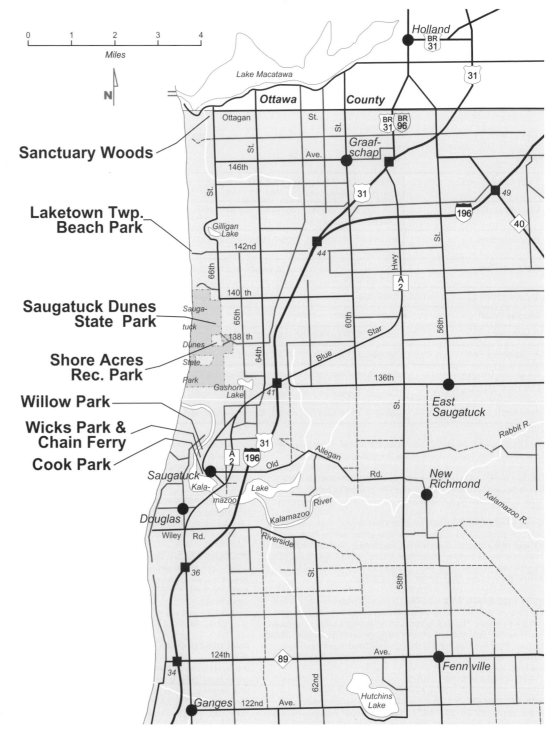

Allegan County

Saugatuck Downtown and Dunes to the North

Name	Location	Entrance Fee	Parking	Modern Restrooms	Vault or Portable Toilet	Stair or Path to Shore	Swimming	Picnic Area	Drinking Water	Campground	Trailered Boat Launch	Kayak / Canoe	Marina	Fishing	Hiking	Biking	X-Country Skiing	Playground	Lighthouse	Beach Strolling	Sandy Beach	Stony or Rocky Shore	Dunes	Bluff	Wetland
Cook Park	Saugatuck, downtown. Culver St. near Butler St.		●		●			●																	
Wicks Park & Chain Ferry	Saugatuck, downtown. Water Street at Main St.		●	●					●																
Willow Park	Saugatuck. Lucy and Water Streets.		●																						
Shore Acres Recreation Park	3 miles N of Saugatuck. 138th Ave., one mile W of 64th St.		●		●	●	●								●		●			●	●		●		
Saugatuck Dunes State Park	3 miles N of Saugatuck. 138th Ave., 1.2 miles W of 64th St.	●	●		●	●	●	●	●						●		●			●	●		●		
Laketown Township Beach Park	4.5 miles N of Saugatuck. 142nd Ave., 0.5 miles W of 66th.		●		●	●	●													●	●		●		
Sanctuary Woods	4 miles W of Holland. 66th Street between Ottogan and 147th Ave.		●												●									●	

Saugatuck is a trendy summer town that hops during the summer. The town's shops and galleries lie within a block of Kalamazoo Lake. Saugatuck Dunes, just north of town, offers quiet shoreline for those willing to hike the mile to shore.

COOK PARK: A small, grassy park along the waterfront and marina area in downtown Saugatuck, it has picnic tables available and shops nearby. Street parking only.
   GPS: 42°39.294'N; 86°12.261'W

WICKS PARK & CHAIN FERRY: Wicks Park is in the midst of Saugatuck's harbor and next to the "chain ferry" which takes pedestrians across the Kalamazoo River in the summer. Here you can view the commotion of this busy tourist town. Across the street are art galleries. Local sculpture enhances the park. A boardwalk lines the channel if you wish to take a short stroll. Parking is limited to the street and difficult to find on prime summer days.
   GPS: 42°39.461'N; 86°12.326'W

WILLOW PARK: Willow Park lies along the Kalamazoo River on the north side of town. It has a small platform with benches and is a good place to view pleasure craft entering and leaving Saugatuck's harbor. Restrooms can be found four blocks south at Wicks Park. Parking is limited to the street and difficult to find in the summer.
   GPS: 42°39.650'N; 86°12.325'W

SHORE ACRES RECREATION PARK: Follow signs for Saugatuck Dunes State Park, then turn off 138th Street when you see the Shore Acres sign. The park is managed by Laketown Township for general recreational purposes. A picnic area as well as basketball, baseball, soccer and sledding facilities form the basis of the park. The area once housed a seminary and later a prison. The 17,000 square foot, 3-story, Felt Mansion, currently being restored, sits on the site.

This park does not lie on Lake Michigan. The large parking lot provides an alternate trailhead for Saugatuck Dunes State Park's trail system. Various trails lead to the Lake Michigan beach or to the dune overlooks. See next listing.

SAUGATUCK DUNES STATE PARK: Saugatuck Dunes is an 1100-acre natural area made of forest, dunes and beach. Thirteen miles of trails traverse the largely undeveloped park. You must do some hiking to use any of its lakeshore. A relatively flat, mile-long path leads to the beach. Be prepared to pack in your food and water if you will be at the beach for the day. Longer paths and loops are available for hikers and skiers. The sandy beach stretches 2.5 miles. Much of it is lined with 200-foot-high dunes. The southern portion of the dunes is a designated natural area. The parking area has vault toilets, tables, grills and a pavilion. Laketown Township's Shore Acres Recreation Park, listed above, is an inholding within the state park area and an alternative for parking. Michigan State Park Motor Vehicle Permit required.
   Telephone: (269) 637-2788
   Web: www.michigan.gov/dnr

LAKETOWN TOWNSHIP BEACH PARK: A beautiful sandy beach accessed by a long stair and boardwalk system characterizes the small park that seems larger than it is. The walkway provides a great overlook of the lake from the tall dune. The beach is about 100 feet wide and quite deep. Private residences bookend the park. Parking is limited to 20 cars with no legal place nearby to park when it is full. This will not be a problem off-season but you may need to get there early on a sunny, summer day. Development has been limited to the paved parking and dune-protecting boardwalk.
   GPS: 42°43.512'N; 86°12.250'W

SANCTUARY WOODS: Sanctuary Woods lies just south of Lake Macatawa. A trail, with a long staircase, circles through the hardwood forest. There are views of Lake Macatawa and beyond to Lake Michigan but no shore access. The vegetation obscures the sight during the summer foliage. The trail is no more than one mile long. The parking lot is paved.

Coastal Cities

Some small towns and a few mid-sized cities rest along the coastline featured in this book. On this side of Lake Michigan, no large urban center exists like Chicago or Milwaukee across the way. Several of these municipalities lie within a block or two of the shore, combining its beach or harbor with shopping and commerce. Art galleries, fudge shops, patio restaurants and boutiques thrive in this environment of tourists and summer residents. Here is a brief overview of the coastal towns, starting from the Indiana border.

Within a short few minutes you can walk from New Buffalo, St. Joseph or South Haven town centers to their beaches. Shops and restaurants make up most of New Buffalo's two-block business district. St. Joseph's downtown sits on a bluff. Walk along the St. Joseph River to Silver Beach and its south breakwater. South Haven also has a nice river

walk ending at South Beach, the breakwater and lighthouse. On the other side of the river is more beach plus the Michigan Maritime Museum, a small but enlightening educational morsel. Saugatuck and Douglas are towns grounded in the visual arts. Galleries make up much of Saugatuck's downtown storefronts and artwork punctuates the town's parks. A hand-cranked, "chain-guided" passenger ferry crosses the Kalamazoo River to the Oval Beach area.

Holland, Grand Haven and Muskegon comprise part of a large population center that reaches inland towards Grand Rapids. Holland celebrates its Dutch heritage with tulips and wooden shoes. The city center lies well to the east of Lake Michigan on the bay-like Lake Macatawa. Grand Haven has small shops along its marina parkland on the Grand River. In the summer, the Music Fountain puts on a nightly music and light show. Muskegon has a number of fine beaches as well as Michigan's largest amusement park, which is within minutes of the lakeshore.

On the central coast, try Pentwater for a neat village with a quiet, relaxed atmosphere. At Ludington, the Lake Michigan Car Ferry Service crosses to Manitowoc, Wisconsin. The city has begun to reshape its waterfront as past industrial sites get converted to recreational use. Manistee stretches along its namesake river down to the shore. A riverfront walkway makes the connection. Unique, small-town shops lie next to the walk. Sitting directly on its waterfront, Frankfort has shed its image as a railroad and ferry terminus. With these transportation functions abandoned, sportfishing and a trendy downtown have reshaped the economy. Each of these towns features a large charter fishing fleet. Fishing has a major impact, especially in the late summer, so prepare for some crowds.

The Leelanau County towns of Suttons Bay, Northport, Leland, Glen Arbor and Empire are small communities that offer a relaxed taste of summer life. As a combination, they make a great day trip when driving Highway M-22 around the Leelanau Peninsula. Suttons Bay has grown the fastest. It features a waterfront arts event and a small jazz festival in July. Several wineries and numerous orchards dot the space between the villages. See the feature, *A Leelanau Day Trip*, on page 126 for more detail.

Traverse City continues its fast-paced growth making it the commerce center of northern Michigan. No longer the sleepy town on the bay, it now blends a portion of the old summer destination with its newer role as a convention and resort center. Numerous hotel rooms line the East Bay. The National Cherry Festival held in early July is one of the largest week-long celebrations in the nation. It consumes the city. Daily parades, national acts, an air show, fireworks and cherry pie eating contests are some of the fun events.

To the north, Elk Rapids, Charlevoix, Petoskey and Harbor Springs have long served the tourist and summer resident. Just far enough away from Traverse City, Elk Rapids keeps a small town atmosphere with nice shops and a bayside park with many features. Charlevoix's shops face Lake Charlevoix and you will enjoy the short walk along the Pine River Channel to its beach on Lake Michigan. Petoskey's shopping area is larger and more varied. Its Bayfront Park lines the entire waterfront offering a variety of activities like walking, biking and in-line skating. Harbor Springs sports a cozy beach, compact shopping district and marina all within a four block area. The galleries are top-notch. Several restaurants, from the swank to the casual, fall into its mix. Old Victorian cottages in Harbor Springs and the Bayview section of Petoskey attest to their long role in "vacation history."

At the end of the trail lies Mackinaw City where the past and present truly meet. Fort Michilimackinac, a colonial restoration, sits next to the nearly 50-year-old, yet still modern, Mackinac Bridge. Passenger ferries ply the Straits of Mackinac to the car-less Mackinac Island and new hotels continue to pop up on the mainland shore. Here, Lake Huron takes on Lake Michigan's flow and with it a future adventure.

The coastal cities have art, shopping and summer festivals ... ... connecting to their primary draw, the beach and waterfront.

Ottawa County

The Ottawa County shore starts at Holland and runs nearly straight north to the Grand Haven area. Holland and Grand Haven are small cities. Dutch immigrants settled the area giving it a dash of flavor from their former homeland. The tourist season starts with the spring tulip blooms and continues through the early fall.

Grand Haven sits along the Grand River a short distance upstream from its mouth. A walk along the south side of the river takes you from the town to the beach. Along the way, you walk past the marina, the Coast Guard Station and a number of shops. The town features a nightly musical light show along the riverfront during the summer. Grand Haven has one of the best town and shore atmospheres on the coast.

Boaters use the channeled harbors located at Holland, Port Sheldon and Grand Haven. Much of the shore is private with public parks regularly sprinkled between strings of lakefront homes. Pure sand forms the beaches. Notable lighthouses mark the breakwaters at Lake Macatawa and the Grand River. The area will satisfy the fisher, swimmer, and sun-worshiper.

Ottawa County has a fine network of bicycle routes connecting virtually all of the local area with the shoreline. One asphalt path follows Lakeshore Avenue connecting Ottawa Beach near Holland to Grand Haven. Along the way, it passes three county parks on the coast. Tunnel Park features numerous recreational activities in addition to its beach. Kirk Park has a natural, wooded environment intermixed with modern conveniences and a sandy shore. Rosy Mound Natural Area blends into the area almost unnoticed just south of Grand Haven. North Park, near Ferrysburg, is a fourth county-operated beach park. It has a dune walk behind the developed portion. Holland and Grand Haven State Parks provide access to adjacent breakwaters. Each has a large sandy beach plus unique, shore-side camping.

As you travel north, US-31 continues as the main transportation artery near the shoreline. Unlike the southwest portion of the coast, it is farther away from the water. Lakeshore Avenue provides the primary shore access in most of the county. North Shore Drive offers access to the shore north of the Grand River near Ferrysburg.

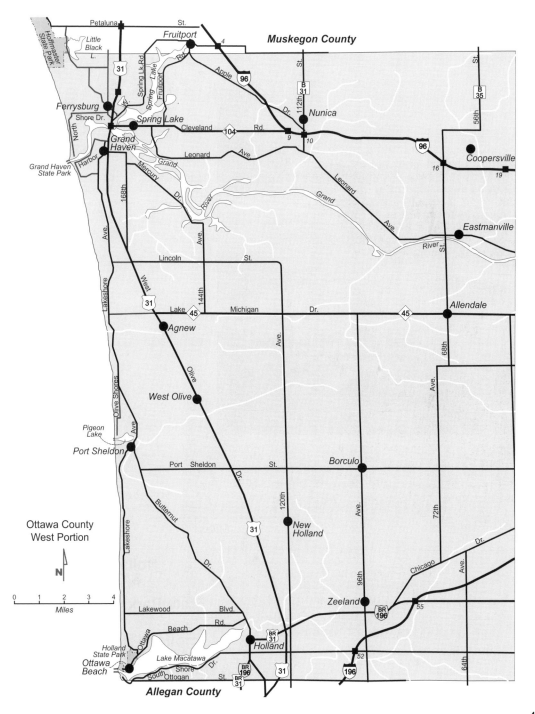

Left: At Kollen Park, "The Immigrants" celebrate Holland's link to the Netherlands.

Above: Dubbed "Big Red," the Holland Harbor Lighthouse is photogenic but hard to visit. See the description for details.

Opposite page: The beach at Holland State Park sits by the channel to Lake Macatawa. The Holland Harbor Lighthouse lies across the channel in good view.

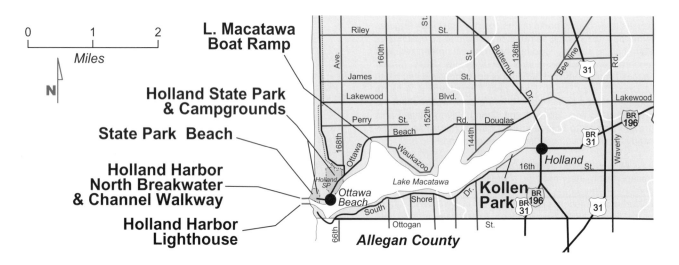

Ottawa County

Lake Macatawa and Holland

Name	Location	Entrance Fee	Parking	Modern Restrooms	Vault or Portable Toilet	Stair or Path to Shore	Swimming	Picnic Area	Drinking Water	Campground	Trailered Boat Launch	Kayak / Canoe	Marina	Fishing	Hiking	Biking	X-Country Skiing	Playground	Lighthouse	Beach Strolling	Sandy Beach	Stony or Rocky Shore	Dunes	Bluff	Wetland
Holland Harbor Lighthouse	7 miles W of Holland at end of South Shore Dr.		●			●													●						
Kollen Park	Holland. Kollen Park Dr. at 12th or 10th & Van Raalke St.		●	●				●	●		●	●		●				●							
Lake Macatawa Boat Ramp	4 Miles W of Holland on Ottawa Beach Rd.	●	●	●							●	●													
Holland State Park	8 mile W of Holland at end of Ottawa Beach Rd.	●	●	●			●	●	●	●		●		●		●					●				
Holland State Park Beach	Holland State Park at end of Ottawa Beach Rd.	●	●	●			●	●	●												●				
Lake Michigan Campground	Holland State Park at end of Ottawa Beach Rd.	●	●	●												●					●				
Lake Macatawa Campground	Holland State Park. Lake Macatawa Unit on Ottawa Beach Rd.	●	●	●		●	●		●	●				●		●		●			●				
North Breakwater & Channel Walkway	8 mile W of Holland at end of Ottawa Beach Rd.	●	●	●		●	●							●							●				

As the city's name implies, Holland features a Dutch heritage to go with its sandy beaches and fine parks. The city and its environs surround Lake Macatawa, its harbor.

HOLLAND HARBOR LIGHTHOUSE: The south breakwater of Holland Harbor can only be accessed through private lands. In recent years, local citizens forged an agreement with the owners to allow some public access for visiting the Holland Harbor Lighthouse affectionately known as "Big Red." Point West Properties provides four, one-hour parking spaces and path access to the lighthouse breakwater. Other restrictions apply. A private security guard provides details and determines admittance. The access agreement is cumbersome, but reduces the controversy produced when the owners prohibited all public access in the mid-1990's. The agreement could be altered at any time, so you should inquire locally before visiting. Generally, the policy is in effect from Memorial to Labor Day. Follow the South Shore Drive along Lake Macatawa until it ends at the security shack for Point West. Contact the security guard for instructions.
GPS: 42°46.136'N; 86°12.253'W (parking lot)

KOLLEN PARK: A large, city park in downtown Holland located at the east end of Lake Macatawa. The park features a large grassy area, picnic grounds and a playground. A concrete, barrier-free, walkway borders the waterfront. The deep boat ramp is located at the west end of the park. Docks for visitors needing temporary mooring can be found at the east end of the park. The channel to Lake Michigan is about 5.5 miles to the west.
GPS: 42°47.194'N; 86°07.430'W (Kollen Park Dr. & 12th)

LAKE MACATAWA BOAT RAMP: This DNR ramp is the closest public boat launch on Lake Macatawa to the Lake Michigan channel. The ramp is equipped to launch large trailered boats. The parking lot has 217 spaces. The channel to Lake Michigan is about 2 miles away. Fee for launching.
GPS: 42°47.505'N; 86°11.235'W

HOLLAND STATE PARK: Holland State Park has a number of things packed into its 143 acres. Beaches and campgrounds comprise the primary development at the very popular park. Access the north breakwater of Holland Harbor from its Lake Michigan beach. The picturesque Holland Harbor Lighthouse can be seen across the channel. Picnic grounds line the channel. Parts of the park lay along Lake Macatawa as well. Michigan State Park Motor Vehicle Permit required.
Telephone: (616) 399-9300
GPS: 42°46.822'N; 86°11.745'W

HOLLAND STATE PARK BEACH: The sandy beach has a large parking lot, concession and changing facilities.
GPS: 42°46.394'N; 86°12.450'W

LAKE MICHIGAN CAMPGROUND: Lake Michigan Campground lies just to the east of the beachhouse. The campground is paved and unshaded accommodating trailers and motorhomes. Shifting sand requires this odd campsite arrangement.

LAKE MACATAWA CAMPGROUND: A separate campground is found at the park's Lake Macatawa Unit a short distance to east. This campground has a more traditional landscape with unpaved sites and shade. Across the road from the campground is a camper's beach on Lake Macatawa. This could be used for a canoe or kayak launch as well. Paddle distance to the channel is short.
GPS: 42°46.736'N; 86°11.929'W

NORTH BREAKWATER & CHANNEL WALKWAY : Located at the south end of Holland Park's Beach, the breakwater is a free, Corps of Engineers facility but the only close-by parking is at the Holland State Park Beach which requires the Michigan State Park Motor Vehicle Permit. To the visitor, the breakwater appears part of the state park. The park's beachhouse facilities are a short walk. Fishing from the breakwater and channel walkway is popular. It also provides a photographic perch for viewing the Holland Harbor Lighthouse, considered by many as the most picturesque and unique lighthouse on the lake. Locally, it is referred to as "Big Red" owing to the color of the gabled-roof structure.

Above: A tunnel through the dune gives Tunnel Park its name.

Left: The covered platform at Kirk County Park is barrier-free and provides a great overlook as the day ends.

Opposite page: The similar beaches at the end of Riley and James Streets provide quiet getaways with no cost.

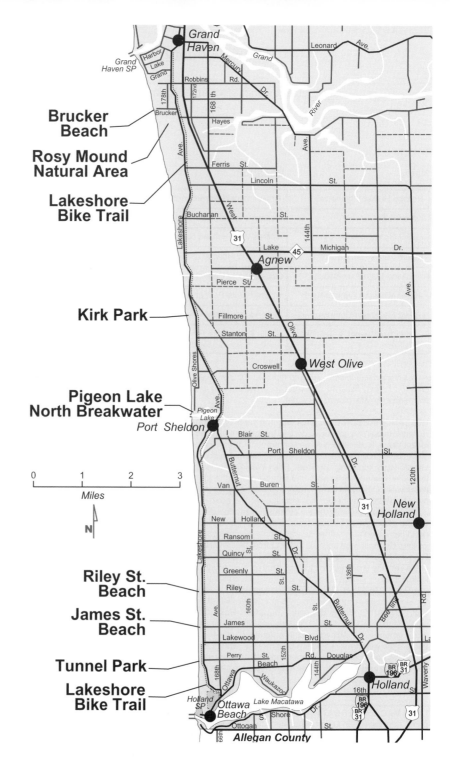

Ottawa County

Lakeshore Avenue Parks

Name	Location	Entrance Fee	Parking	Modern Restrooms	Vault or Portable Toilet	Stair or Path to Shore	Swimming	Picnic Area	Drinking Water	Campground	Trailered Boat Launch	Kayak / Canoe	Marina	Fishing	Hiking	Biking	X-Country Skiing	Playground	Lighthouse	Beach Strolling	Sandy Beach	Stony or Rocky Shore	Dunes	Bluff	Wetland
Lakeshore Bike Trail	Along Lakeshore Ave. from Holland State Park to Grand Haven.														●	●									
Tunnel Park	7 miles W of Holland. Lakeshore Ave. just S of Lakewood Ave.	●	●	●		●	●	●	●									●			●		●		
James Street Beach	7 miles W of Holland. James St. at just W of Lakeshore Ave.		●			●	●														●			●	
Riley Street Road End	7 miles W of Holland. Riley St. at just W of Lakeshore Ave.		●			●	●														●			●	
Pigeon Lake Boat Launch	Port Sheldon. Lakeshore Ave. north side of highway bridge.	●	●		●						●	●													
Pigeon Lake Channel North Breakwater	4 miles W of West Olive in Port Sheldon area. End of Olive Shores Dr. W of Lakeshore Dr.		●			●								●											
Kirk Park	8 miles S of Grand Haven on Lakeshore Drive N of Stanton St.	●	●	●		●	●	●	●						●		●	●		●	●		●	●	
Rosy Mound Natural Area	3 miles S of Grand Haven on Lakeshore Drive.		●			●	●								●					●	●		●		
Brucker Beach Access	End of Brucker St. just W of Lakeshore Ave. 2.5 miles S of Grand Haven.					●	●														●				

The shore from the Ottawa Beach Area to the Grand Haven city limit is mostly private. Lakeshore Drive parallels the coast but offers no lake views. The Ottawa County Parks and the Lakeshore Trail are highlights.

LAKESHORE BIKE TRAIL: A nearly 20-mile-long paved bike path parallels Lakeshore Drive connecting Ottawa Beach with Grand Haven. A number of spur routes join this pathway from the east. A brochure is available locally that maps the western Ottawa County bike routes. The pathway directly passes most of the other listings on this page.

TUNNEL PARK: Tunnel Park gets its name from the tunnel cut through the dune between the parking lot and beach. To the west of the dune is a pure sand beach. The beach is very wide and several hundred feet long. Swimming is excellent. The east side of the dune has a picnic area, two shelters, several beach volleyball courts, changehouse and concession. A large playground next to the dune gives the children plenty to do. There is a stairway up the dune as well. Parking fee is charged from late-May to mid-September. Some free street parking is available in the area. The park is closed in winter. Administered by Ottawa County.
GPS: 42°47.882'N; 86°12.405'W

JAMES STREET BEACH: This is a sandy beach in a residential area. A short path leads to the beach. Parking is limited to a couple of cars.

RILEY STREET ROAD END: Like James Street Beach just to the south, Riley Street has no facilities, requires a short walk to the beach and has limited parking.
GPS: 42°48.722'N; 86°12.035'W

PIGEON LAKE BOAT LAUNCH: Small craft can launch at the DNR access site on Pigeon Lake. Lake Michigan can be accessed through the channel about one mile to the west.
GPS: 42°54.261'N; 86°11.885'W

PIGEON LAKE CHANNEL NORTH BREAKWATER: Public access to Lake Michigan in the Port Sheldon area is poor at best. Port Sheldon Township Park, listed on some maps, has been posted for township residents only. Consumers Energy, however, has an unusual access point for the public at its Campbell Generating Plant. Unusual, because you constantly move from an industrial setting to a more natural one. It begins by winding through a fenced-in drive. Very soon you are staring at the smokestacks of the plant. After parking, a boardwalk leads to the north breakwater. To your left is Pigeon Lake. To the right is the fencing separating you from the private lands to the north. Once on the breakwater, industry reappears as you share the breakwater with a large pipeline. There is no shore access, but you can fish or view a sunset. To their credit, Consumers Energy has done the best they could. The boardwalk is first-rate with benches and platforms along the way. The atmosphere is unusual and like no other along the lakeshore!
GPS: 42°54.299'N; 86°12.302'W

KIRK PARK: Part of the Ottawa County park system, Kirk is in a pleasant, natural setting of wooded dunes and bluffs. The development is new and modern. The third-of-a-mile-long beach is sandy and easily accessed down a paved path. The concession is open in the summer. Hiking and ski trails pass through the woods with views of Lake Michigan. A lodge building is also available. Parking fee is charged from late May to mid-September.
GPS: 42°59.180'N; 86°13.475'W

ROSY MOUND NATURAL AREA: Recently, Ottawa County finished its new park at Rosy Mound. It is a natural area development of the 160-acre parcel with designated path-stairway system to reach the 3400 feet of sandy beach. The walk to the shore is about 0.7 miles through hardwoods and over Rosy Mound. Area includes about 2.5 miles of hiking trails.

BRUCKER BEACH ACCESS: This park is essentially a road end two blocks west of Lakeshore Ave. The shore is sandy with limited beach width. Parking is limited to the street, however no parking is allowed along the road near the road end so you will need to walk some. A narrow sandy path leads a few hundred feet to the beach.
GPS: 43°02.008'N; 86°14.171'W

Below left: Grand Haven's Lighthouses guard the South Breakwater at Grand Haven State Park.

Below right: Grand Haven's Municipal Marina sits amid shops and along the waterfront walkway on the Grand River. During the summer, the world's largest musical fountain puts on a nightly light show.

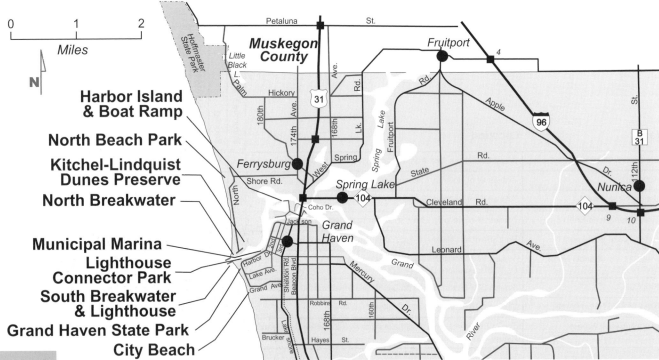

Harbor Island & Boat Ramp

North Beach Park

Kitchel-Lindquist Dunes Preserve

North Breakwater

Municipal Marina

Lighthouse Connector Park

South Breakwater & Lighthouse

Grand Haven State Park

City Beach

Name	Location	Entrance Fee	Parking	Modern Restrooms	Vault or Portable Toilet	Stair or Path to Shore	Swimming	Picnic Area	Drinking Water	Campground	Trailered Boat Launch	Kayak / Canoe	Marina	Fishing	Hiking	Biking	X-Country Skiing	Playground	Lighthouse	Beach Strolling	Sandy Beach	Stony or Rocky Shore	Dunes	Bluff	Wetland
City Beach	Grand Haven. Harbor Drive about 1 mile SW of downtown.		●				●					●								●	●				
Grand Haven State Park	Grand Haven. Harbor Drive about 1 mile SW of downtown.	●	●	●			●	●	●	●				●				●	●	●	●		●		
Grand Haven South Breakwater and Lighthouse	Grand Haven. Harbor Drive about 1 mile SW of downtown.						●							●					●		●				
Lighthouse Connector Park	Grand Haven. Downtown to Grand Haven State Park along Harbor Dr. & south side of Grand River.													●	●										
Grand Haven Municipal Marina	Grand Haven. Harbor Drive.		●	●				●	●				●												
Harbor Island & Boat Ramp	Grand Haven. Harbor Island. Enter via Coho Drive near US-31 drawbridge. From downtown, enter via 3rd Street. (see listing)		●	●	●				●		●	●		●	●	●									
Grand Haven North Breakwater	From Ferrysburg, follow North Shore Rd. to end.		●		●									●											
Kitchel-Lindquist Dunes Preserve	From Ferrysburg, North Shore Rd to Berwyck St.		●	●					●						●								●		
North Beach Park	Ferrysburg. North Beach Rd. at North Shore Dr.	●	●	●			●	●	●						●				●			●		●		

Grand Haven and Ferrysburg wrap around the Grand River's outflow into Lake Michigan. Sportfishing, boating and beach-going share top billing. Grand Haven's business district revolves around the waterfront.

CITY BEACH: Located on the south edge of Grand Haven State Park, City Beach essentially adds another couple hundred feet of public beach frontage to the larger park to its north. Aside from the parking lot, there are no facilities as part of this park. State Park facilities are close by.
  GPS: 43°03.072'N; 86°14.683'W

GRAND HAVEN STATE PARK: Grand Haven is a small, unique park on the south side of the Grand River's channel to Lake Michigan. It, along with the adjoining breakwater and City Beach Park, form the primary Grand Haven lakerfront. The park is literally the beach and the beach is pure sand. The concession and beachhouse harken back a few decades as this beach has drawn swimmers and sunworshippers for many years. It has camping, geared to trailers, in a paved, parking-lot-like setting. The pavement keeps some of the sand tacked down but the westerly winds move the sand constantly, drifting it in to the lot, camping area, roadways and every crack and crevice. Sunny, summer days make for a packed house. The Harbor Trolley bus operates from town to the park Memorial to Labor Day. This is a good way to avoid the parking hassle, and motor vehicle fee, on those crowded days. A separate parking lot is available for fishermen using the breakwater. State Park Motor Vehicle Permit required.
  GPS: 43°03.369'N; 86°14.871'W

GRAND HAVEN SOUTH BREAKWATER AND LIGHTHOUSE: Grand Haven's south breakwater has two classy lights connected to the shore by the south breakwater and a lighted catwalk. The breakwater is a favorite of fishermen and walkers. It abuts Grand Haven State Park. Technically free, the closest parking is at the state park, which has a motor vehicle fee. Park restroom facilities are convenient to the breakwater. The state park swimming beach lies next to the breakwater as well. The Lighthouse Connector Park walkway leads east to downtown, about one mile away.

LIGHTHOUSE CONNECTOR PARK: Grand Haven has constructed a fine walkway to connect the town to the Grand Haven Lighthouse on the south breakwater. The length is a bit more than a mile. It passes the marina, the Waterfront Stadium, the new Coast Guard Station and continues on to end at Grand Haven State Park. The stadium hosts a number of summer events including the nightly "Musical Fountain," a display of music, lights and water choreography.

GRAND HAVEN MUNICIPAL MARINA: This is a modern public marina along the Grand River a short distance from the channel to Lake Michigan. It has 51 slips available.
  GPS: 43°03.270'N; 86°15.260'W

HARBOR ISLAND & BOAT RAMP: Harbor Island sits in the Grand River near downtown Grand Haven. A picnic shelter, walkway and benches are located at its southwest end. Here a paved linear park starts heading east along the river providing a path for bicyclists, skaters and walkers. The north side of the island has a major boat ramp capable of handling large trailered boats. From here it is a short distance down river to Lake Michigan. A launch fee is charged. Near the ramp is a new restroom building and a pier. Kayak launching is easy and free near the pier. If traveling north on US-31, turn right just before the Grand River Bridge and follow the road under the bridge to the park. From US-31 southbound, take the first right after crossing the bridge. From downtown, travel 3rd Street to the north.

GRAND HAVEN NORTH BREAKWATER: There is no public access to the beach around the north breakwater but you can fish or stroll on the pier. There is a good view of the Grand Haven Lights on the south breakwater. The Old Coast Guard buildings, which are in private ownership, are also in view.
  GPS: 43°03.539'N; 86°14.967'W

KITCHEL-LINDQUIST DUNES PRESERVE: A 112-acre sand dune preserve located near the north breakwater area, it features a self-guided trail that points out many of the hardy dune plants.
  GPS: 43°03.539'N; 86°14.731'W

NORTH BEACH PARK: A 20-acre park with 745 feet of sandy shore, North Beach facilities are relatively new. The park has two parts, the shore and the sand dune interpretation area. The beach side of the road has nice playground equipment, a picnic area and a covered pavilion. There is a seasonal concession as well. A series of boardwalk, trail and stairway leads to the top of a dune blow-out. A barrier-free beach walkway makes this one of the friendlier beach parks for special-needs access. A parking fee is charged from late May until mid-September.
  GPS: 43°04.908'N; 86°15.136'W

Winter Fun

Winter along the shore means drifting snow, natural ice sculpture and few people. For years, the lake's winter has drawn me to the coast to walk the frozen sand, ski the open dunes and enjoy the solitude that the colder months bring.

Ice formations catch the eye first. In early winter, crashing waves coat the beach, icing it down. Layer-by-layer, the ice builds. Small sculptures appear along the sand as a hardened, icy lip forms along the water's edge. Waves, slapping against this developing wall, toss spray into the air shaping a mound as it freezes on the ground. The mounds grow taller. Sometimes a "blowhole" develops spouting water up like lava from a volcano. As the winter progresses, more and more hills take shape stretching farther out. During the extreme winters, the lake ices over halting the process. It is a progression unique to the freshwater sea.

Piers, breakwaters and jetties offer a human twist to the ice formation. Crashing water flings against these man-made structures coating them with ice. Breakwater lighthouses are not immune to the process and they are often partially encapsulated in a thick frost. Be careful! The slick piers are no place to walk.

Muskegon State Park features a unique experience just a few yards from Lake Michigan. The Muskegon Winter Sports Park has one of North America's few luge runs. You can learn to use these sleds on a beginner track and then work your way up to an Olympic-style run. The track is open to the public on winter weekends. Other winter activities include groomed cross-country skiing, ice-skating and hockey. The Lake Michigan Campground lies across the road offering the chance to see the winter shore and its ice mounds.

Try cross-country skiing off-the-track. Many of the larger parks have wide open places where you can divert off the trail for a quick, downhill schuss on the small dunes. A good snow base is needed to ski the dunes. While this side of Lake Michigan gets volumes of "lake effect" snow, most of it generates a few miles inland. Winds on the mostly bare dunes often blow much of the snow into drifts leaving bare spots or a sand-snow mixture good for wax removal and quick stops! But when it is right, usually later in the ski season, it is fun beyond belief. If you are a skate-style skier, look for a cold spell following a thaw. You can ski fast on top of the dunes,

traveling almost anywhere. Ski nirvana is a fresh inch of snow on top of a frozen snow pack. Make sure you stop the fun long enough to enjoy the view! Remember that some of the best places require good physical conditioning. If you do not know the area well, take a compass and map. The winds can cover your tracks with snow, making backtracking difficult. If you do not ski, snowshoes make a great alternative.

The charts list numerous shoreline ski locations. Some favorite ski and snowshoe places are highlighted below.

Muskegon SP	Groomed track plus luge and ice skating.
Platte Plains, SBNL	For those in good shape; great dunes and views.
Saugatuck Dunes SP	Dunes and rolling terrain.
Stocking Drive, SBNL	Ski or snowshoe the unplowed, 7-mile drive for great views of the Sleeping Bear.
Wilderness SP	Ski or snowshoe out to Waugoshance Pt. or on the park's inland trails; rustic cabins to rent.

Clockwise from the near right:
• Ski or snowshoe the Pierce Stocking Scenic Drive at the Sleeping Bear Dunes for winter views of South Manitou Island and the drifts of sand and snow.
• Frankfort Lighthouse and breakwater gets its winter coat of ice.
• A winter "blowhole" and ice mounds formed at Point Betsie.
• Sand mushrooms formed from iced sand in early winter.

Muskegon County

Muskegon County presents both great variety and long stretches of public shore. Hoffmaster and Muskegon State Parks have several miles of coast, wooded terrain, dunes, great sand beaches and swimming. The City of Muskegon adds another long stretch of waterfront when you add together its string of parks south of the Muskegon Lake Channel. Several city, county and state parks of similar quality enhance the coastal appeal.

The City of Muskegon and surrounding suburbs comprise the most populous area of the coast covered in this book. Muskegon has the largest concentration of industry as well. Most is found along the shore of Muskegon Lake, which forms the city's harbor. Large ships serve the needs of these plants. Dwellers in metropolitan areas like Chicago, Detroit or Cleveland will think of Muskegon as small, but that may be the most amazing part of traveling this shore. Large cities do not exist here.

Hoffmaster State Park stands out as a great starting point for travelers. Displays at its Gillette Visitor Center provide an educational glimpse of the coast. Here you learn about the sand dunes, how they form and about their unique life forms. The interpretation includes both indoor and outdoor exhibits. For free parks and beaches, try Lake Harbor Park in Norton Shores, Kruse Park or Marquette Beach in Muskegon. Each has a sandy shore. Lake Harbor requires a walk to the beach where you will find small dunes and the Mona Lake Channel. Kruse includes an extensive dune boardwalk and picnic area. Marquette Beach connects with the Muskegon lighthouses and harbor entrance. In addition, lighthouse seekers should visit the White River Lighthouse farther north at the White Lake Channel.

Muskegon provides other unique activities. Muskegon State Park has one of the few luge runs in North America. You can try this Olympic sledding sport during the winter months. *Michigan Adventure*, the state's largest amusement park located just north of the city, features a number of roller coasters and a large waterpark. Board the World War II era submarine, *U.S.S. Silversides*, at its permanent mooring on the south side of the Muskegon channel.

Highway US-31 continues north serving as the main artery for the coast. Several secondary roads follow close to the lake. At the south of the county, follow Lake Harbor Road to travel near the shore. Mid-county, Scenic Drive goes from Muskegon Lake to White Lake where scenic views are offered along the stretches in Muskegon and Duck Lake State Parks.

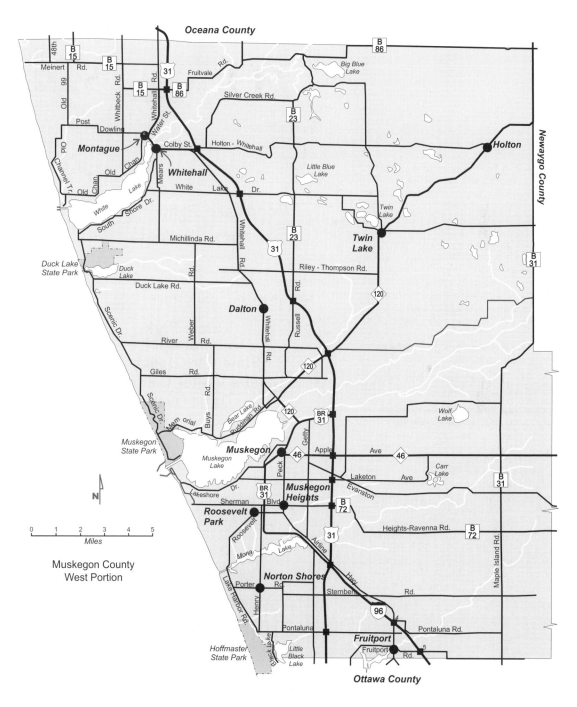

Muskegon County
West Portion

53

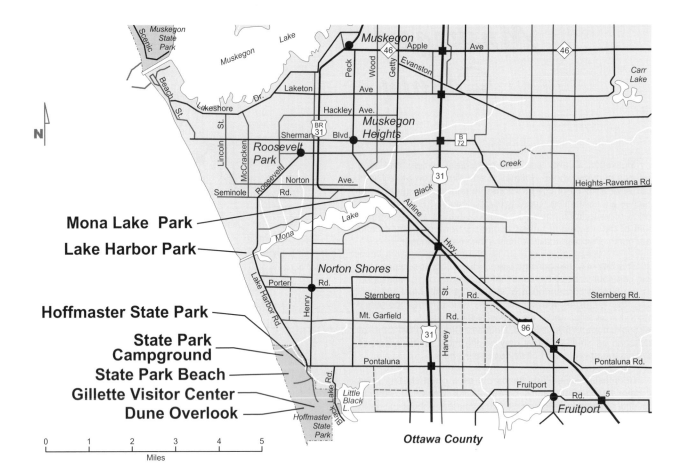

Mona Lake Park

Lake Harbor Park

Hoffmaster State Park

State Park Campground

State Park Beach

Gillette Visitor Center

Dune Overlook

Ottawa County

Below left: Early morning fog along the beach at Hoffmaster State Park.

Below right: The boat channel from Mona Lake at Lake Harbor Park.

Opposite page: The path from the Gillette Visitor Center ends at Lake Michigan.

Hoffmaster State Park and Lake Harbor

Name	Location	Entrance Fee	Parking	Modern Restrooms	Vault or Portable Toilet	Stair or Path to Shore	Swimming	Picnic Area	Drinking Water	Campground	Trailered Boat Launch	Kayak / Canoe	Marina	Fishing	Hiking	Biking	X-Country Skiing	Playground	Lighthouse	Beach Strolling	Sandy Beach	Stony or Rocky Shore	Dunes	Bluff	Wetland
P.J. Hoffmaster State Park	Norton Shores. West Pontaluna Rd. and Lake Harbor Dr.	●	●	●		●	●	●	●	●		●			●		●			●	●		●		
Hoffmaster State Park Beach	Hoffmaster State Park.	●	●	●	●	●	●	●	●											●	●		●		
Gillette Visitor Center	Hoffmaster State Park.	●	●	●					●						●					●	●		●		
Dune Overlook	Hoffmaster State Park.	●	●	●					●						●								●		
Hoffmaster State Park Campground	Norton Shores. Lake Harbor Dr. just N of West Pontaluna Rd.	●		●		●	●		●	●										●	●		●		
Lake Harbor Park	Norton Shores. Lake Harbor Drive at Mona Lake.		●			●	●	●	●					●							●		●		
Mona Lake Park	Muskegon Heights. BR US-31 on NE side of Mona Lake.		●	●			●	●	●		●	●						●			●				

A blend of education, dunes and fine beaches awaits you at these facilities. The Gillette Visitor Center prepares you to fully experience all the shore found in this book.

P.J. HOFFMASTER STATE PARK: With more than a thousand acres and over two miles of beach and dunes, Hoffmaster State Park is a gem. Facilities include a major campground found a short walk from Lake Michigan, a large nature center, numerous trails, dune overlooks, dune climbs and a beachhouse with concession. Away from the beach and dunes is a tall, hardwood forest. The picnic areas are found in the shady woods. The parking lots and other developed portions are nicely segregated from the beach. Most of the shore is undeveloped. A path leads to the pure sand beach. Large dunes parallel the shore. Even on busy days, those willing to walk can get away from the crowd. The walk itself is peaceful exercise here. Motorized vehicles require the Michigan State Park Vehicle Permit.
   Telephone: (231) 798-3711
   Web: www.michigan.gov/dnr
   GPS: 43°07.994'N; 86°15.959'W

HOFFMASTER STATE PARK BEACH: A changehouse, concession and modern restrooms are a short distance down the path and stairway from the sandy Lake Michigan beach. Other than these few improvements, the park's shore is generally undeveloped.

GILLETTE VISITOR CENTER: Set in the woods a short walk from Lake Michigan, the Gillette Visitor Center provides exhibits and programs about the geology, flora and fauna of Michigan's dune coast. Part of the interpretive trail near the building is barrier-free. The Visitor Center is also the trailhead for the dune overlook mentioned below. In the summer, the building is open daily. Hours vary during the off-season. The park motor vehicle fee provides admittance. A picnic area is nearby.

DUNE OVERLOOK TRAIL: The dune overlook trail starts at the Gillette Visitor Center. A series of walks and stairs ascends to the top of a dune. Interpretative signs, describing dune vegetation, are found along the way. There is also a trail spur that leads to the Lake Michigan shore. Dunes, dune "blow-outs," and beautiful hardwood forest make up the trail area. The overlook rises nearly 200 feet above Lake Michigan providing distant views on clear days and a colorful sight during the fall foliage season.

HOFFMASTER STATE PARK CAMPGROUND: Located just north of the park's main entrance, the camping area has 333 campsites with modern restroom and shower facilities. Paths lead through forest and dunes to Lake Michigan.
GPS: 43°08.209'N; 86°16.106'W

LAKE HARBOR PARK: Located on the north side of the Mona Lake Channel, Lake Harbor Park is an uncommon slice of shore. Once resort property, some of the old foundations and sidewalks are still visible. The City of Norton Shores now operates it. A large picnic area with shelter and grills is located near the parking lot. A quarter-mile path parallels the narrow channel on its way to Lake Michigan. The outlet channel is lined with rudimentary steel and rock rip-rap. Some sections are adequate as a fishing platform. The park's sandy beach is a few hundred feet long. Swimming is excellent. A boardwalk-stair system leads to the top of small dunes for an overlook.
   GPS: 43°10.146'; 86°17.474'

MONA LAKE PARK: A city park on Mona Lake, it has swimming and a good, hard-surfaced boat launch about 2.5 miles from Lake Michigan through the Mona Lake Channel.

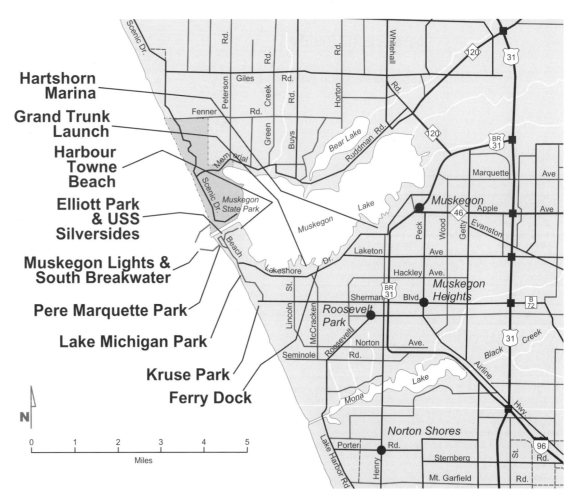

Hartshorn Marina

Grand Trunk Launch

Harbour Towne Beach

Elliott Park & USS Silversides

Muskegon Lights & South Breakwater

Pere Marquette Park

Lake Michigan Park

Kruse Park

Ferry Dock

Above: Sailing into the Muskegon Harbor past the South Breakwater Light.

Below right: The beach at Kruse Park has a long, wood ramp down from the dunes.

Far Right: World War II submarine "USS Silversides" moored in Muskegon Channel.

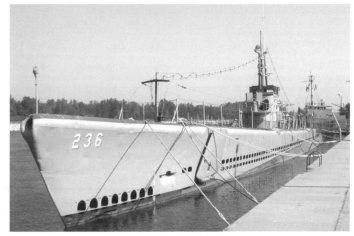

Muskegon County

City of Muskegon, South

Name	Location	Entrance Fee	Parking	Modern Restrooms	Vault or Portable Toilet	Stair or Path to Shore	Swimming	Picnic Area	Drinking Water	Campground	Trailered Boat Launch	Kayak / Canoe	Marina	Fishing	Hiking	Biking	X-Country Skiing	Playground	Lighthouse	Beach Strolling	Sandy Beach	Stony or Rocky Shore	Dunes	Bluff	Wetland
Kruse Park	Muskegon. West end of Sherman Blvd.		●	●		●	●	●	●			●		●	●			●		●	●		●		
Lake Michigan Park	Muskegon. Beach St. between Lakeshore Dr. and Sherman Blvd.		●		●		●					●			●					●	●		●		
Pere Marquette Park	Muskegon. Beach St. at the west end of Muskegon Channel.		●	●			●	●	●			●		●				●	●	●	●		●		
Muskegon Lights	Muskegon at Pere Marquette Park.		●	●		●			●					●						●	●				
Elliot Park	Muskegon. Beach Street just W of Pere Marquette Park.		●	●				●	●					●	●			●		●					
USS Silversides	Muskegon. W of Pere Marquette and Drake Parks.	●	●																						
Harbour Towne Beach	Muskegon. E of Elliot Park. From Beach St. go NW on Fulton St..		●		●		●					●									●				
Grand Trunk Boat Ramp	Muskegon. Lakeshore Dr. near McCracken St.	●	●		●						●	●													
Ferry Dock	Muskegon. 1920 Lakeshore Dr.	●	●	●																					
Hartshorn Marina	Muskegon. Lakeshore Dr.		●	●							●														

The City of Muskegon provides a series of interconnected parks along 2 miles of Lake Michigan shore south of the Muskegon Lake Channel. Choose from the "high energy" classic Marquette Beach to the family oriented Kruse Park. Add a little history by visiting a World War II submarine. Stroll the shore, the channel or out on the south breakwater.

NORMAN F. KRUSE PARK: Once called Bronson Park, Kruse makes up the southern terminus of a series of parks along Muskegon's Lake Michigan shore. This park has a number of assets; high dunes, great swimming, sandy beach and nicely developed picnic grounds. Other park facilities include a basketball court, playground and first-rate restrooms. A long series of boardwalk and stairs traverses the dunes going from Old Bronson Park to the newer section of Kruse Park to the north. These walkways provide high vantage points overlooking both the beach and developed park area. The Muskegon South Breakwater Light can be seen several miles to the northwest. A long, barrier-free, boardwalk-type ramp leads to a platform at beach level. Beach walkers will find miles of shore to stroll. Kayakers willing to make a reasonably short carry could put in here as well.
  Web: www.ci.muskegon.mi.us
  GPS: 43°12.315'N; 86°19.231'W

LAKE MICHIGAN PARK: Between Marquette Beach on the north and Kruse Park to its south, Lake Michigan Park is simply a long, wide, flat, sandy beach. It is perfect for the minimalist who just wants to park along the road and get out the blanket. There are no buildings on this undeveloped beach. Fly a kite, surfcast a line, soak up the sun or swim. You make your own fun here. A walkway travels along Beach Street connecting the park with others in the area.
  Web: www.ci.muskegon.mi.us

PERE MARQUETTE PARK: This is a traditional, urban-style beach with changehouse, concession, restaurant and other amenities. It is also the access point to the south breakwater where you can walk out to the Muskegon South Breakwater Light and also view the Muskegon Inner Harbor Light. The primary beach is on the Lake Michigan side of the breakwater. The inner harbor beach, next to the Coast Guard Station, is sandy as well. It is an easy kayak or canoe carry from the north end of the parking lot to the calm, harbor water.
  Web: www.ci.muskegon.mi.us
  GPS: 43°13.458'N; 86°20.172'W

MUSKEGON LIGHTS: There are two Muskegon historic navigation lights. One is on the south breakwater the other on the south channel pier. Access to the South Breakwater Light is made from Pere Marquette Park.

MARGARET DRAKE ELLIOT PARK: The Margaret Drake Elliott Park borders the Muskegon Lake Channel on its north and Pere Marquette Park on its west. The WW II submarine "Silversides" exhibit is moored just to its east. Elliott Park provides great access to the south channel walkway where viewing boats and ships is a favorite activity. Fishing along the channel is also common. Benches provided. Away from the channel, tall trees shade its fine picnic, playground and restroom facilities.
  Web: www.ci.muskegon.mi.us

USS SILVERSIDES: The Silversides submarine was part of the World War II fleet. Today, it is a tribute to Navy sailors. Tours are given regularly. Youth groups have educational sleepovers on the craft year-round. You can view the moored ship from the channel area without charge. There is a fee for touring below deck.

HARBOUR TOWNE BEACH: This is a small beach located on Muskegon Lake near the channel to Lake Michigan. It is sandy and offers a warmer water alternative to the big lake. This is a good kayak launch point for entering the channel or plying Muskegon Lake.
  GPS: 43°13.981'N; 86°15.761'W

GRAND TRUNK BOAT RAMP: A major boat ramp approximately two miles from the Muskegon Channel. The launch is hard-surface and deep for large boats.
  GPS: 43°12.896'N; 86°17.696'W

FERRY DOCK: Lake Express began a seasonal passenger car ferry service to Milwaukee in 2004. The trip takes about 2.5 hours with three sailings each way per day.
  Telephone: (231) 724-6785
  Web: www.lake-express.com

HARTSHORN MARINA: A major marina with fuel, slips and boat launch. Fee for services and launching
  Telephone: (231) 724-6785
  GPS: 43°13.760'N; 86°15.837'W

Heritage Landing
Pioneer Park
Winter Sports Complex
Lake Michigan Campground
Blockhouses
Snug Harbor Facilities
Muskegon SP Beach
Channel Campground

0   1   2   3   4   5
Miles

Above left: The staircase at Lake Michigan Campground leads to miles of sand beach.

Below left: The Muskegon Lake Channel opens to Lake Michigan and has a barrier-free fishing platform seen at the left of the picture.

Muskegon County

Muskegon State Park Area

Name	Location	Entrance Fee	Parking	Modern Restrooms	Vault or Portable Toilet	Stair or Path to Shore	Swimming	Picnic Area	Drinking Water	Campground	Trailered Boat Launch	Kayak / Canoe	Marina	Fishing	Hiking	Biking	X-Country Skiing	Playground	Lighthouse	Beach Strolling	Sandy Beach	Stony or Rocky Shore	Dunes	Bluff	Wetland
Heritage Landing	Muskegon downtown. M-120 near US-31 BR.		●	●				●	●					●				●							
Muskegon State Park	Scenic Drive, 6 miles W of Muskegon.	●	●	●	●		●	●	●	●	●	●		●	●	●	●	●		●	●		●	●	
Snug Harbor Facilities	Muskegon State Park.	●	●	●			●	●	●		●	●		●	●	●					●				
Channel Campground	Muskegon State Park.	●	●	●		●	●		●	●		●		●	●	●					●				
Channel Walkway	Muskegon State Park.	●			●	●								●	●										
Muskegon State Park Beach	Muskegon State Park.	●	●	●				●		●										●	●				
Blockhouse	Muskegon State Park.	●	●												●									●	
Lake Michigan Campground	Muskegon State Park.	●	●	●			●	●		●					●					●	●			●	
Winter Sports Complex	Muskegon State Park.	●	●	●					●						●		●								
Pioneer County Park	Scenic Drive just N of Giles Rd., 7.5 miles NW of Muskegon.	●	●	●			●	●	●	●				●							●			●	

Muskegon State Park dominates the immediate shore north of the Muskegon Lake Channel. North of the park, private cottages take over until you reach the Duck Lake area.

HERITAGE LANDING: A major county park located on Muskegon Lake near downtown Muskegon. Walkways, pier, picnic tables and concert stages are some of the features of this newly renovated area.
> Web: www.co.muskegon.mi.us/heritage.htm
> GPS: 43°13.981'N; 86°15.761'W

MUSKEGON STATE PARK: Here is a mix of developed and natural park with campgrounds, a unique winter sports area and both inland and Great Lakes shore. The park rates high for use and appeal. The choice of the warmer Muskegon Lake or cooler Lake Michigan waters provides variety to the beachgoer. Enjoy the walk along the Muskegon Channel or through wooded, inland trails. Motorized vehicles require the Michigan State Park Vehicle Permit. Campground reservations can be made by calling 1-800-44PARKS.
> Telephone: (231) 744-3480
> Web: www.michigan.gov/dnr

SNUG HARBOR FACILITIES: Snug Harbor is part of Muskegon Lake. This portion of Muskegon State Park has a very good boat launch in a well-protected bay. The channel to Lake Michigan is about one mile away. A large, grassy picnic ground with tables, grills and a sandy beach lie along the relatively warm waters of Snug Harbor.
> GPS: 43°14.958'N; 86°19.996'W

CHANNEL CAMPGROUND: A modern campground located along Muskegon Lake and the channel to Lake Michigan. Facilities include showers, modern restrooms and an RV sanitation station.
> GPS: 43°13.839'N; 86°20.142'W

MUSKEGON LAKE CHANNEL WALKWAY: The blue-railed, concrete walk runs the entire length of the north side of the Lake Muskegon Channel. At one end is Muskegon Lake and the Channel Campground. At the other end is the harbor's North Inner Pier. Views include the Muskegon lighthouses and the submarine *USS Silversides* all located on the south channel side. Numerous craft from pleasure boats to large ships ply the channel from lake to lake. A barrier-free fishing platform is found at the channel walk parking area about midway along its length.

MUSKEGON STATE PARK BEACH: Here is a great, sandy beach with bathhouse and concession located near the entrance to Muskegon's harbor channel. The beach stretches for nearly 3 miles north of the main facilities. The crowd thins as you walk north. Small dunes, wooded bluffs and wonderful swimming make this one of the best beaches along the central coast.
> GPS: 43°14.196'N; 86°20.494'W

Note: You can take in views of Lake Michigan along Scenic Drive near the intersection of Memorial Drive. Many park along the road shoulder to access the lake.

THE BLOCKHOUSE: A log, fort-like "blockhouse," designed as a scenic lookout, sits atop the bluff along Muskegon State Park's Scenic Drive. View Lake Michigan and the surrounding forest from the blockhouse. The view is especially pretty during the fall color change. Two stories high, it makes an interesting sight and a fun stop for children.
> GPS: 43°15.315'N; 86°21.000'W

LAKE MICHIGAN CAMPGROUND: This campground occupies the north shore of Muskegon State Park. It sits on a wooded bluff above Lake Michigan. Access the sandy beach by stairway from the camp. For the walker or beach enthusiast, there are miles of public shoreline south to the channel. Facilities are modern. The Winter Sports Complex is across the highway.

WINTER SPORTS COMPLEX: The Winter Sports Complex at Muskegon State Park features the popular luge run, one of the few in North America. During winter weekends, the public can try their hand at luge, the seemingly daring sled trip through an iced trough. Novices start at the small, "Lower Luge" until they prove their skill. The longer "Upper Luge" comes next! Other activities include cross-country skiing, skating and hockey. Each of these has a fee separate from the park entrance permit.
> Telephone: (231) 744-9629
> Web: www.msports.org

PIONEER COUNTY PARK: The park, located a little over a mile north of Muskegon State Park, has a number of facilities on its 145 acres. The campground has 213 wooded sites. Tennis, beach volleyball, basketball and baseball can be played. Down the bluff from the camping and picnic area is the sandy beach. There is a fee for entrance and camping.
> Telephone: (231) 744-3580
> Web: www.co.muskegon.mi.us/parks/pioneer.htm

**Whitehall Marina &
Goodrich Park**

**Scenic Dr. Road
End Launch**

**South Channel
Walkway & Breakwater**

**White River Lighthouse
and Museum**

Duck Lake State Park

Scenic Dr. Pull-offs

Marcus Park

Above: The outlet stream from Duck Lake changes depending on Lake Michigan's action. It often forms a long sand bar between itself and the lake as seen above.

Right: The White River Lighthouse and Museum.

Muskegon County

Duck Lake and South Side of White Lake

Name	Location	Entrance Fee	Parking	Modern Restrooms	Vault or Portable Toilet	Stair or Path to Shore	Swimming	Picnic Area	Drinking Water	Campground	Trailered Boat Launch	Kayak / Canoe	Marina	Fishing	Hiking	Biking	X-Country Skiing	Playground	Lighthouse	Beach Strolling	Sandy Beach	Stony or Rocky Shore	Dunes	Bluff	Wetland
Marcus Park	SW of Whitehall. Scenic Drive near Duck Lake Rd. on Duck Lake.						●	●						●							●				
Scenic Drive Pull-offs	West end of Duck Lake State Park on Scenic Drive.						●					●		●							●	●			
Duck Lake State Park	Michillinda Rd. 5.5 miles SW of Whitehall.	●	●	●	●	●	●	●	●		●	●		●							●	●			
White River Lighthouse & Museum	5.5 miles SW of Whitehall on Murray Rd about 1 mile N of Scenic Dr. and South Shore Dr. intersection.	●	●		●														●						
South White Lake Channel Walkway and Breakwater	5.5 miles SW of Whitehall on Murray Rd about 1 mile N of Scenic Dr. and South Shore Dr. intersection.		●		●	●	●							●						●	●				
Scenic Drive Road End Launch	4.5 miles SW of Whitehall at end of Scenic Drive 1 block N of South Shore Dr.											●													
Whitehall Marina and Goodrich Park	Whitehall. 1 block W of business district.		●	●				●	●				●	●				●							

From the Duck Lake outlet flows a small amount of water through a sand bar to Lake Michigan. In contrast, the engineered White Lake Channel allows boat navigation from the inland towns of Montague and Whitehall. In a few short miles, you have a choice of the natural or the modern.

MARKUS PARK: Marcus Park is a small bit of public land on Duck Lake at a curvy portion on Scenic Drive. The park is generally in a natural state with a couple of picnic tables and grill. Parking is a problem. None is designated and parking on the road shoulder is hazardous because the curves make it difficult for drivers to see pedestrians. The park is very close to the popular stretch of Scenic Drive that travels along Lake Michigan to the west of Duck Lake.

SCENIC DRIVE PULL-OFFS: The west end of Duck Lake State Park has frontage on Lake Michigan. Scenic Drive runs close to the lake here and some shoulder parking is available without charge. Parking is not allowed along part of the highway. The south portion of this stretch sits high and it is difficult to access the beach because stone rip-rap was placed at the bottom of the bluff for erosion control. The north end is lower, reaching beach level where the road crosses the Duck Lake outlet. Be careful of traffic, especially in the summer.

An alternative is to enter Duck Lake State Park proper where a Michigan State Park Vehicle Permit is required. A parking lot and short walkway is near the Duck Lake outlet. The entrance to the park is 2 miles away and the drive to the parking lot is another 2 miles. See the Duck Lake Park listing for more information.

DUCK LAKE STATE PARK: Duck Lake State Park is a day-use park with both Lake Michigan and Duck Lake shoreline. Beaches are located on both lakes. The Duck Lake beach has a change building.

At the west end of Duck Lake is a boat launch. The Duck Lake outlet to Lake Michigan is too shallow for boats but canoes and kayaks can make way, although this may require dragging the craft over occasional shallows. The outlet's sand bar shifts depending on the wind and waves. Once past the highway bridge, it is easier to carry a kayak over the sand to Lake Michigan. At the west end is the parking lot for the Lake Michigan beach. A vault toilet at the parking lot is the closest facility to the Lake Michigan beach area. A short path leads to Scenic Drive at the Duck Lake Outlet. Children love playing in the warm, shallow water of the outlet where wet sand for sandcastles is abundant and there always seems to be something to catch their interest.

> Telephone: (231) 744-3480
> Web: www.michigan.gov/dnr
> GPS: 43°20.556'N; 86°24.474'W'

Note: To reach the White River Lighthouse and the adjoining channel walkway (next two listings) turn at Murray Road at the intersection of Scenic and South Shore Drives. Murray narrows near the lighthouse area making it difficult for large vehicles or those with trailers to negotiate.
> *Murray Rd. intersection GPS: 43°21.646'N; 86°24.741'W*

WHITE RIVER LIGHTHOUSE AND MUSEUM: Narrow Murray Road winds through old cottages on the west side of White Lake leading to the beige brick White River Lighthouse. The lighthouse contains a small museum open during summer afternoons except Monday. Appointments can be made during the off-season.
> Telephone: (231)-894-8265
> Web: www.whiteriverlightstation.org
> GPS: 43°22.482'N; 86°25.428'W

SOUTH WHITE LAKE CHANNEL WALKWAY AND BREAKWATER: To the north of the lighthouse is the channel from White Lake to Lake Michigan. The paved, barrier-free walkway is accessible from the lighthouse parking lot. Fishing is common along its blue railing. Sandy beach is available from the walkway in front of the lighthouse. The parking lot, shared with the museum, is not very large.

SCENIC DRIVE ROAD END LAUNCH: This is a shallow launch within a mile of the White Lake Channel to Lake Michigan. Parking is limited but it provides the closest channel access for kayaks from the south side of White Lake.

WHITEHALL MARINA AND GOODRICH PARK: These two facilities adjoin each other on Whitehall's waterfront. The marina has 50 boat slips and is about 4 miles from the White Lake Channel to Lake Michigan.
> Telephone: (231) 894-4048
> GPS: 43°22.500'N; 86°25.850'W

Below: Little Flower Creek empties to Lake Michigan at Meinert County Park

Opposite Page: A sailboat passes the north breakwater on the White Lake Channel.

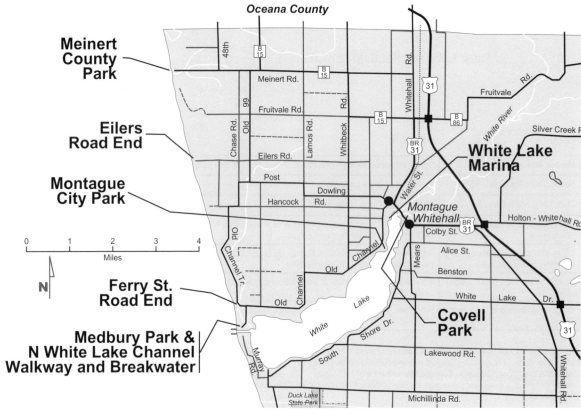

Name	Location	Entrance Fee	Parking	Modern Restrooms	Vault or Portable Toilet	Stair or Path to Shore	Swimming	Picnic Area	Drinking Water	Campground	Trailered Boat Launch	Kayak / Canoe	Marina	Fishing	Hiking	Biking	X-Country Skiing	Playground	Lighthouse	Beach Strolling	Sandy Beach	Stony or Rocky Shore	Dunes	Bluff	Wetland
Covell Park	Whitehall. BR US-31 at bridge over White River.		●		●						●	●		●	●	●									●
White Lake Marina & Ramp	Montague. 2 blocks S of business district.	●	●	●							●	●	●												
Montague City Park	1.5 S of Montague on Old Channel Trail.		●	●			●	●	●			●		●				●			●				
Medbury Park & North Channel Walkway and Breakwater	6 miles SW of Montague. Follow Old Channel Trail, turn S on Lau Rd.		●		●	●	●					●		●							●				
Ferry Street Road End	6 miles SW of Montague off Old Channel Trail.						●														●		●		
Eilers Road End	W of Montague 5.5 miles. Go N on Whitehall Rd. then W on Eilers Rd.		●				●	●													●		●		
Meinert County Park	7 miles W of US-31 exit Fruitvale Rd. follow B-15 to Meinert Rd.	●	●	●			●	●	●	●		●		●	●			●			●		●		

Public access to Lake Michigan is very limited north of the White Lake Channel and into southern Oceana County.

COVELL PARK: The grassy park has a boat ramp on the White River. The Hart-Montague Rail Trail, a state linear park, has a trailhead here. The asphalt bikeway does not pass along the Lake Michigan shore but affords an additional recreational opportunity for those inclined. The trail in this area provides views of the White River Marsh.
GPS: 43°24.781'N; 86°21.035'W

WHITE LAKE MARINA & RAMP: Excellent boat ramp for larger craft boating on White Lake or making the five mile voyage to Lake Michigan.

MONTAGUE CITY PARK: A small beach and picnic park on White Lake.
GPS: 43°24.217'N; 86°21.623'W

MEDBURY PARK AND NORTH WHITE LAKE CHANNEL WALKWAY AND BREAKWATER: Medbury Park provides access to the White Lake Channel's north side. A concrete walkway lines the channel and leads to the short breakwater and small navigation light at its end. It is barrier-free. Fishing from the breakwater is popular. The park's beach is sandy with small dunes. The picturesque White River Lighthouse can be seen across the channel.
GPS: 43°22.985'N; 86°25.450'W (Lau Rd. turn location)

Note for kayakers: Lau Road splits near Medbury Park's entrance. The dirt lane to the left leads to a shallow launch spot usable for kayaks or canoes. Parking is very limited at the road end but the walk to the Medbury Park lot is not far. This is the closest launch point to the White Lake Channel.

FERRY STREET ROAD END: Parking is about non-existent here. There is room for maybe one car. No parking is allowed along the street. Biking to the area might be the best prospect, especially on nice days. The White River Township Dune Sanctuary lies to the south of the street.
GPS: 43°23.174'N; 86°25.627'W

EILERS ROAD END: Park at the large turn-around area at the end of Eilers Road. A short path leads over the dune and between two residences to the beach. It is a pleasing place with a sandy beach. No facilities.
GPS: 43°25.792'N; 86°26.774'W

MEINERT COUNTY PARK: A big sandy beach and small dunes are the primary attraction of this park. There are modern restrooms, concession, picnic and playgrounds. A view platform is wheelchair-accessible. The shallow, Little Flower Creek flows into Lake Michigan attracting young children for creative play. The campground has modern facilities and 67 sites.
Telephone: (231) 894-4881
Web: www.co.muskegon.mi.us/parks/meinert.htm
GPS: 43°27.552'N; 86°27.395'W

Dune Forms

Lake Michigan dunes owe much to the glaciers formed during the ice age. Glacial action ground rock into fine grains. Melting ice formed rivers that transported material towards the Great Lakes. Many of the smallest sand particles stayed suspended until the water flow slowed at the rivermouth. Lake currents spread the sand along the coast. Large quantities of these tiny grains were deposited when the current slowed at embayments. The material was then in place for building dunes.

As lake levels lowered, more and more sand became exposed. Winds transported the sand inland until reaching an object that slowed the flow of air, dropping the grains. Vegetation provided the primary collection points. Dune-adapted plants, such as marram grass, trapped sand and eventually became covered. These plants sent up rhizomes and again surfaced to the top of the sand. The collection continued and slowly a dune formed. The process continues today.

Generally, a series of ridges form separating the dune area into natural zones. The beach extends only a short way inland from the lake but it provides for a variety of life. Dead insects and fish wash onto the *wet beach* where shorebirds feed. Some of the insect and fish remains, along with aquatic vegetation, get blown just past the wet area to the *storm beach*. Many insects find this habitat to their liking. At the *back beach,* plants like marram start to take hold.

The first and usually short dune ridge is referred to as the *foredune*. Here the grasses and small plants struggle to stabilize the dune in a harsh environment. The extremes of summer heat and bitter winter winds challenge life in this zone.

A *trough* of low, wet areas often lies behind foredune. Water level fluctuations can shift the character of these swales. In times of high lake levels, ponds form, hosting an abundance of aquatic species. Frogs and cattails mark this as a wetland. Jack pine, a scraggly conifer, finds a place along the edge. Low water levels might completely dry the area. These patches form a unique micro-environment within the dune complex.

The *backdune* lies behind the foredunes. Vegetative decay develops a shallow, fragile soil on the sand. Here the forest further protects the dune from large scale wind erosion. Shade contributes a cooler environment. The plant and wildlife patterns begin to look like those further inland.

Clockwise from the left:

- Sand gathers at the base of a wormwood plant at Grand Mere State Park demonstrating part of the dune building process.
- The back beach and a small foredune fronts this blowout on North Manitou Island.
- A graphic sampling of some dune forms and terms used to define them.

Blow-outs, also called parabolic dunes, are found within this mix in the larger dune complexes. These U-shaped forms develop when erosion exposes part of the dune face. Wind, working with stabilizing grasses, restarts the build-up process, pushing inland and piling sand up to 250 feet high.

Perched dunes, such as the Sleeping Bear in Leelanau County, are sand piles found on the top of glacial moraines (hills). When the moraine sits along the coast, high winds pick up fine material from its lakeside surface and moves it to the top. Over time, a dune forms. Most of the perched dune looks like a giant sand pile, but the sand is just the frosting.

Blowout

Backdune

Trough Pond

Foredune

Beach

Oceana County

With beautiful sandy beaches and a rural life, Oceana County marks the beginning of a slower pace as you travel north. The center of Oceana County contains Little Sable Point, the larger of the two "knobs" found along the middle of the Michigan mitten. Here, the Silver Lake Dunes rise above Lake Michigan, creeping east as they gradually fill Silver Lake. The dune area embodies the center of the county's tourist activity as well. Little Sable Point Lighthouse juts from small dunes, a favorite photography spot. Mac Wood's Dune Rides take visitors onto the rolling sand dunes. Also, a unique, Off-Road-Vehicle (ORV) area allows the dune buggy set to operate their machines on a portion of the bald, silicon-beaded hills. You can hike, climb or roll down the dunes too! All this takes place in and around Silver Lake State Park near the town of Mears.

In the north of the county, the pretty town of Pentwater attracts those interested in the boating life. Its harbor on Pentwater Lake affords good refuge for boaters as well as fishing on both Lake Michigan and the inland water. The harbor channel walkway provides a picturesque stroll or a good fishing spot. South of the Silver Lake Dunes, access is limited to a couple of township parks. Orchards, farms and forests fill in the scenery.

Many of the county's parks on Lake Michigan have entrance fees. If you want a quiet swimming spot with no fee, try Cedar County Park between Silver Lake and Pentwater. The Golden Township Park Beach, near the dunes, is free, but crowded on nice days, so get there early. Mears and Silver Lake State Parks require the Michigan State Park Vehicle Permit but have great beaches plus camping.

The US-31 Freeway remains the main coastline route as you continue north. County Road B-15, however, follows closer to the shore. It makes for a pleasant drive through the rural county and connects with all the important sites listed here. Stop at a farmer's fruit stand, witness the fall foliage and eye the always inspiring Silver Lake Dunes as you putt your way to Pentwater. Highway B-15 is not fast, but if you want speed, you are in the wrong place!

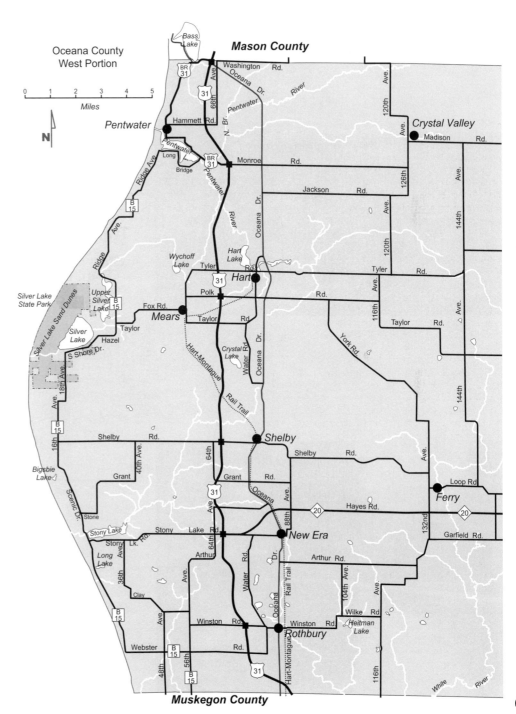

Benona Twp. Park

Knoll Twp. Park

Stony Lake Twp. Park

Park Road End

Claybanks Twp. Park

N

0   1   2   3   4   5
Miles

Muskegon County

Above left: Stony Creek fights it way to Lake Michigan at Benona Township Park

Below left: A dock and grassy bank greet you at Knoll Park on Stony Lake.

Opposite page: At Claybanks, a sandy trail down a small bluff leads through the dune grasses to the shore

Oceana County

Claybanks and Benona Townships

Name	Location	Entrance Fee	Parking	Modern Restrooms	Vault or Portable Toilet	Stair or Path to Shore	Swimming	Picnic Area	Drinking Water	Campground	Trailered Boat Launch	Kayak / Canoe	Marina	Fishing	Hiking	Biking	X-Country Skiing	Playground	Lighthouse	Beach Strolling	Sandy Beach	Stony or Rocky Shore	Dunes	Bluff	Wetland
Claybanks Township Park	7.5 miles W of Rothbury on Scenic Dr.		●		●	●	●	●	●	●										●	●			●	
Park Road End	7.5 miles W of Rothbury. 0.1 miles W of Scenic Dr. on Park Rd.						●														●				
Stony Lake Township Park	7 miles W New Era on Stony Lake Rd.		●		●		●	●			●	●		●							●				
Knoll Township Park	Scenic Drive at the west end of Stony Lake.		●		●		●					●		●							●				
Benona Township Park	9 miles W of New Era. 0.5 Miles W of Scenic Dr. at Stony Lake townsite. (see listing)	●	●		●		●					●		●							●				

Public access to Lake Michigan is limited along the southern half of Oceana County's coast. Only a couple of small, shoreline parks are available in this area of cottages, farms and forest.

CLAYBANKS TOWNSHIP PARK: Claybanks Park is a throwback to earlier days of travel. The campground is basic with hand pumps, vault toilets and a functional picnic shelter. The camp sits on the high bank above Lake Michigan. A platform allows viewing along the shore. A steep path leads down the bluff to the natural, sandy beach below. There is a fee for camping. The surrounding area is rural; a mix of woods and farms.
  GPS: 43°31.839'N; 86°29.099'W

PARK ROAD END: Park Road heads west just north of the Claybanks Park, ending where Whiskey Creek meets Lake Michigan. The road is a sandy two-track lane with a single residence at the end as well. Take care not to get stuck in the soft sand. Parking is limited to about one vehicle. A short path leads to the sandy beach.
  GPS: 43°32.049'N; 86°29.253'W

STONY LAKE TOWNSHIP PARK: Located on the south shore of Stony Lake, most of the park sits on forested land high above the water. A lane descends down to the lake where a boat ramp and small swim area are found.
  GPS: 43°33.340'N; 86°28.629'W

KNOLL TOWNSHIP PARK: Found just north of the highway bridge that crosses the Stony Lake outlet stream, Knoll Park has two sections. East of Scenic Drive is a beach with a dock on Stony Lake. The area has a grassy shoreline and sand bottom for good swimming. The extensive dock furnishes plenty of space to fish. Canoes or kayaks can be carried easily to the shore. Basketball and baseball facilities are on the west side of the road.
  GPS: 43°33.597'N; 86°29.839'W

BENONA TOWNSHIP PARK: Located at Stony Lake's outlet to Lake Michigan, low water has made the park's boat launch on the small creek unusable for all but small craft like canoes and kayaks. Fishing in the creek is common during fall fish runs. The beach is sandy. There are no signs to direct users to the park. A convenience store is located where Scenic Drive makes a sharp curve just north of Stony Lake and Knoll Park. Look for the narrow asphalt road that heads west.
  GPS: 43°33.575'N; 86°30.502'W (park); 43°33.633'N; 86°29.966'W (turn location at Scenic Drive)

Top left: The historic Mac Wood's Dune Rides use specially modified vehicles to tour portions of the Silver Lake Dunes.

Below left: Little Sable Point Light sits precariously close to the water.

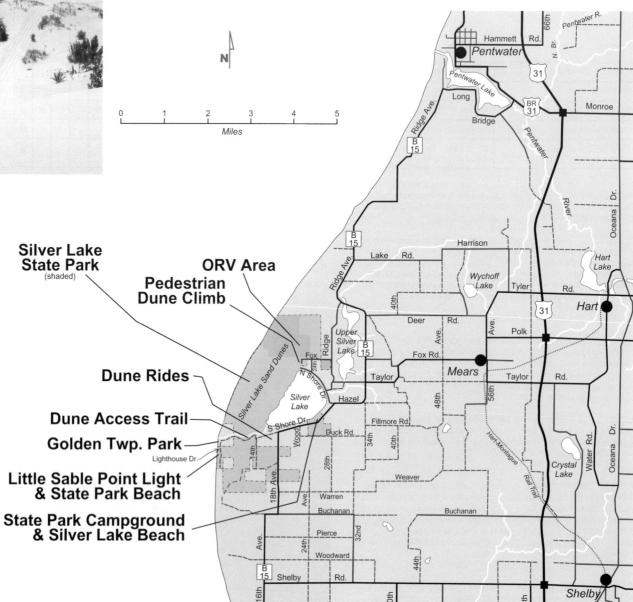

N

0   1   2   3   4   5
Miles

Silver Lake State Park
(shaded)

ORV Area

Pedestrian Dune Climb

Dune Rides

Dune Access Trail

Golden Twp. Park

Little Sable Point Light & State Park Beach

State Park Campground & Silver Lake Beach

Pentwater

Hammett Rd.

Long Bridge

Harrison

Lake   Rd.

Wychoff Lake

Deer   Rd.

Tyler   Rd.

Hart

Hart Lake

Fox Rd.

Mears

Taylor   Rd.

Polk

Upper Silver Lake

Silver Lake Sand Dunes

Ridge

Fox

N Shore Dr.

Taylor

Hazel

S Shore Dr.

Silver Lake

Fillmore Rd.

Duck Rd.

Weaver

Hart-Montague Rail Trail

Crystal Lake

Water Rd.

Oceana Dr.

Lighthouse Dr.

Warren

Buchanan

Buchanan

Pierce

Woodward

Shelby   Rd.

Shelby

Ridge Ave.

Pentwater Lake

Pentwater R.

Monroe

River

Oceana Dr.

Name	Location	Entrance Fee	Parking	Modern Restrooms	Vault or Portable Toilet	Stair or Path to Shore	Swimming	Picnic Area	Drinking Water	Campground	Trailered Boat Launch	Kayak / Canoe	Marina	Fishing	Hiking	Biking	X-Country Skiing	Playground	Lighthouse	Beach Strolling	Sandy Beach	Stony or Rocky Shore	Dunes	Bluff	Wetland
Golden Township Park	6.5 miles SW of Mears on Lighthouse Dr. Travel 1 mile W of the intersection of 18th and South Shore Rd. (Hwy B-15).		●		●		●					●									●				
Silver Lake State Park	4.5 miles SW of Mears on South Shore Dr. (Hwy B-15).	●	●	●	●	●	●	●	●	●	●	●		●	●			●	●	●	●		●		
Little Sable Point Light and Beach	Silver Lake State Park. Lighthouse Dr. 1.5 mile W of intersection of 18th and South Shore Rd. (Hwy B-15).	●	●		●		●												●		●		●		
Dunes Access Trail	Silver Lake State Park. Lighthouse Drive, 0.5 miles W of 14th Ave.	●				●	●								●					●	●		●		
Mac Wood's Dune Rides	5.5 miles SW of Mears on South Shore Rd. (Hwy B-15) at 18th.	●	●	●																	●		●		
State Park Campground & Beach	4.5 miles SW of Mears on South Shore Dr. (Hwy B-15).	●	●	●			●	●	●	●	●	●		●				●			●				
Pedestrian Dune Climb	Silver Lake State Park. End of Fox Rd., 1/2 mile W of Ridge Rd.	●	●		●	●	●	●							●					●	●		●		
Off-Road-Vehicle Area	Silver Lake State Park. Fox Rd. 1/2 mile W of Ridge Rd.	●	●	●																			●		

The Silver Lake Sand Dunes provide the view, the activities and the excitement of this area. The vivid tan sand contrasts with the greens of the surrounding forests and the blues of the lakes and sky. Within a few miles, you will find fine beaches, great scenery and plenty for all ages to do.

GOLDEN TOWNSHIP PARK: A paved parking area of about 20 spaces can be found on Lighthouse Drive where it makes its curve south towards the Little Sable Point Light. Park here, cross the road and you will be at the small, sandy park on the south side of Silver Creek. There is no development in the park but plenty of residences nearby. Good swimming. The creek is shallow and a good place for small children to play.

SILVER LAKE STATE PARK: A scenic gem along the central coast, the park has about 3.5 miles of Lake Michigan frontage, a picturesque lighthouse, miles of perched sand dunes and a nice inland lake. Dune climbing is a favorite activity. In addition, it has a unique dune ride concession and one of the few remaining places for dune ORV use. A campground is located on Silver Lake.

Silver Lake State Park is busy in the summer. Much of the park's dunes are difficult to access, making for some quiet areas for those willing and able to find them. All the shores are sandy and excellent for swimming. Geography, geology and land ownership divides the park into several areas described below.
Telephone: (231) 873-3083
Web: www.michigan.gov/dnr

LITTLE SABLE POINT LIGHT & BEACH: A lonely exclamation mark along the shore, Little Sable Lighthouse juts 107 feet out of the sand. It stands as a solitary, red-brick tower following the demolition of the keeper's dwelling in the 1950's. Aside from the light and parking lot, this section of Silver Lake State Park is undeveloped. To the north and south of this half-mile public beach are summer residences.
GPS: 43°39.065'N; 86°32.293'W

DUNE ACCESS TRAIL: A hiking trail bridge crosses Silver Creek from the east-west portion of Lighthouse Drive. The trailhead is well marked. The road near the trailhead is narrow with little shoulder and parking is poor at this site. Traveling north leads to the Silver Lake Dunes. Expect to walk a minimum of one mile and traverse several dunes to reach the shore.
GPS: 43°39.401'N; 86°31.527'W

MAC WOOD'S DUNE RIDES: Mac Wood's Dune Rides are a concession operated under agreement with Silver Lake State Park. These "dune buggy" excursions are a piece of history that started in 1930. The open-passenger, modified vehicles take a scenic trip over the dunes and along the waterfront. Trips cover about 7 miles and take about 40 minutes. The tour can accommodate the physically disabled. The operating period is mid-May through the first week in October.
Telephone: (231) 873-2817
Web: macwoodsdunerides.com
GPS: 43°39.471'N; 86°30.777'W

SILVER LAKE STATE PARK CAMPGROUND & BEACH: Located on the shores of Silver Lake, the campground has modern restrooms, showers, electricity and a sanitation station for RV's. The sandy beach on Silver Lake has restrooms, a picnic pavilion and a boat ramp as well. A beautiful view of the Silver Lake Dunes lies across the way, framed by the sky and lake.

Silver Lake continues to get smaller as the dune edges slowly eastward with each grain blown by the westerly winds. Boats, canoes or kayaks can make the one-mile crossing to the dunes on the west shore of Silver Lake. This is a good way get to the dunes for hiking and climbing while avoiding some of the summer crowds at dune climb parking areas.
GPS: 43°39.401'N; 86°29.672'W

PEDESTRIAN DUNE CLIMB: The dune climb is a strenuous activity. A tall stairway starts you out but soon you will trek up and down loose sand on the high dunes. That said, what fun! Children will love this place, careening down the dunes, making giant leaps as if on the moon! Access to Silver Lake and Lake Michigan shores is possible. A straight walk to Lake Michigan is about one mile away. Silver Lake is a little shorter hike. Take water and a compass if you attempt it. Shifting sand can cover footprints in a short period, so do not expect that you can backtrack your steps on this landmark-free sand pile. A drawback is the noise generated at the adjacent ORV area to the north.
GPS: 43°40.925'N; 86°29.876'W

OFF-ROAD-VEHICLE AREA: The Silver Lake ORV area is famous as the last remaining place for a dune buggy or ORV to frolic on large Lake Michigan dunes. A portion of the dunes has been designated for this use at the north end of the park. It is a busy place with long lines and a permit (voucher) system to control and limit this access. Orange signs in the area direct you to the ORV Voucher Area. Contact the park for the use rules.
GPS: 43°40.898'N; 86°29.411'W

Top left: The beach at Mears State Park provides the backdrop to Pentwater's North Breakwater, a fine fishing spot.

Below left: Modern facilities and relaxing views of the waterway characterize Channel Lane Park.

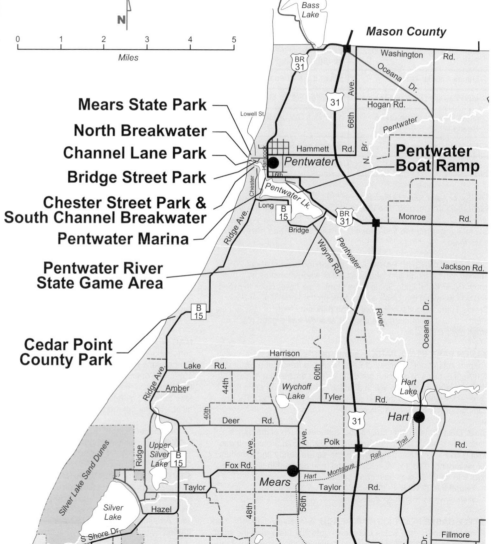

Oceana County

Pentwater Area

Name	Location	Entrance Fee	Parking	Modern Restrooms	Vault or Portable Toilet	Stair or Path to Shore	Swimming	Picnic Area	Drinking Water	Campground	Trailered Boat Launch	Kayak / Canoe	Marina	Fishing	Hiking	Biking	X-Country Skiing	Playground	Lighthouse	Beach Strolling	Sandy Beach	Stony or Rocky Shore	Dunes	Bluff	Wetland
Cedar Point County Park	3.5 miles S of Pentwater Lake on Hwy B-15 (Ridge Ave.).		●			●	●	●													●			●	
Chester Street Park & Pentwater Channel South Breakwater	Pentwater at south side of Pentwater Channel, Chester St. N of Long Bridge Rd. (B-15).		●		●	●								●											
Pentwater State Game Area	1.5 miles SW of Pentwater on B-15 (Long Bridge Rd.) just S of Monroe Rd. (US-31 BR).		●									●		●											●
Pentwater Boat Ramp	Pentwater. From US-31 BR turn S on Bean St. 1 block.	●	●	●							●	●													
Pentwater Marina	Pentwater. Hancock St. (US-31 BR) between 5th and 6th Streets.		●	●					●	●			●												
Bridge Street Park	Pentwater. South end of Bridge St. one block S of Lowell St.		●			●								●											
Channel Lane Park	Pentwater. Take W Lowell St. then S on Bridge St. then W on Channel Lane.		●	●		●		●	●																
Pentwater Channel North Breakwater	Pentwater at end of W Lowell Street.		●					●						●					●		●				
Charles Mears State Park	Pentwater at end of W Lowell Street.	●	●	●			●	●	●	●		●		●				●	●		●				

Pentwater is a small community that thrives on its Lake Michigan location. The summer months bring tourists and summer residents for a variety of interests. Sportfishing dominates in the spring and fall.

CEDAR POINT COUNTY PARK: Cedar Point Park is a small, wooded park sitting on a bluff above a broad, sandy beach. The picnic tables and grills are up on the bluff with the parking. Stairs lead down to the shore. Development is kept to a minimum. No pavement, no pavilion or playground, the park is nearly natural in most respects. The beach is its drawing point.
GPS: 43°43.998'N; 86°29.876'W

CHESTER STREET PARK & PENTWATER CHANNEL SOUTH BREAKWATER: Chester Park leads to the concrete walkway along the south side of Pentwater Channel and out to the south breakwater. There is no beach access. Benches are located near the Pentwater Lake end. Fishing from the walkway or breakwater is popular. The park is barrier-free
GPS: 44.46.758'N; 86°26.244'W

PENTWATER STATE GAME AREA: The Pentwater State Game Area is mostly wetland used for fishing and hunting. It is located at the east end of Pentwater Lake. Fishing without a boat can be accomplished in the Pentwater River at the bridge on Highway B-15 just south of the US-31 Business Route (Monroe Rd.). Limited parking is found on the shoulder near the bridge.
GPS: 43.45.794'N; 86.24.556'W

PENTWATER BOAT RAMP: Located on Pentwater Lake near downtown Pentwater, the channel to Lake Michigan is about 1 mile from the ramp.
GPS: 43°46.491'N; 86°25.740'W

PENTWATER MARINA: Located on the edge of the village, this is a full service public marina. Restrooms are available to the public. The fish cleaning station will be busy during the late summer and fall fish runs. Fees are charged for boat mooring and some boating services.
Telephone: (231) 869-7028
GPS: 43°46.617'N; 86°26.033'W (marina), 43°46.950'N; 86°26.65'W (Pentwater Channel entrance)

Note: A barrier-free, concrete walkway along the north side of the Pentwater Channel connects the four listings that follow. To reach these listings, turn west from Hancock Street onto Lowell Street.

BRIDGE STREET PARK: A very small, clean park on the north side channel near Pentwater Lake. Parking is limited to four spaces, one handicapped-designated. The concrete channel walkway heads west from here to the end of the north breakwater. The channel walk and breakwater are wheelchair-accessible facilities.
GPS: 43°46.828'N; 86°26.243'W

CHANNEL LANE PARK: Channel Lane Park is a small and modern facility along the Pentwater Channel. It has first-rate facilities including restroom, tables, grills and two pavilions. Landscaping and lawn are immaculate. There are 18 parking spaces. The channel walkway passes through on the park on its route from the north breakwater to Pentwater Lake. Wheelchair-accessible. *Note: Channel Lane is a narrow residential side street one block south of West Lowell Street near the lakeshore.*
GPS: 43°46.898'N; 86°26.397'W

PENTWATER CHANNEL NORTH BREAKWATER: Access the north breakwater via the channel walkway from Bridge Street or Channel Lane Park or by parking at Mears State Park. Parking at the state park requires a permit, the other locations are free. A modern-style navigation light tower is at the end of the breakwater. Fishing, walking and sunset-watching top the activities.

CHARLES MEARS STATE PARK: Mears is about 50 acres large with about 1500 feet of sandy Lake Michigan Beach. It has full services such as beachhouse, concession, modern restrooms and camping. The north breakwater is just to its south. Mears Park provides the closest parking to the breakwater. Motor vehicle entry requires a Michigan State Park Motor Vehicle Permit.
Telephone: (231) 869-2051
Web: www.michigan.gov/dnr
GPS: 43°46.993'N; 86°26.421'W

Car Ferries

The Great Lakes provided an efficient highway for early transportation. Native Americans could travel long distances with heavy loads in their canoes. Later the French fur traders and explorers used the waters for trade as well as to search for a shipping route to the orient. But for newer forms of transportation, first the railroad and then the automobile, the lakes became an impediment. The long and wide expanses of these waters meant time consuming circumnavigation by land.

In the 1850's, railroad ferries began crossing the Niagara River from Buffalo, New York to Ontario. Service across the Detroit River between Detroit and Windsor soon followed. Around 1880, the movement of ore and timber from Michigan's Upper Peninsula prompted the construction of railroads in the area. The railroads started ferry service to connect the state's two peninsulas at the Straits of Mackinac. The service remained until 1984 when railroad decline made the crossing unneeded. Each of these locations required a relatively short route but they had obstacles, particularly in winter, when the freshwater froze, requiring ice breaking. Keeping docks open and avoiding dangerous pack ice were common winter challenges.

During the mid-1800's, railroads were built to the Lake Michigan shore cities of Grand Haven, Ludington and Frankfort as well as to port cities in Wisconsin and the Upper Peninsula. Cargo arriving by rail was shipped between the shores on freighters. In 1892, the Toledo, Ann Arbor & North Michigan Railroad hatched an ambitious plan to ferry the loaded rail cars from a Frankfort (Elberta) terminus to Kewaunee, Wisconsin. The route traversed 60 miles making this the first car ferry service to cross a wide body of open water. To make the operation reliable for shippers, year-round sailing was necessary. Like the shorter river crossings, winter posed a major problem. Normally, Lake Michigan does not freeze completely but its harbors do. Daily use helped to keep the channel open. Ferry design required a bow capable of cutting ice. The original Ann Arbor ferries had bow propellers to churn the water ahead of the bow, helping to break the ice. During deep cold spells, the ice won the battle, marooning ferries.

The open waters also required a special system to secure the railcars. In heavy seas, the cars would sway on their suspension, called trunks. The rocking motion of the unstable cargo could cause instability for the ferry. In 1893, the Ann Arbor engineered a method

of jacking the load off the trunks, then chained them to hold the load firm. The boats were loaded and unloaded from the stern because open bow-type ferries were unsuitable for use on the lake.

The Wisconsin Central Railroad built a slip at Manitowoc, Wisconsin in 1896 which was first used by the Ann Arbor ferries from Frankfort. The Pere Marquette Railroad, later part of the Chesapeake & Ohio (C&O), began car ferry operations from Ludington to Manitowoc in 1897 and afterwards added service to Milwaukee and Kewaunee, Wisconsin. In 1903, the Grand Trunk Railroad began car ferry service from Grand Haven to Milwaukee. It became a Muskegon to Milwaukee route some thirty years later.

Times changed as highways developed. The service expanded to carry trucks, automobiles and their passengers. As roads improved and the Mackinac Bridge opened in 1957, cargo and cars could move around the lake easier. By the 1970's, rail traffic began to suffer. In 1982, Frankfort operations stopped. In 1990, Ludington service ceased. Railcars no longer take the trip across the lake.

The Lake Michigan Car Ferry Service revived seasonal service for automobiles and passengers in 1992 from Ludington to Manitowoc. Its modern ship transports tourists in comfort from May to October. It gives a glimpse of the past during the 4-hour voyage. In 2004, a new high-speed ferry established Muskegon to Milwaukee runs. Again the service looks to tourists and their automobiles as its primary revenue. Time will tell whether demand can keep two ferry services afloat. The finance of such operations has been as perilous as the early ferry crossings.

• *Left:* Ships of the past lay moored and idle in Ludington. The *Arthur K. Atkinson* (front) served Frankfort and the Ann Arbor Railroad from 1958 until its demise. Originally built as the *Ann Arbor No. 6* in 1917, it was later lengthened and renamed. The *Spartan*, built in 1952 and seen at the back of the photo, serviced Ludington for the C&O. Its twin ferry, the now refurbished *Badger,* still travels the Ludington to Manitowoc route for the Lake Michigan Car Ferry Service.

• *Below:* Car ferry routes connected a number of Lake Michigan ports during their roughly hundred-year heyday. Today, only two routes survive. Neither carry rail cars anymore, instead they focus on tourist travel during the warmer months only.

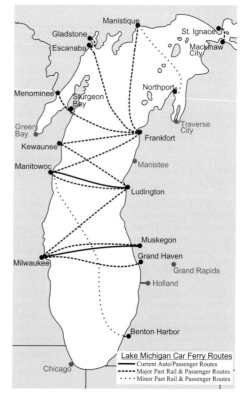

Lake Michigan Car Ferry Routes
— Current Auto/Passenger Routes
--- Major Past Rail & Passenger Routes
···· Minor Past Rail & Passenger Routes

Mason County

With some of the longest public shore anywhere on the coast, you can find whatever you are looking for in Mason County. If you seek solitude, try the Nordhouse Dunes, a unique wilderness of endless beach and forested dune. Want a large recreational area? Visit Ludington State Park. It has sandy beach on both Lake Michigan and the inland Hamlin Lake. Great fishing abounds, especially when the fall spawning run sends chinook salmon up the Big Sable River. Take a hike and find a solitary lighthouse stuck out in the sand dunes more than a mile from any development. An interpretive center, hiking trails, forests and camping create other opportunities.

Ludington, one of the larger cities north of Muskegon, marks the center of the coast. Ferry service to and from Wisconsin anchors here. Several marinas and a number of boat ramps occupy the shores of Pere Marquette Lake, Ludington's harbor. Several blocks of shops lie close to the harbor. Stearns Park, with the adjoining breakwater area, offers a city beach experience.

Private owners possess most of the shore south of the city. A notable private site is the Ludington Pumped Storage Plant whose role in the nation's energy grid is explained in the section *Industry on the Lake (p.38)*. Consumers Energy allows limited public access to view portions of the facility. Stop here to overlook Lake Michigan while learning about power generation and energy storage. Several small parks offer free beach access in the area. One is Summit Township Park which provides a nice setting for those desiring an excellent beach, fewer users and a shaded picnic area.

For those heading north, the freeway portion of US-31 ends east of Ludington. Two-lane US-31 continues north, farther away from the shore, until reaching the City of Manistee. Along the south county coastline, Lakeshore Drive offers occasional lake views especially near the Pumped Storage Plant and on the peninsula heading to the Ludington South Breakwater. Highway M-116 takes visitors from downtown Ludington to Ludington State Park. In the north portion of the county, no highway parallels the shore. Here you venture into the Huron-Manistee National Forest via Forest Trail (paved) or Nurnberg Road (gravel) where the Lake Michigan Recreation Area and Nordhouse Dunes lie at the end.

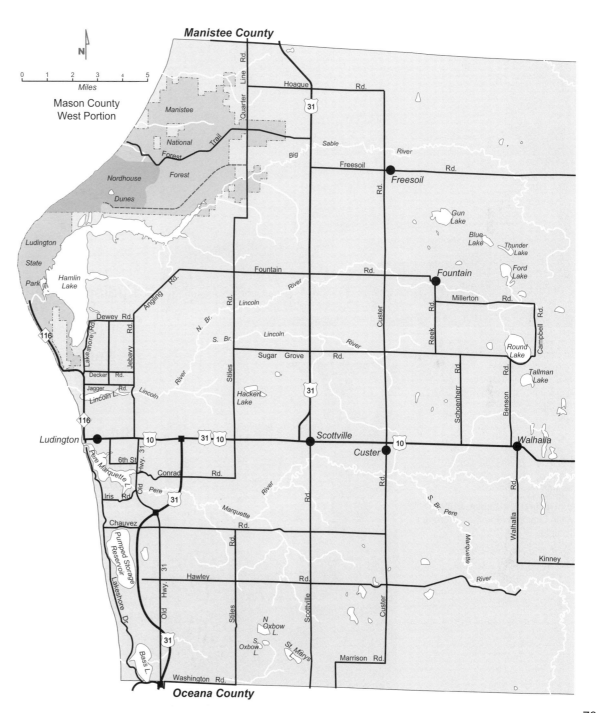

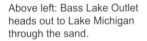

Above left: Bass Lake Outlet heads out to Lake Michigan through the sand.

Above right: The turbine station at the Ludington Pumped Storage Complex

Right: The beach at Summit Township Park.

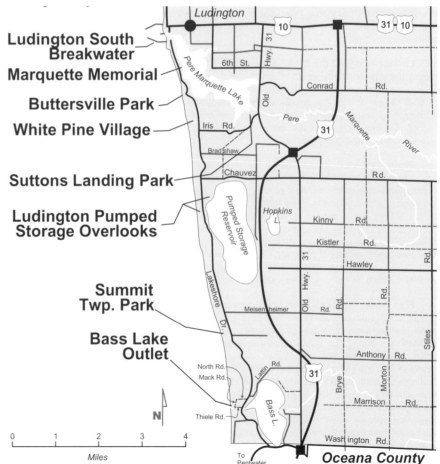

Ludington

Ludington South Breakwater

Marquette Memorial

Buttersville Park

White Pine Village

Suttons Landing Park

Ludington Pumped Storage Overlooks

Summit Twp. Park

Bass Lake Outlet

Oceana County

0 1 2 3 4
Miles

Mason County

Oceana County Line to Ludington

Name	Location	Entrance Fee	Parking	Modern Restrooms	Vault or Portable Toilet	Stair or Path to Shore	Swimming	Picnic Area	Drinking Water	Campground	Trailered Boat Launch	Kayak / Canoe	Marina	Fishing	Hiking	Biking	X-Country Skiing	Playground	Lighthouse	Beach Strolling	Sandy Beach	Stony or Rocky Shore	Dunes	Bluff	Wetland
Bass Lake Outlet	3 miles N or Pentwater. From Lakeshore, W on Thiele Rd.		●			●	●					●		●							●		●		
Summit Township Park	5 miles N of Pentwater on Lakeshore Drive.		●	●		●	●	●				●									●			●	
Ludington Pumped Storage Overlooks	Lakeshore Dr., 5 mi. S of Ludington. Exit US-31 at Old US-31 exit, travel S 0.5 mi then W on Chauvez Rd. Turn S on Lakeshore Dr.		●			●	●																	●	
White Pine Village	Lakeshore Drive 0.2 miles N of Iris Rd.	●	●	●				●																	
Buttersville Park	Lakeshore Drive one mile N of Iris Rd.		●	●			●	●	●	●		●									●				
Pere Marquette Memorial	Lakeshore Drive 1.5 miles N of Iris Rd.		●								●	●													
Ludington South Breakwater	Lakeshore Drive 2.5 miles N of Iris Rd.		●				●	●				●		●							●				
Suttons Landing Park	4 miles SE of Ludington. Iris Rd. just W of Old US-31.		●	●	●			●						●											●

The shore between Pentwater and Ludington is rural and lightly developed by housing. The Ludington Pumped Storage facility owns much of the shore, limiting access in the middle of this stretch.

BASS LAKE OUTLET: The undeveloped park at Bass Lake's outlet stream is poorly marked. A short, sandy trail to the creek mouth and Lake Michigan starts at the end of Thiele Road where it ends at Mack Road. This is a very short distance west of Lakeshore Drive and is the first road to the north of the creek. Parking can be found along Mack Road a few hundred feet north of Thiele. Look for the small, aging sign designating the parking area to avoid blocking private drives. The park has small dunes, lots of sand and a choice of swimming in the lake or stream. Children will find the creek's moving water a treat. The public parcel is relatively small. Prevailing winds normally turn the creek's flow towards the north before it empties into Lake Michigan. Because of this, accessing the public portion of Lake Michigan may require crossing the creek. A kayak carry to the creek is relatively short.
  GPS: 43°50.028'N; 86°25.721'W

SUMMIT TOWNSHIP PARK: Most of Summit Township Park sits high on a bluff overlooking Lake Michigan. Tennis courts, a baseball field and the picnic area sit on the highland. There is some play equipment and modern restrooms as well. A path leads down a relatively gradual slope to the beach. A small creek borders the beach area to the south. The beach is generally sandy with some stone.
  GPS: 43°51.404'N; 86°25.828'W

LUDINGTON PUMPED STORAGE OVERLOOKS: The Ludington Pumped Storage Hydroelectric Plant is a unique facility. An 842-acre, man-made reservoir sits on the east side of Lakeshore Drive. During periods of low electric demand, reversible turbines use electricity to pump water from Lake Michigan uphill 363 feet to the reservoir. When electric demand is high, water released back to the lake through the turbines generates hydroelectric power. Electricity is thus stored as potential energy in the reservoir for use when most needed. The facility is a vital component of the northeast power grid.

North of the generator station is a parking area with walking paths to two viewing areas. The lower overlook is west of Lakeshore Drive and looks down at the generating complex and Lake Michigan from a couple hundred feet high. The second viewing platform is much higher, at the rim of the reservoir, some 13-stories above the lake level. Distant views of the lake are found here. The path up to the reservoir is paved but relatively steep. For some people, it is an arduous hike. The Ludington Pumped Storage Complex owns much of lakeshore in this area limiting shoreline access.
  GPS: 43°53.876'N; 86°26.598'W

Note: Reach the next four listings by continuing on Lakeshore Drive north of Iris Road.

WHITE PINE VILLAGE: The "Village" is a historical recreation of the Ludington area from the lumber era around the start of the 19th century to later periods. History in action and special events highlight the visit. An antique auto exhibit plus lumber and maritime museums are other features. The chapel provides a beautiful view of Lake Michigan. Admission fee. Normally open from the end of April to mid-October and usually closed Sundays and Mondays. Contact the museum for actual dates and hours.
  Telephone: (231) 843-4808
  Web:www.historicwhitepinevillage.org
  GPS: 43°55.653'N; 86°23.700'W

BUTTERSVILLE PARK: This county park includes camping and picnicking on a wooded highland. The beach below the bluff is sandy. A separate parking area for day-use beachgoers is available north of the campground area on Lakeshore Drive. Surfcasting is popular particularly in the fall. Fee for camping.
  GPS: 43°56.141'N; 86°27.060'W (camping area entrance)
  GPS: 43°56.258'N; 86°27.158'W (beach along Lakeshore Dr.)

PERE MARQUETTE MEMORIAL: Pere Marquette, a French explorer and missionary is a legendary figure of the upper Great Lakes; so much so that more than one community has claimed the site of his death. He died somewhere along the Lake Michigan shore on May 18, 1675 while attempting to return to St. Ignace from his Mississippi River exploration. This location is one place that meets the description of his passing and has managed a state historical marker to mark it. Frankfort, Michigan, a short way up the coast, has been able to claim the same. A large cross sits on top of the hill with overlooks of Lake Michigan and Pere Marquette Lake. A very good boat ramp on Pere Marquette Lake is located behind the memorial hill.
  GPS: 43°56.500'N; 86°27.204'W

LUDINGTON SOUTH BREAKWATER: Find the south breakwater for Ludington Harbor at the north end of Lakeshore Drive. Look for the paved parking lot on the left where the public road ends at the condominium complex. A sandy path leads to the small beach and the concrete breakwater. The Ludington Lighthouse can be seen on the north breakwater across the way and a city view lies directly to the east. Canoes or kayaks could be carried to either the harbor or the lake side of the breakwater for launch. Use caution. This breakwater is narrow and runs mostly south-to-north making it fully exposed to prevailing winds and waves.
  GPS: 43°56.905'N; 86°27.373'W

SUTTONS LANDING PARK: Sutton's Landing sits along the wetland where the Pere Marquette River empties into Pere Marquette Lake. Fishing is a major activity. Picnic pavilion.
  GPS: 43°55.558'N; 86°25.136'W

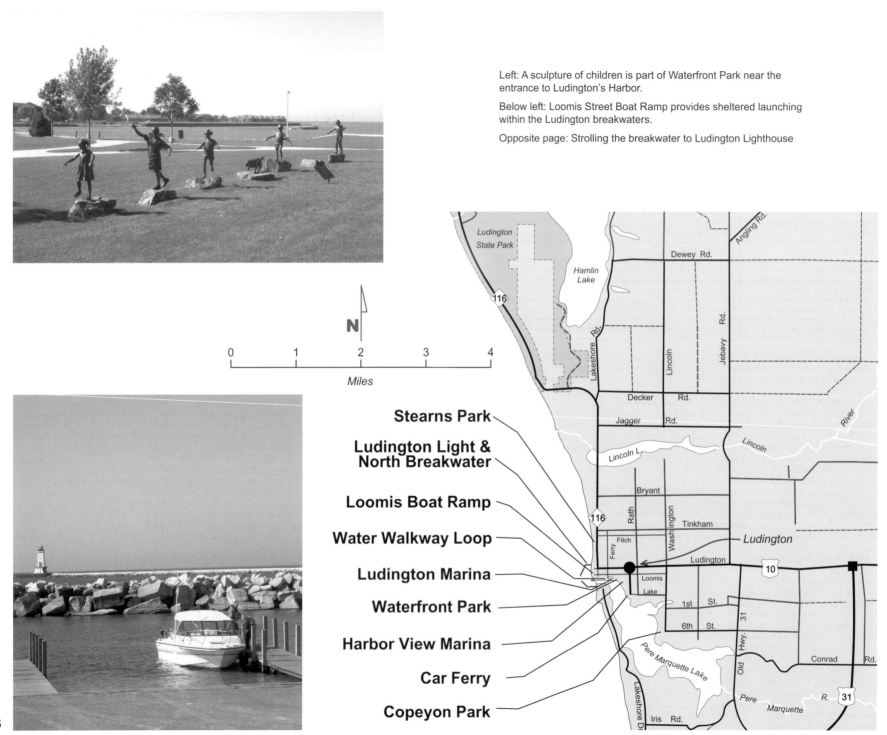

Left: A sculpture of children is part of Waterfront Park near the entrance to Ludington's Harbor.

Below left: Loomis Street Boat Ramp provides sheltered launching within the Ludington breakwaters.

Opposite page: Strolling the breakwater to Ludington Lighthouse

Stearns Park

Ludington Light & North Breakwater

Loomis Boat Ramp

Water Walkway Loop

Ludington Marina

Waterfront Park

Harbor View Marina

Car Ferry

Copeyon Park

N

0   1   2   3   4
Miles

Mason County

Ludington

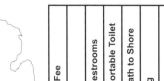

Facilities   **Environment**

Name	Location	Entrance Fee	Parking	Modern Restrooms	Vault or Portable Toilet	Stair or Path to Shore	Swimming	Picnic Area	Drinking Water	Campground	Trailered Boat Launch	Kayak / Canoe	Marina	Fishing	Hiking	Biking	X-Country Skiing	Playground	Lighthouse	Beach Strolling	Sandy Beach	Stony or Rocky Shore	Dunes	Bluff	Wetland
Peter Copeyon Park & 2nd Street Boat Ramp	Ludington. Second at Washington Streets		●					●	●		●	●						●							
Lake Michigan Car Ferry	Ludington. US-10 ferry dock terminus. James at Dowland Streets.	●	●	●					●																
Ludington Harbor View Marina	Ludington. Rath at Fisher Street.		●	●									●												
Waterfront Park	Ludington. Filer at William Street.		●	●				●	●					●				●							
Ludington Municipal Marina	Ludington. William at Filer Street.		●	●				●	●				●												
Water Walkway Loop	Ludington. Ferry Street, S of Loomis St.		●	●		●			●						●	●				●					
Loomis Street Boat Ramp	Ludington. W end of Loomis Street.	●	●								●	●								●					
Ludington Light & North Breakwater	Ludington. Lakeshore Drive (M-116) near W end of Ludington St.		●			●								●						●		●			
Stearns Park	Ludington. Lakeshore Dr. with auto entrance near Fitch St.		●	●			●	●	●			●						●		●	●	●			

Downtown Ludington sits on the north side of Pere Marquette Lake, the city's harbor. The car ferry service to Wisconsin keeps the port feeling of the town. Beach life and fishing share the traveler's attention.

PETER COPEYON PARK & 2ND STREET BOAT RAMP: A city park located on the east side of Pere Marquette Lake, Copeyon contains a major boat ramp roughly one mile from Lake Michigan. A picnic and playground park adjoins the ramp area.

LAKE MICHIGAN CAR FERRY: The seasonal car ferry service across Lake Michigan to Wisconsin leaves from the Ludington docks near downtown. The ferry is large, comfortable and takes about 4 hours for the crossing to Manitowoc. Food service, movies and other amenities are available. The season runs from mid-May to mid-October. Two crossings each way during the summer. Reservations are advised.
 Telephone: (800) 841-4243.
 Web: www.ssbadger.com.
 GPS: 43°56.715'N; 86°26.365'W

LUDINGTON HARBOR VIEW MARINA: A new marina with a number of amenities, Harbor View is located just north of the ferry terminal. The marina, built with state waterway funds, is operated as a private entity making it an interesting monument to the politics of its time. It is included here because a few transient boat slips are available.
 Telephone: (231) 843-6032
 GPS: 43°56.950'N; 86°27.067'W

WATERFRONT PARK: Located a block from downtown on Pere Marquette Lake, this is a nice, new facility with a large playground, clean, modern bathrooms and walkways leading to other waterfront areas. A bandshell has been added completing the area's renovation from rail yard to park.
 GPS: 43°57.197'N; 86°27.121'W

LUDINGTON MUNICIPAL MARINA: The marina is located next to Waterfront Park and is primarily for boaters. It includes 150 boat slips located a short distance from the Lake Michigan harbor entrance. Picnic tables are located along the harborfront.
 Telephone: (231) 843-9611
 GPS: 43°57.133'N; 86°27.333'W

WATER WALKWAY LOOP: The sidewalks bordering Marina Street, the Ludington Channel, Inner Harbor waterfront and Loomis Street form a short walking loop near the Ludington North Breakwater. It is a good place to watch boats leaving and entering Pere Marquette Lake. One corner of the rectangular loop intersects the inner harbor pier. Stearns Park and the primary Ludington waterfront lie adjacent to the walking loop. Street parking is available on Marina Street.
 GPS: 43°57.199'N; 86°27.374'W

LOOMIS STREET BOAT RAMP: Located on the Lake Michigan shore inside the breakwater is a deep launch a short distance from the harbor opening to the big lake. Stearns Park and the North Breakwater abut to the north.

LUDINGTON LIGHT & NORTH BREAKWATER: The largest parking area near the breakwater is at Stearns Park but local streets provide additional spaces within an easy walk. Ludington's white, squarish lighthouse stands at the end of the breakwater.

STEARNS PARK: Stearns Park is the home of the city's major beach. There are 2500 feet of sand beachfront. The north breakwater with the Ludington lighthouse lies at the south end of the beach. Concession, beachhouse and tables are available. The American Legion playground adjoins it at the south end. Shuffleboard, mini-golf and volleyball are other activities.
 GPS: 43°57.530'N; 86°27.605'W

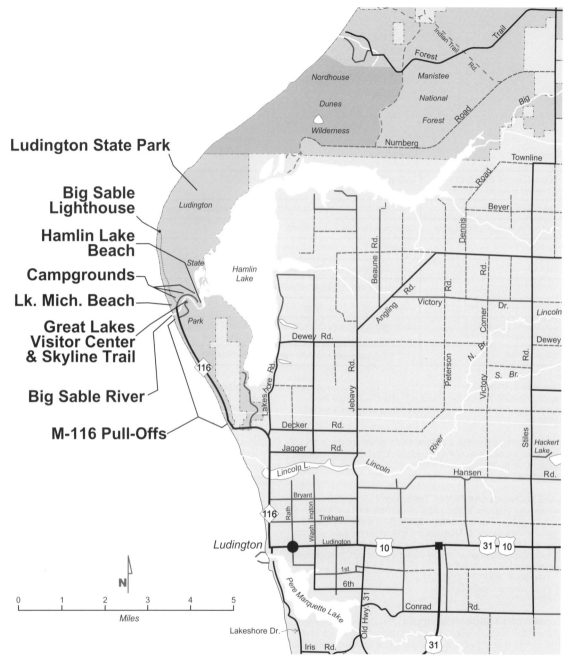

Ludington State Park

Big Sable Lighthouse

Hamlin Lake Beach

Campgrounds

Lk. Mich. Beach

Great Lakes Visitor Center & Skyline Trail

Big Sable River

M-116 Pull-Offs

Above left: Big Sable Point Lighthouse looms ahead after the mile stroll down from the park's beachhouse.

Near left: Fishing lineup at the Hamlin Lake Dam during the fall salmon run.

Mason County

Ludington State Park

Name	Location	Entrance Fee	Parking	Modern Restrooms	Vault or Portable Toilet	Stair or Path to Shore	Swimming	Picnic Area	Drinking Water	Campground	Trailered Boat Launch	Kayak / Canoe	Marina	Fishing	Hiking	Biking	X-Country Skiing	Playground	Lighthouse	Beach Strolling	Sandy Beach	Stony or Rocky Shore	Dunes	Bluff	Wetland
Ludington State Park	4 miles N of Ludington on M-116.	●	●	●			●	●	●	●	●	●		●	●	●	●	●	●	●	●		●		
M-116 Pull-Offs	3 miles N of Ludington on M-116.		●				●					●								●	●		●		
Great Lakes Visitor Center:	Ludington State Park.	●	●	●					●					●											
Skyline Trail	Ludington State Park at Great Lakes Visitor Center.	●	●	●					●						●								●		
Lake Michigan Beach	Ludington State Park. North end of M-116.	●	●	●			●							●						●	●				
Big Sable Point Lighthouse	Ludington State Park.	●				●	●							●	●				●	●	●		●		
State Park Campgrounds	Ludington State Park. North end of M-116.	●	●	●		●				●	●			●	●										
Hamlin Lake Beach	Ludington State Park. North end of M-116.						●		●	●	●	●		●	●	●					●				
Big Sable River	Ludington State Park. North end of M-116.	●	●	●			●	●	●			●		●	●						●				

Ludington State Park, the northern of the two knobby points along the central coast, offers a variety of activities. Young children, teens and adults all find this destination to their liking.

LUDINGTON STATE PARK: Ludington is one of Michigan's largest state parks. It protects 7 miles of Lake Michigan shore and dunes. It adjoins a portion of the Huron-Manistee National Forest to the north combining for a total of 12 miles of continuous public shore. All of it is easily hiked, sandy beach making this one of the finest, undeveloped shore accesses on Lake Michigan. The park beachhouse and Big Sable Lighthouse are the only buildings along the way.

Sand dunes parallel the coast in this area. Big Sable Point Lighthouse presents the shore's most visible destination. Hamlin Lake forms the park's east border providing considerably more shore and a warm, calm water alternative to the big lake. The Big Sable River flows between the lakes. The beachgoer, hiker, skier, snowshoer, fisher, boater, canoeist and kayker will find their place at this popular destination. State Park Permit required beyond the park entrance.
Telephone: (231) 843-8671
Web: www.michigan.gov/dnr

M-116 PULL-OFFS: North of Ludington a few miles, M-116 returns to its parallel course along Lake Michigan. Short dunes obscure the lake for the most part. Three pull-offs accommodate a few cars each. The beach is sandy along this stretch. Below are coordinates for three pull-off points.
GPS: 43°59.638'N; 86°28.662'W
GPS: 44°00.879'N; 86°29.627'W
GPS: 44°01.691'N; 86°30.293'W

GREAT LAKES VISITOR CENTER: This Michigan State Park interpretive center focuses on the geological and human history of the Great Lakes, along with the diverse life forms found in the park. In addition to exhibits depicting the Great Lakes, displays tell the early history of Ludington State Park and its unique resources.

SKYLINE TRAIL: One of many trails within Ludington State Park, Skyline Trail is highlighted here for its views of Lake Michigan. This hiking loop starts at the Great Lakes Visitor Center area. The lower trail sits in the shade of tall trees below the ridge. Tall, wooden stairs take you to the ridge top for views of the dunes to the south, Lake Michigan to the west and Big Sable River to the north. The wooden "ridge-way" has an opening for accessing the steep dune on the south side.

LAKE MICHIGAN BEACH: One of the finest beaches on Lake Michigan, the sandy shore stretches for miles each way from the beachhouse. Concession, change room and restrooms are found at this location. The area has been kept natural and the beachhouse building blends pleasantly into the dunes. Walk north 1.75 miles along the beach to the Big Sable Lighthouse.
GPS: 44°01.957'N; 86°30.344'W

BIG SABLE POINT LIGHTHOUSE: Big Sable's black and white tower rises 112 feet from the sands. Originally made of brick, the lighthouse was encased in steel during 1902 to protect it from further deterioration. Prior to the encasement, the Little Sable Point Light in Oceana County was a twin. Unlike Little Sable Light, the connected keeper's residence still exists here. Tours are available at scheduled times. Big Sable Point Lighthouse's uniqueness owes much to its isolated site. Miles of undeveloped beach and small dunes border its north and south flanks. The visit requires a 1.75-mile hike from the

south via the beach or trail. About halfway through the beach trek, the top of the tower begins to appear. A much longer hike is required if entering from Nordhouse Dunes to the north (see p.81). Pack a lunch and towel, then swim and stay a while.
GPS: 44°03.404'N; 86°30.887'W

STATE PARK CAMPGROUNDS: Three campgrounds with a total of 344 sites lie between Hamlin Lake and Lake Michigan. Each has electricity and modern restrooms with showers. These campgrounds fill frequently and reservations are wise during the summer season. Fishing season extends their extensive use past Labor Day. Campground reservations: 1-800-44-PARKS

HAMLIN LAKE BEACH: Hamlin is a large lake whose outlet is less than a mile from Lake Michigan. The park has a sandy beach on a small bay. The water is relatively warm. The islands and small bays make for interesting canoeing and kayaking. A boat ramp is also available. Changehouse, concession and picnic area are also available. Unlike the Lake Michigan shore, there is plenty of shade.

BIG SABLE RIVER: A short but relatively wide river flows through Hamlin Lake to Lake Michigan. Paths and boardwalk line each side of this popular site to hike. A high dam, located just south of Hamlin Lake Beach, controls the level of Hamlin Lake. Foot traffic can cross the dam and walk downstream to the Great Lakes Visitor Center and Skyline Trail. Paddlers can portage the dam on the river's left. The stream teems with salmon during the fall spawning run. Fishermen line the banks up to the dam. Most of the parking is along the north side of the river with the Hamlin Beach area providing the largest parking area.

Above: Study nature's traces in the sand at Nordhouse Dunes.

Below: Looking south from the Lake Michigan Recreation Area towards Nordhouse Dunes and Big Sable Point.

Opposite page: Scenic views and relative solitude characterize the isolated Nordhouse Dunes.

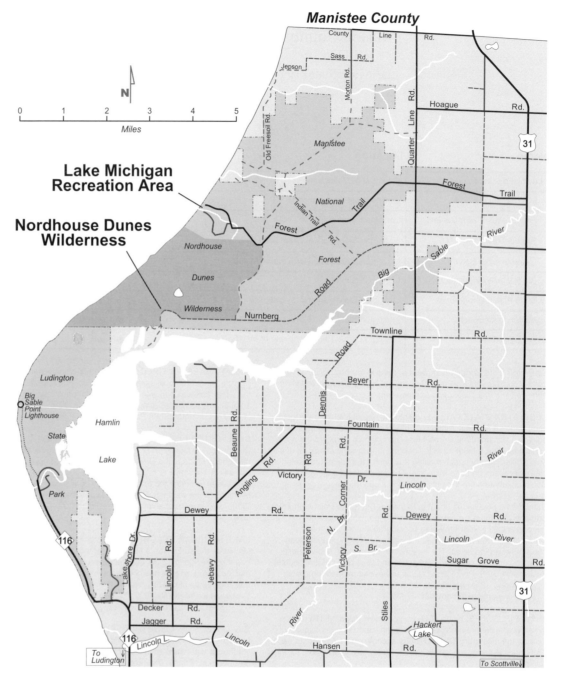

Manistee County

Lake Michigan
Recreation Area

Nordhouse Dunes
Wilderness

80

Mason County

Manistee National Forest - Nordhouse Dunes

Name	Location	Entrance Fee	Parking	Modern Restrooms	Vault or Portable Toilet	Stair or Path to Shore	Swimming	Picnic Area	Drinking Water	Campground	Trailered Boat Launch	Kayak / Canoe	Marina	Fishing	Hiking	Biking	X-Country Skiing	Playground	Lighthouse	Beach Strolling	Sandy Beach	Stony or Rocky Shore	Dunes	Bluff	Wetland
		Facilities																			**Environment**				
Nordhouse Dunes Wilderness	12 miles SW of Manistee. Primary access via Nurmberg or Forest Trail Roads.	●	●		●	●	●							●		●				●	●		●		
Lake Michigan Recreation Area	12 miles SW of Manistee. From US-31, turn W on Forest Trail Rd. then about 8 miles.	●	●	●	●	●	●	●	●	●		●		●	●		●	●		●	●		●		

Little of the Huron-Manistee National Forest lands lie along the coast but what does provides the public some of the nicest real estate available. Those seeking peace and willing to walk will enjoy Nordhouse Dunes. The Lake Michigan Recreation Area has easier access plus a few facilities. Towns and development keep a distance here.

NORDHOUSE DUNES WILDERNESS: The Nordhouse Dunes, part of the Huron-Manistee National Forest, is a federally managed wilderness area. It encompasses 3450 acres and nearly 3.5 miles of Lake Michigan sand shore. When combined with Ludington State Park to its south and additional US Forest Service lands to its north, the public shore extends about 12 miles. Little of it is developed.

As its name implies, much of the wilderness is composed of dunes. Forests and vegetation cover the backdune. Camping is allowed by permit and wilderness rules must be followed. Latrines are available at the primary trailheads, one located on Nurmberg Road and the other at Lake Michigan Recreation Area. Once inside the wilderness area, you are on your own. Carry water or a water purifier. Trails are limited, with few if any signs. A compass and map should be used. Fees are collected by self-serve pay envelopes. Have exact cash or check. Map and rules are posted on the website. Print a copy in case the map box at the trailhead is empty.

Telephone: Manistee Ranger District (231) 723-2211
Web: www.fs.fed.us/r9/hmnf/pages/nordhouse.htm.
GPS: 44°05.240'N; 86°26.689'W (Nurmberg Road Trailhead)

LAKE MICHIGAN RECREATION AREA: The Lake Michigan Recreation Area encompasses the developed portions of the Huron-Manistee National Forest along the lakeshore at Portage Creek. Several campsite loops, a picnic area and observation platforms round out the development. Access to the beach is provided via short paths. Small dunes line the shore. The beach is sandy with a few stones and swimming is very good. Development is generally kept to a minimum here. The roadway in is paved. There is an access fee. This area is very popular in summer especially on weekends.

Telephone: Manistee Ranger District (231) 723-2211
GPS: 44°07.254'N; 86°25.534'W

Salmon and Steelhead

Not many things top the excitement of a big fish snatching a lure, running with the line, then breaking out of the water to display its contempt. Sportfishing along Lake Michigan is big fun and big business. Coho and chinook salmon, brown and steelhead trout lead the excitement. The fish can easily weigh 10 pounds with record fish up to 30 or 40 pounds. Every major port has a fleet of charter boats whose captains live and breathe fishing and rarely leave you without success. It is a good way to get familiar with the sport and its methods. What kind of rod and reel should you use? What size line do you need? What kind of bait works? It helps to have an expert to get you started.

If your pocketbook isn't ready for a charter, try shore fishing. It is productive and inexpensive, but it requires more knowledge on your part. Check page 14 for a map of public breakwaters, piers and fishing platforms. They are spaced regularly along the coastline and most sit at rivermouths where the fish come to spawn. The relatively warm river outflow sets up a temperature gradient where it meets the lake. Fish often feed near this line, where food is plentiful and the darker-colored river water provides protective cover.

Try fishing along the riverbank during the spawning run. With polarized glasses you can see the fish as they lay in holes and maybe as they attack your lure. You won't be alone, but you can pick up on techniques used by the others in the crowd. The beach is another simple fishing spot. Surfcasting works in spring or fall especially near a creekmouth. A section of PVC pipe tapped into the sand makes a nice rod holder. Bring a chair for relaxing and some waders in case you need to get into the water. Often, you will have the beach to yourself.

Most of the action will occur near the lake bottom. If still-fishing, weight live baits just off the bottom. Spawn bags, cut baits and various worm types are typical baits depending on specie or conditions. Casting spoon-type lures is another method. Contact the local bait and tackle shops to see what's hot and what's attracting the fish.

The pier fisherman has all sorts of other gear. A long-handle net for snatching your catch out of the water is a necessity at high docks, piers and breakwaters. Bring a chair or pail to sit on and a pack or cart to carry your stuff. Prepare for the weather. The piers and shore can be cool. The wind can change a warm day into a cold one quickly. Coveralls, long underwear, warm coat, hat and gloves are often welcome in fall and spring, the most productive fishing seasons.

Clockwise from the bottom left:
- After a day on the big lake, the fishing boat heads into St. Joseph Harbor.
- A lone fisherman casts from the breakwater during the fall season.
- Stream fishing during the fall salmon run.
- A calm day brings out the local fishermen at Grand Haven.
- Peacefully, two fishermen enjoy the end of the day on the Big Sable River.

Manistee County

High bluffs line most of the Manistee County coast. They fade away at a few places such as the three harbors located at Manistee, Portage Lake and Arcadia. You will not find many large parks. Private shore dominates but small beaches are interspersed regularly along the way. Of the beaches, only Orchard Beach State Park charges for entrance.

The City of Manistee features a lively downtown with charming shops and restaurants. The business district sits on the south side of the Manistee River. The "Riverwalk" travels 1.5 miles from town to Douglas Park, a multi-purpose facility located at the harbor entrance on Lake Michigan. Manistee emphasizes its historic roots, featuring a Victorian character and a deep connection to the logging era of a hundred years ago. By contrast, a new casino pumps money into the economy, helping to keep the local business atmosphere strong.

Highway US-31 continues to serve as the primary artery for the lakeshore counties, but north of Manistee, a second highway starts its journey. M-22 heads towards Portage Lake and the towns of Onekama and Arcadia. It then follows close to the coast through parts of four counties. It is one of the state's most scenic roads, meandering north, wrapping around the Leelanau Peninsula and then reversing to the south, ending in Traverse City. This drive is a must. During the summer and fall harvest season, numerous fruit stands dot the highway shoulder, selling strawberries, cherries, peaches and apples. Be sure to stop.

Here are some other suggestions. If you seek a quiet place to swim or picnic, try the Magoon Creek Natural Area south of Manistee. It combines woodlands, trails and bluff views with a sandy beach. The Portage Point area provides a glimpse of the past with its summer cottage atmosphere and picturesque Portage Point Inn. Its beautiful beach sits next to the Portage Lake Channel. The small town of Arcadia enjoys a relaxed setting with a nice beach and good boating facilities. The Fifth Avenue Beach on the north side of the Manistee Channel is a bit difficult to find and provides a chance to mix with a more local crowd.

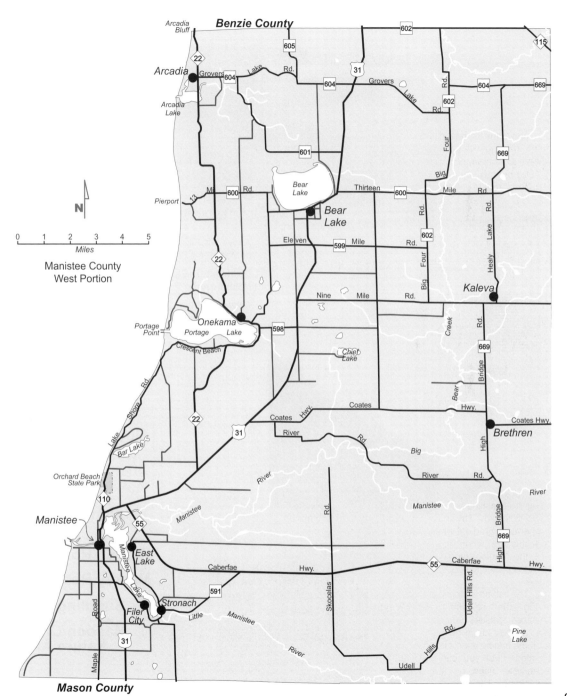

Manistee County
West Portion

Above left: First Street Beach stretches on both sides of Manistee's South Breakwater.

Below left: The beach and bluff at Magoon Creek Natural Area.

Above right: In Douglas Park, some of the Manistee nautical heritage provides foreground for the channel and lighthouse.

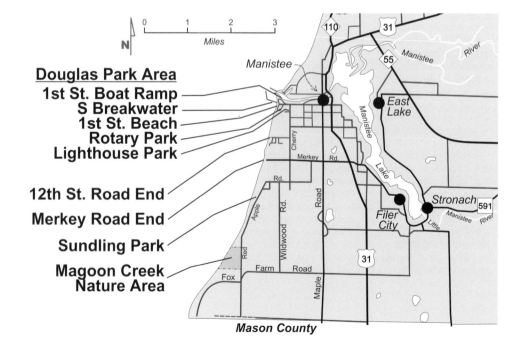

Douglas Park Area
1st St. Boat Ramp
S Breakwater
1st St. Beach
Rotary Park
Lighthouse Park

12th St. Road End

Merkey Road End

Sundling Park

Magoon Creek Nature Area

Mason County

Manistee County

Mason County Line to Manistee City South

Name	Location	Entrance Fee	Parking	Modern Restrooms	Vault or Portable Toilet	Stair or Path to Shore	Swimming	Picnic Area	Drinking Water	Campground	Trailered Boat Launch	Kayak / Canoe	Marina	Fishing	Hiking	Biking	X-Country Skiing	Playground	Lighthouse	Beach Strolling	Sandy Beach	Stony or Rocky Shore	Dunes	Bluff	Wetland
Magoon Creek Natural Area	5 miles SW of Manistee on Red Apple Rd. From US-31, W 3 miles on Fox Rd. then 0.5 mile N on Red Apple.		●		●	●	●	●	●			●			●	●	●				●			●	
Sundling Park	3.5 miles SW of Manistee on Red Apple Rd.					●	●														●			●	
Merkey Road End	2 miles SW of Manistee. From US-31, Merkey Rd. W for 2.5 miles.																							●	
12th Street Road End	1.5 miles SW of Manistee. From Cherry St., 12 blocks S of Manistee Channel to 12th, then W 0.5 miles.																							●	
Douglas Park	Manistee. W end of First Street.		●	●			●	●	●		●	●		●	●			●			●				
First Street Beach	Douglas Park, Manistee. W end of First Street.		●	●			●														●				
Manistee South Breakwater & Pier	Douglas Park, Manistee. W end of First Street.		●	●			●	●	●					●							●				
First Street Boat Ramp	Douglas Park, Manistee. W end of First Street.	●	●	●							●	●													
Rotary Park	At Douglas Park, Manistee. W end of First Street.		●	●					●																
Lighthouse Park	Manistee. Cherry Rd. S of First Street.		●	●														●							

The south portion of the county is a mix of forests, residences and parks. The public has plenty of free access along the Manistee River and the Lake Michigan beaches of the City of Manistee.

MAGOON CREEK NATURAL AREA: Magoon Creek is a lightly developed 90-acre park with about 1/4-mile of Lake Michigan frontage. Hiking and ski trails are prominent features. The wooded picnic area sits on a steep bluff and has tables, grills, hand water pump and vault toilets. Trails lead to the beach and the Magoon Creek outlet. The shore is generally sandy with some small stone. The Manistee breakwater can be seen in the distance. Note: Kayaking requires a carry of several hundred yards from parking lot to shore.
　GPS: 44°11.828'N; 86°22.265'W

SUNDLING PARK: This is a narrow, township park with limited parking. There is a path to the beach down a small bluff. The beach is sand with some stone and sits between residences.
　GPS: 44°12.426'N; 86°21.659'W

MERKEY ROAD END: A lake view from a high bluff. Limited parking.
　GPS: 44°13.714'N; 86°21.051'W

12TH STREET ROAD END: A lake view from a steep bluff with limited shoulder parking.
　GPS: 44°14.135'N; 86°20.873'W

The following facilities form a contiguous block of public parkland.

DOUGLAS PARK: Found at the west end of First Street, Douglas Park and the surrounding area contains a number of recreational and lakefront facilities. The variety mixes swimmers and walkers, tennis players and fishermen, boaters and picnickers. Near its First Street entrance is the west terminus of Manistee's Riverwalk. The walkway follows the Manistee River east into downtown Manistee. See page 87 for more information about the Riverwalk.

FIRST STREET BEACH: Manistee City's largest beach, the beachhouse fronts Lake Michigan proper. Additional beach with slightly warmer water lies inside the south breakwater. Covered picnic tables and modern restrooms are some of the facilities.

MANISTEE SOUTH BREAKWATER & PIER: Manistee is prime salmon fishing territory and the concrete breakwaters are busy with people fishing during the fall fish run. The north side of the park borders on the Manistee River Channel which provides another fishing platform. It is fun to watch the activity during late August and September, even if you are not fishing. Fish-cleaning house available. Also, view the north breakwater's light from the channel walk.
　GPS: 44°14.924'N; 86°20.567'W

FIRST STREET BOAT RAMP: Located at the entrance to Douglas Park is an excellent boat launch on the Manistee River just inside the channel to Lake Michigan. It gets very heavy use during fall fish runs but the large ramp is capable of launching 12 boats at a time.

ROTARY PARK: Tennis, baseball, basketball and playground areas are found off the lake and adjacent to First Street Beach.

LIGHTHOUSE PARK: This is a children's park containing a large, wood structure playground along Cherry Street near First Street. Nautical name but no lighthouse here.
　GPS: 44°14.676'N; 86°20.362'W

Bar Lake Outlet

Lake Bluff
Audubon Center

Orchard Lake
State Park

5th Ave. Beach
Picnic Area

N Breakwater
& Lighthouse

Riverwalk Park

Historical Museum

Manistee Marina

Above: A child takes a sunset frolic on the sands at Bar Lake Outlet.

Below left: Manistee North Breakwater and Lighthouse.

Below right: Manistee's Riverwalk Park lines the south side of the Manistee River. A good place to watch vessel traffic, here the drawbridge opens for a sailboat heading towards Lake Michigan.

Manistee County

More Manistee City and Orchard Beach

Name	Location	Entrance Fee	Parking	Modern Restrooms	Vault or Portable Toilet	Stair or Path to Shore	Swimming	Picnic Area	Drinking Water	Campground	Trailered Boat Launch	Kayak / Canoe	Marina	Fishing	Hiking	Biking	X-Country Skiing	Playground	Lighthouse	Beach Strolling	Sandy Beach	Stony or Rocky Shore	Dunes	Bluff	Wetland
Manistee County Historical Museum	Manistee. 425 River Street, also 1st St. at Tamarack St.	●	●	●																					
Riverwalk	Along Lower Manistee River. Douglas Park to US-31 bridge area.		●					●				●	●	●											
Manistee Marina	Manistee. Water Street at Spruce.		●	●				●					●												
Fifth Avenue Beach	Manistee. Lakeshore Drive near north breakwater.		●	●			●	●										●			●				
Lake Michigan Free Picnic Area	Manistee. W end Fifth Avenue at north breakwater.		●					●																	
Manistee North Breakwater & Lighthouse	Manistee. W end of Fifth Avenue.		●											●					●		●				
Orchard Beach State Park	2 miles N of Manistee. M-110 one mile N of US-31	●	●	●		●	●	●	●	●				●	●		●	●		●	●			●	
Lake Bluff Audubon Center	2.5 miles N of Manistee. Lakeshore Drive (M-110) 1.5 mile N of US-31.	●	●	●		●									●									●	
Bar Lake Outlet	3 miles N of Manistee. From US-31 N on M-110 which becomes Lakeshore Dr.		●		●		●					●									●	●			

The Riverwalk and an active downtown business area lie east of Lake Michigan along the south channel. Small parks and the lighthouse highlight the area north of Manistee's channel. Farther north, high bluffs prevail until reaching Bar Lake.

MANISTEE COUNTY HISTORICAL MUSEUM: It consists of two buildings; one located in the former Lyman Drugstore on River Street and the other on 1st Street. The museum features replications of rooms from the past two centuries. It has a large photo collection, civil war mementos, pioneer exhibits plus maritime and genealogy information. Open Tuesday-Saturday, 10-5. Small fee.
  Telephone: (231) 723-5531
  GPS: 44°14.792'N; 86°20.001'W

RIVERWALK: The Riverwalk travels along the south side of the Manistee River from Douglas Park at Lake Michigan to just past the US-31 drawbridge near Manistee Lake. The west end is constructed from wooden planks on pilings over the riverbank. Here, it passes numerous docks until it meets with the city marina downtown. It continues as a paved walkway along the river next to the downtown business district, ducking under both of the town's drawbridges. The length totals about 1.5 miles. Trialheads are at each end and throughout the downtown business area. One central access point with easy parking is behind the Manistee Historical Museum at 1st and Tamarack Streets. A stairway at the end of Tamarack Street takes you down to the walk. One barrier-free access point is at the end of Spruce Street near the Marina. Picnic tables are available along the grassy knoll at the marina.

MANISTEE MARINA: Located at the Riverwalk Park on the Manistee River, the marina has 36 slips, 24 for transient use.
  Telephone (231) 723-1552
  GPS: 44°14.900'N; 86°19.370'W (Marina), 44°15.133'N; 86°20.967'W (Channel)

FIFTH AVENUE BEACH: Finding Fifth Avenue Beach would seem straight forward, "drive down Fifth Avenue until it ends at the lake," right? That once worked but the addition of a housing complex has made it more of an adventure. Turn west on Memorial Drive found just north of the Manistee River drawbridge on US-31. Memorial bends becoming Fifth Avenue. Near the end of Fifth Avenue is the "Harbor Village" housing complex. Take a right into Harbor Village and follow the "beach" signs. Like many new residential developments, the streets twist and wind creating a slalom course for traffic. The park has about 1000 feet of lake frontage and modern restrooms. Its plain, tan brick building and steel playground equipment is reminiscent of the 1950's. To the south, the breakwater and lighthouse look largely the same as they did when built. All this sits behind the contrasting 1990's condominiums of Harbor Village.
  GPS: 44°15.101'N; 86°20.420'W

LAKE MICHIGAN FREE PICNIC AREA: Across from the Coast Guard Station in the shadows of the North Breakwater is a tattered sign designating the picnic park sponsored by the "Northside Improvement Association." The Fifth Avenue Beach sits next door. There is street parking by the picnic area. The log building forms the center of the north side public beach area, a locale that is a throwback to past times.

MANISTEE NORTH BREAKWATER & LIGHTHOUSE: At the north end of the Manistee River Channel, the north breakwater juts into Lake Michigan. The concrete breakwater has a white lighthouse tower and a black, elevated catwalk used in the past by lightkeepers during storms. Many fishermen will line the breakwater during the fall fish runs.

ORCHARD BEACH STATE PARK: As the name implies, the park is at the site of an old fruit orchard. The campground and picnic areas sit on a high bluff. A tall, multiple-landing, wooden stairway leads to the sandy beach below. From either the beach or bluff you can see south to the Manistee Lighthouse and north to Arcadia Bluffs (p.95). Hiking and ski trails are on the east side of the highway. The park's campground remains busy through the fall sportfishing season, as the Manistee area is one of the primary ports for that activity.
  GPS: 44°17.058'N; 86°18.893'W

LAKE BLUFF AUDUBON CENTER: A 60-acre arboretum located a short distance north of Orchard Beach State Park, the sanctuary has over a quarter-mile of bluff overlooking Lake Michigan. Plant species include California redwood, ginkgo, weeping beech, and English holly as well as a woodlot of maple, beech, hemlock, birch and oak regrowth. A foot trail leads along the shore bluff.

BAR LAKE OUTLET: Bar Lake is one of many lakes having short outlets to Lake Michigan. At the outlet, is a small, largely unmarked roadside access to the beach. The shore is sand with some rocky bottom. The beach is very close to the road, making for a short canoe or kayak carry to the water. Parking is limited to about 20 cars.

Above left: The sandy, natural beach at 13 Mile Road and the Burnam Street Access.

Below left: Portage Point picnic shelter, its sandy beach and the newly rebuilt Portage Lake Breakwaters.

Opposite page: At the Portage Point Area, road end access points to Portage Lake and Lake Michigan are well marked by signs like these.

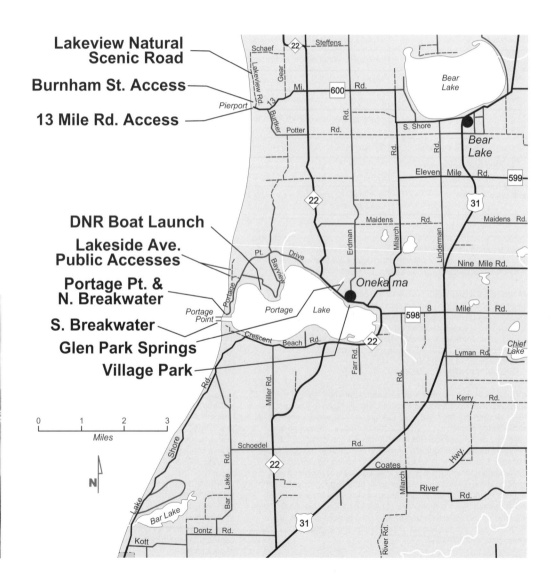

Lakeview Natural Scenic Road

Burnham St. Access

13 Mile Rd. Access

DNR Boat Launch

Lakeside Ave. Public Accesses

Portage Pt. & N. Breakwater

S. Breakwater

Glen Park Springs

Village Park

Name	Location	Entrance Fee	Parking	Modern Restrooms	Vault or Portable Toilet	Stair or Path to Shore	Swimming	Picnic Area	Drinking Water	Campground	Trailered Boat Launch	Kayak / Canoe	Marina	Fishing	Hiking	Biking	X-Country Skiing	Playground	Lighthouse	Beach Strolling	Sandy Beach	Stony or Rocky Shore	Dunes	Bluff	Wetland
Portage Lake Channel South Breakwater	4 miles SW of Onekama at W end of Crescent Beach Rd. 1.5 miles W of M-22.		●			●								●											
Onekama Village Park	Onekama. M-22 and Park St.		●	●			●	●	●		●	●		●				●			●				
Glen Park Springs	Onekama. From M-22 travel N on 4th St. a short distance.		●												●										
Portage Point Beach & North Breakwater	3.5 miles W of Onekama. From M-22, W on Portage Pt. Dr. to its end then W on 2nd Ave.		●			●	●	●				●		●							●		●		
Lakeside Ave. Public Accesses	3 miles W of Onekama. From M-22, W on Portage Pt. Dr. then W on Lake Isle to Lakeside Ave.					●	●															●				
DNR Portage Lake Boat Launch	3 miles W of Onekama. From M-22, W on Portage Pt. Dr. then E on Seymour to Lake Park Dr.		●		●							●										●				
13 Mile Road Access	6 miles N of Onekama, 1.5 miles west M-22.		●				●					●										●				
Burnham Street Access	5 miles S of Arcadia 1 block west of Lakeview Rd.		●				●					●										●				
Lakeview / Schaef Natural Scenic Road	3 miles S of Arcadia. Turn off M-22 on Gear Rd at sharp curve. Then west on Schaef Rd. (0.1 miles).																									

Onekama lies on the northeast edge of Portage Lake a couple of miles from its Lake Michigan channel. Access to Lake Michigan is limited to small parks and road ends.

PORTAGE LAKE CHANNEL SOUTH BREAKWATER:
Access the breakwater by walking 1/4 mile from the unpaved parking area at the end of Crescent Beach Road. Part is on a cement walkway with the last part on sand and rubble. This is a hard-to-find access for fishing.

ONEKAMA VILLAGE PARK: Located on Portage Lake, the Village Park has a variety of activities including tennis and basketball. It has the best boat ramp for large craft wishing to reach Lake Michigan through the Portage Lake Channel. The channel lies about three miles to the west. Portage Lake offers a warmer swimming alternative to Lake Michigan. The park has a changehouse and sandy beach. Many picnic grills and tables plus a pavilion are available.
GPS: 44°21.791'N; 86°12.425'W

GLEN PARK SPRINGS: Glen Park is a pretty, wooded area in the hills just north of Portage Lake. Nestled in a small subdivision, Glen Creek flows from a number of small springs. The trails and pathways make for a good change of pace.
GPS: 44°22.134'N; 86°12.552'W

Note: The next 3 listings are reached by turning west on Portage Point Drive from M-22. GPS: 44°22.313'N; 86°13.113'W.

PORTAGE POINT BEACH & NORTH BREAKWATER:
A bit hard to find, Portage Point Beach is tucked a few blocks behind the Portage Point Inn, a large historic, vacation hotel. Follow Portage Point Drive to the 3-way stop at the Inn. Continue straight. At this point, the road narrows dramatically and winds behind the Inn. It makes a 90-degree turn at 2nd Street ending at the beach. The North Portage Lake Channel Breakwater forms the south end of the beach. The water depth is great for swimming and the beach is very sandy. There is not a great amount of parking, so it may be difficult to get a spot on a sunny, summer afternoon.
GPS: 44°21.680'N; 86°15.792'W

LAKESIDE AVENUE PUBLIC ACCESSES: There are several narrow road end public access points off Lakeside Ave. A street sign marks each. One is at the end of Lake Isle Avenue another is at Avenue F. These are squeezed between residences and parking is limited to what you can find on the narrow gravel roads of this area. Portage Point is a better choice, but if the parking is full there, these are alternatives.
GPS: 44°22.445'N; 86°15.577'W

DNR PORTAGE LAKE BOAT LAUNCH: Small boats and kayaks can put in here a short distance from the Portage Lake Channel to Lake Michigan. There is a good view of Portage Lake Inn, a historic tourist resort.
GPS: 44°22.178'N; 86°14.858'W

13 MILE ROAD ACCESS: A sandy beach lies at the end of 13 Mile Road. A short carry makes canoe and kayak launching possible. Parking is generally adequate even during holiday periods.

BURNHAM STREET ACCESS: This is a sandy beach accessed by a hard to find two-track road. Look for the street sign with street name and words "public access." There is very limited parking and turn-around space. A short path makes canoe and kayak launching possible. If full, try 13 Mile Road access 0.25 mile to the south.

LAKEVIEW / SCHAEF NATURAL SCENIC ROADS: These are narrow, curvy, tree-lined, gravel roads with some overlook views of Lake Michigan. They will get you off-the-beaten-track for a short, scenic drive.

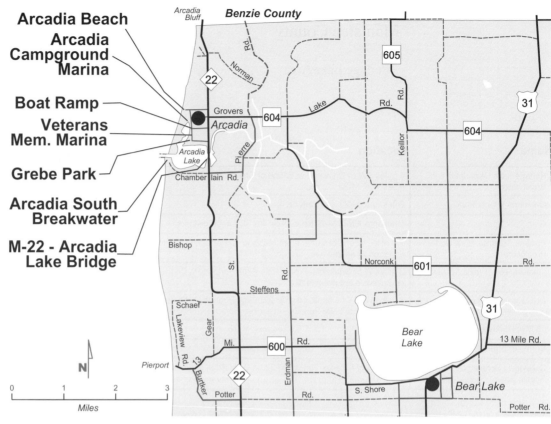

Arcadia Beach

Arcadia Campground Marina

Boat Ramp

Veterans Mem. Marina

Grebe Park

Arcadia South Breakwater

M-22 - Arcadia Lake Bridge

Benzie County

Arcadia Bluff

Norman Rd.

605

31

Grovers

604

Lake

Rd.

Rd.

604

Arcadia

Keillor

Arcadia Lake

Pierre

Chamberlain Rd.

Bishop

Norconk

Rd.

601

Steffens Rd.

Schael

31

Lakeview Rd.

Gear St.

Mi.

600

Rd.

Bear Lake

13 Mile Rd.

Pierport

13 Burtker

22

Erdman Rd.

Potter

Rd.

S. Shore

Bear Lake

Potter Rd.

N

0   1   2   3

Miles

Above: Arcadia Beach Natural Area has a long, sandy beach.

Right: The rubble-filled South Arcadia Breakwater is reachable via Chamberlain Road.

Opposite page: The marina on Arcadia Lake is small, well-maintained and a short run through the channel to Lake Michigan.

Manistee County

Arcadia Area

Name	Location	Entrance Fee	Parking	Modern Restrooms	Vault or Portable Toilet	Stair or Path to Shore	Swimming	Picnic Area	Drinking Water	Campground	Trailered Boat Launch	Kayak / Canoe	Marina	Fishing	Hiking	Biking	X-Country Skiing	Playground	Lighthouse	Beach Strolling	Sandy Beach	Stony or Rocky Shore	Dunes	Bluff	Wetland
Arcadia South Breakwater	1.5 SW of Arcadia. From M-22, turn W on Chamberlain Rd. to end.		●			●	●							●							●				
M-22 / Arcadia Bridge	Just north of Arcadia on M-22.											●		●											●
Grebe Park	Arcadia. 4 blocks W of M-22 on 1st Street.		●		●			●						●				●							
Arcadia Township Veteran's Memorial Marina	Arcadia. 4 blocks W of M-22 at the end of Pine St.		●	●				●	●		●	●	●												
Arcadia Dock Boat Ramp	Arcadia. 4 blocks W of M-22 at the end of Pine St.		●								●	●													
Arcadian Campground Marina	Arcadia. 4 blocks W of M-22, Lake Street at !st.	●		●						●	●														
Arcadia Beach Natural Area	Arcadia. 6 blocks W of M-22 at the end of Lake Street.		●		●	●	●	●										●			●				

Arcadia is a small town and harbor oriented to the summer resident and vacationer. The town has a pretty swimming beach and very good boating facilities yet less summer congestion than larger coastal towns.

ARCADIA SOUTH BREAKWATER: Access is poor to Arcadia's breakwaters. Reach the south breakwater by traveling from M-22 to the end of Chamberlain Road. The road changes to two-track. When it ends, you will need to walk 0.5 mile over sand. Parking is limited to the road end. The beach is natural and sandy. Note: The north breakwater is located along private property.

M-22 / ARCADIA BRIDGE: Canoes or kayaks could be launched at this crossing on the east end of Arcadia Lake. The Lake Michigan outlet is clearly seen about 0.5 mile away. Limited parking.

Note: The following listings are located four blocks west of M-22 in the town of Arcadia. They form a nearly continuous series of parks and public facilities on the northeast and north side of Arcadia Lake.

GREBE PARK: A barrier-free fishing dock and picnic overlook sits on the east side of Arcadia Lake. The T-shaped fishing platform is located in 10 to 15 feet of water. Picnic shelter and grills. A modern, barrier-free public restroom is located at the marina next door.

ARCADIA TOWNSHIP VETERAN'S MEMORIAL MARINA: The marina has 36 slips, of which half are held for transient use. It also has boat launch access to Arcadia Lake which has a Lake Michigan outlet about 0.75 miles away. The launch is capable of handling large, trailered boats. A fee is charged for boat mooring and launching. Marina restrooms are open to the public.
  Telephone: (231) 889-9653
  GPS: 44°29.270'N; 86°14.210'W (marina); 44°29.017'N; 86°15.067'W (channel)

ARCADIA DOCK BOAT RAMP: This is another boat launch providing access to Arcadia Lake. The Lake Michigan outlet is about 0.75 miles away.

ARCADIAN CAMPGROUND MARINA: A grass field located on the north side of Arcadia Lake serves as a campground. The Arcadia Beach is a short distance to the west and the marina area can be seen from the campground shores.
  Telephone: 231-889-3301

ARCADIA BEACH NATURAL AREA: A lightly developed beach area is located at the end of Lake Street. Here, you will find parking, some playground equipment, tables and grills. The view is wonderful from the barrier-free platform referred to as the "Sunset Station." A short stairway leads to the shore. The beach is mostly sand and extends several hundred feet to the south. Swimming is very good. A chemical toilet is the only restroom.
  GPS: 44°29.643'N; 86°14.485'W

Non-Native Species

In 1959, the United States and Canada completed the Saint Lawrence Seaway, allowing ocean ships to directly enter the Great Lakes basin. The ships brought more than trade goods. Freighters take on or discharge ballast water to adjust their weight when they load or unload their cargo. Organisms from other parts of the globe were pumped into the ballast tanks and later discharged into Great Lakes waters. Other species hitch-hiked on ship hulls. A number of these organisms found the new waters accommodating and some have become a nuisance. A few threaten the ecological balance of the Great Lakes.

The sea lamprey, an eel-like organism, was the first to strike hard. The parasite attaches to a fish, then literally sucks the life from its host. The Great Lakes had no natural predator for the lamprey. Within a few decades, it, along with increased fishing pressure, had decimated the populations of whitefish and lake trout. Efforts to control the lamprey ensued, including the use of chemical larvicide and barriers to prevent the lamprey from reaching streams to spawn. Today, the controls must remain to keep the lamprey population in check.

More recently, the zebra mussel and various foreign fish have found their way here. The zebra mussel likely came from the Caspian Sea in ship ballast water. It has been a prolific spreader, attaching itself to fixed objects such as rocks and piers. The mussel filters food from the water, reducing the food available for native species. It clogs the intake pipes of municipal water plants increasing maintenance costs for these facilities. The sharp shells of dead mussels present a hazard for the barefoot beachgoer. With zebra mussel establishment in the Great Lakes a done deal, concerns have turned to the thousands of nearby inland lakes. Mussel colonies have started in many of these. Because these lakes are smaller, the ecological impact may be more dramatic.

The introduction of the non-native alewife, a small, silvery fish, first provided additional food for the larger fish like lake trout. Increased commercial fishing, the lamprey and other changes caused the lake trout population to drop dramatically. As this happened, the alewife numbers increased immensely. Without a predator to manage their population, large die-offs of the alewife occurred, timed by their natural life-cycle. During some years, Lake Michigan beaches became awash with the rotting fish. The seagulls were happy, but people were not. Tourism suffered during these periods. At great expense, cities used equipment to scoop and rake the smelly remains from their shores. More remote coasts just lived with it.

Ironically, the Michigan Department of Natural Resources introduced another non-native species, in part, to relieve the alewife situation. Coho salmon ,released into the Platte River (Benzie County) in 1966, made their way to Lake Michigan and fed voraciously on the nuisance fish. Two years later, the coho returned to the Platte to spawn. The transplant was successful. Sportfishing spiked, as fisherman returned to the Platte each fall to hunt this salmon which took a liking to its new freshwater habitat. The coho were planted in other streams and by other states. The larger chinook salmon was introduced soon after. Today, the fishery provides an economic boost to coastal towns and alewife populations have come under control.

Ballast water discharge remains a hot topic. Environmental groups and some government officials from the states and provinces of the Great Lakes basin have reissued their calls to regulate shipping operations to prevent the inadvertent introduction of more species. It remains to be seen if their efforts will pay off.

• *Top:* Zebra Mussel shells cover this stretch of beach on North Manitou Island.
• *Right:* Introduced to Lake Michigan in 1967, the chinook salmon can weigh 40 pounds or more.

Benzie County

South of Benzie County, the shoreline stretches nearly north-to-south as a continuous strand of sand. No islands lay off the shore. A number of channeled harbors exist but no natural bays for mariners to seek refuge. Heaps of sand greet one at the shore but nary a stone or rock. From here north, it changes. The Point Betsie and Platte Bay areas form the first bit of east-west beach. Look north from the bay and spy South Manitou, the first island. Small, flat, rounded stone begins to mix in with the sand. You start to find the occasional fossilized coral named Petoskey Stone.

M-22 continues its winding course near the shore. The view from the Arcadia Bluff welcomes you to the county at the south. Frankfort and Elberta, maritime towns from the past, now retooling for the tourist, have large, free, sandy beaches. Fish from their breakwaters, piers or charter boats. From Elberta Bluff, gaze out across the water with the harbor entrance below. Enjoy Frankfort's shopping area along its waterfront or travel a few miles north to visit the Point Betsie Lighthouse, one of the lake's most scenic. For an exhilarating experience, hop down to Frankfort Airport and take a glider ride. The price is reasonable, the view terrific and the feeling like no other.

Benzie County is the southern gateway to the Sleeping Bear Dunes National Lakeshore. The park incorporates much of Benzie's shore, offering numerous opportunities for lakeside recreation. It includes the only free-flowing, naturally-kept rivermouth on the east Lake Michigan shore. The Platte River challenges winds and waves as it fights its way through the dunes before spilling into the big lake. This is what the Galien, the Kalamazoo, the Manistee and similar rivers had to do before man channeled their outflow to benefit navigation. Canoe the Platte, a popular activity, and end at the long, dune-covered Lake Michigan beach. Canoe liveries are available.

As one of the busiest national parks, Sleeping Bear's popular sites get plenty of use in the summer season. Want to get away? The Platte Plains area provides a bit of solitude. The more you are willing to hike, the lonelier you will get. Plenty of trails lead to small dunes and miles of natural beach buffered by acres of forest land. Otter Creek, on the north edge is a popular swimming spot, long a favorite of local residents.

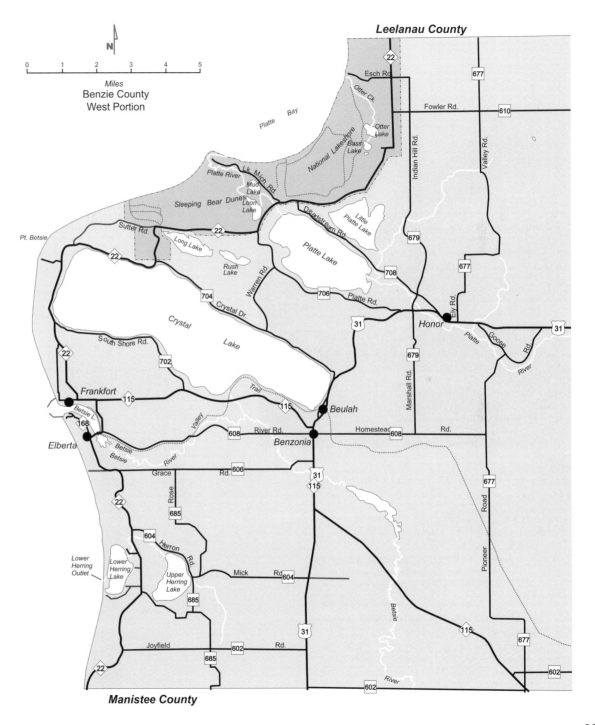

Benzie County
West Portion

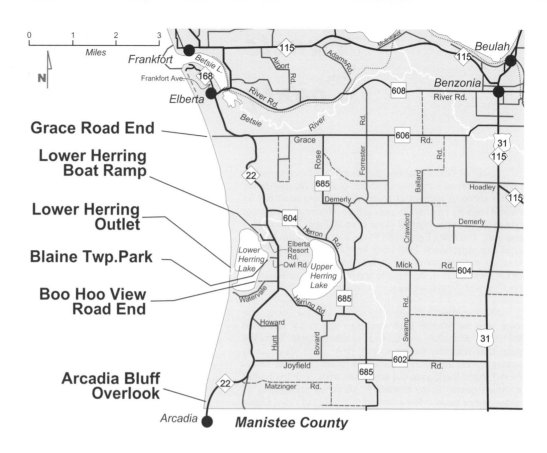

Grace Road End

Lower Herring Boat Ramp

Lower Herring Outlet

Blaine Twp. Park

Boo Hoo View Road End

Arcadia Bluff Overlook

Manistee County

Above: The MDOT highway rest area offers views of Arcadia and the Manistee County coastline from atop the Arcadia Bluff.

Right: A kayak venture can swing pass the Herring Lake Outlet and surrounding dunes. Bordering land is private, restricting its access.

Arcadia Bluff and Herring Lakes

Name	Location	Entrance Fee	Parking	Modern Restrooms	Vault or Portable Toilet	Stair or Path to Shore	Swimming	Picnic Area	Drinking Water	Campground	Trailered Boat Launch	Kayak / Canoe	Marina	Fishing	Hiking	Biking	X-Country Skiing	Playground	Lighthouse	Beach Strolling	Sandy Beach	Stony or Rocky Shore	Dunes	Bluff	Wetland
Arcadia Bluff Overlook	Along M-22, 1 Mile N of Arcadia.		●		●			●																●	
Boo Hoo View Road End	4.5 miles S of Elberta. From M-22, W on Watervale Rd. 0.25 mi. then on Boo Hoo View Rd.		●			●						●									●				
Blaine Township Park	0.25 mile W of M-22 on Owl Rd. 4 miles S of Elberta.		●		●			●				●									●				
Lower Herring Outlet	Via watercraft from Lower Herring Lake launch sites.					●	●					●		●							●		●		
Lower Herring Lake Boat Ramp	0.25 mile W of M-22 on Elberta Resort Rd., 3.5 miles S of Elberta.		●								●	●													
Grace Road End	1 mile S of Elberta. From M-22, W on Grace Rd. 0.3 miles.		●			●	●														●			●	

Summer cottages and resorts dominate the landscape near Herring Lake limiting public access. The outlet from Herring Lake to Lake Michigan provides a unique adventure for kayakers and those with small boats.

ARCADIA BLUFF OVERLOOK: A popular stop with motorists, the roadside park lies along M-22 just north of the Manistee County line. The parking lot is located about midway up the bluff. From here the scenery is beautiful and barrier-free. Climb the 126 step stairway to the bluff top for a spectacular Lake Michigan view. Picnic tables and vault toilets are available at the parking level.
  GPS: 44°31.178'N; 86°13.958' W

BOO HOO VIEW ROAD END: Watervale Road serves the south end of Lower Herring Lake. A short distance to the west of M-22, Watervale Road curves south. At the curve, Boo Hoo View Road, a short gravel trail, heads directly west to the southeast corner of the shore. There is a turnaround with shoulder parking. The shore is great for launching canoes or kayaks. Swimming is okay as well. Lower Herring has an outlet about 0.5 miles to Lake Michigan. The outlet is about 0.5 miles from this point making the big lake easy to access by canoe or kayak.
  GPS: 44°33.461'N; 86°12.576' W (park), 44°33.462'N; 86°12.056'W (M-22 / Watervale Rd. turn)

BLAINE TOWNSHIP PARK: Located near the center of the east shore of Lower Herring Lake. This park has a shallow ramp suitable for launching canoes and kayaks. The Lower Herring outlet to Lake Michigan is directly across from the park and no more than a 0.5-mile paddle.
  GPS: 44°33.884'N; 86°12.315' W (park), 44°33.919'N; 86°12.033'W (M-22 / White Owl Rd. turn)

LOWER HERRING OUTLET: Hills and dunes separate Lower Herring Lake from Lake Michigan. The distance between the two is minimal. A small outlet stream connects the two. Small boats can navigate the outlet a few hundred feet until reaching the spillway that maintains the level of Lower Herring Lake. Canoes and kayaks could pull around to finish the last hundred feet to Lake Michigan. It is likely that you will need to pull your craft over some sandbars below the spillway. The land at the outlet is owned by the Watervale Inn. Navigation on and walking of the bottom lands of the stream and Lake Michigan is public privilege, but use of this area is limited unless you have permission from the Inn. This is a popular destination with boating visitors.

Note: Hand-carried craft can be launched at Boo Hoo View Road End and Blaine Township Park. Trailered boats should use Lower Herring Lake Boat Ramp listed below. To find the outlet, look for the sand blowout near the southwest end of Herring Lake. The outlet is a short distance north of the blowout.

LOWER HERRING LAKE BOAT RAMP: This public boat access site is at the northeast corner of Lower Herring Lake. Most small, trailered boats can use this ramp without problem. The outlet of Lower Herring Lake is less than 0.75 miles from this boat launch.
  GPS: 44°34.255'N; 86°12.116' W (M-22 / Elberta Resort Rd. turn)

GRACE ROAD END: Like many road ends, the one at Grace Road is located between a couple of residences. There are several places to park on the bluff which overlooks the beach. A steep, not easily traversed, path leads you down. Very sandy and good swimming.
  GPS: 44° 36.289'N; 86° 13.760'W (road end), 44° 36.269'; 86°N 13.096'W (M-22 / Grace Rd. turn)

Below: The Betsie Lake Fishing Platform at Elberta Historic Waterfront Park provides easy access for anglers.

Right: Elberta Breakwater and Elberta Beach as seen from the Elberta Bluff.

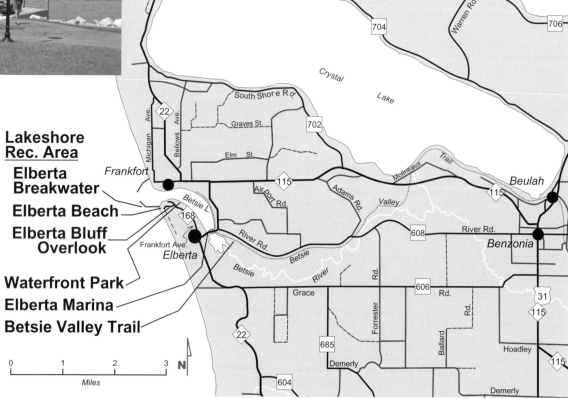

Lakeshore
Rec. Area

Elberta
Breakwater

Elberta Beach

Elberta Bluff
Overlook

Waterfront Park

Elberta Marina

Betsie Valley Trail

Benzie County

Elberta

Name	Location	Entrance Fee	Parking	Modern Restrooms	Vault or Portable Toilet	Stair or Path to Shore	Swimming	Picnic Area	Drinking Water	Campground	Trailered Boat Launch	Kayak / Canoe	Marina	Fishing	Hiking	Biking	X-Country Skiing	Playground	Lighthouse	Beach Strolling	Sandy Beach	Stony or Rocky Shore	Dunes	Bluff	Wetland
Lakeshore Recreation Area	Elberta. Take Frankfort Ave. (M-168) then turn left at the steep climb near the road's end.		●		●	●						●		●						●	●		●	●	
Elberta Bluff Overlook	Elberta. Lakeshore Recreation Area. Take Frankfort Ave. (M-168) then turn left at the steep climb near the road's end.		●																					●	
Elberta Beach	Elberta. Lakeshore Recreation Area. Continue down road from Elberta Bluff Overlook.		●		●	●						●		●						●	●				
Elberta Breakwater	Elberta. Lakeshore Recreation Area, at Elberta Beach.		●		●	●	●							●							●				
Elberta Historic Waterfront Park	Elberta. Take Frankfort Ave. (M-168). On right near the road's end.		●		●			●						●				●							
Elberta Village Marina	Elberta. M-22 just E of Frankfort Ave. (M-168) along Lake Betsie.		●								●	●	●												
Betsie Valley Trail	Trailheads in Elberta on M-22 and Frankfort on 10th near Main St.		●												●	●									●

Elberta and Frankfort are small towns that together surround the harbor called Betsie Lake. Elberta once had a thriving maritime economy and the port served as a ferry service hub to Wisconsin and the Upper Peninsula. Rail and ferry service ended in the 1980's and the town has struggled to reshape its identity. Its waterfront is a favorite with those who find it.

To visit the first four listings, turn north on M-168 (Frankfort Ave.) from M-22 in Elberta. The intersection is at the southwest corner of Lake Betsie. GPS: 44°31.178'N; 86°13.958'W

LAKESHORE RECREATION AREA: The next three sites are found within the Lakeshore Recreation Area of Elberta Village. It is found near the end of M-168, which starts as Frankfort Avenue and then becomes Furnace Street about midway down. A sign designates the left turn up a steep hill towards the park area.
   GPS: 44°37.657'N; 86°14.212'W (entrance road)

ELBERTA BLUFF OVERLOOK: The first stop within the Lakeshore Recreation Area, Elberta Bluff rises well above Lake Michigan. Ascending air currents created by the wind buffeting this highland have launched many a hang-glider. The beach below served as the landing strip. A parking area atop the north end of the bluff provides a great view of the sunset and the entrance to Frankfort Harbor.

ELBERTA BEACH: Located below the Elberta Bluff, Elberta Beach has minimal facilities, great scenery and a natural feel. From the bluff, the road descends steeply to Lakeside Boulevard and the shore. A parking area at the bottom serves the beach and the Elberta Breakwater. Past the primary beach parking area, the road continues to the south. The farther you drive south, the worse the road gets and the more remote the beach. If continuing on, watch that you do not

get stuck in the sand! Normally, high ground clearance, all-wheel-drive vehicles will find it passable.

ELBERTA BREAKWATER: Use the parking area at the Elberta Beach. During calm seas, you can walk the breakwater for a nice view of Frankfort to the east and the Frankfort Bluffs to the north. Fishing from the breakwater can be fruitful as well. Elberta Breakwater is oriented to take the brunt of prevailing southwest winds so be careful.

ELBERTA HISTORIC WATERFRONT PARK: This park, located along Lake Betsie near the opening to Lake Michigan, pays tribute to the past maritime heritage of Elberta. Located near the old ferry docks that served several Wisconsin and Michigan towns in the past, a planned museum will provide the details. Fishing dock, playground and picnic areas round out the facilities. It is a pleasant, grassy stop with a view of Frankfort across the lake.
   GPS: 44°37.648'N; 86°14.173'W

ELBERTA VILLAGE MARINA: Located on Betsie Lake, the Elberta Marina has seen better days. It is adjacent to the Betsie Valley Trail and thus a good trailhead. It also has tables, grills and a pavilion. It is a good place to launch a kayak for a paddle in Betsie Lake. Use it for parking and a take-out point for canoeing the Betsie River.

BETSIE VALLEY TRAIL: Most of the pathway follows the abandoned Ann Arbor Railroad route from Frankfort and Elberta to Thompsonville in southeast Benzie County. The western end actually starts at 10th near Main Street in Frankfort but a good trailhead is found in Elberta at the south end of Betsie Lake. The trail, designated for non-motorized use, is asphalt until reaching the Crystal Lake area except for the wooden boardwalks at Betsie River crossings. The southeast portion, roughly from Beulah to its Thompsonville terminus, is gravel.

Below left: Frankfort Beach looks out to the harbor entrance. Quite large, it has frontage both inside and outside the harbor offering different water temperatures for swimming.

Below right: Winter encroaches on Point Betsie Lighthouse, one of the most picturesque and accessible along the shore.

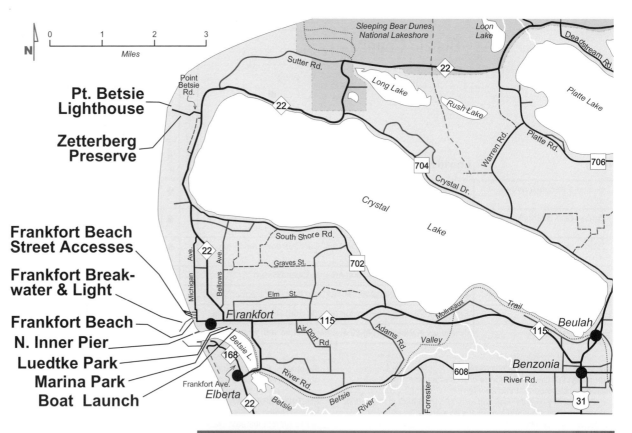

Pt. Betsie Lighthouse

Zetterberg Preserve

Frankfort Beach Street Accesses

Frankfort Break-water & Light

Frankfort Beach

N. Inner Pier

Luedtke Park

Marina Park

Boat Launch

Benzie County

Frankfort and Point Betsie

Name	Location	Entrance Fee	Parking	Modern Restrooms	Vault or Portable Toilet	Stair or Path to Shore	Swimming	Picnic Area	Drinking Water	Campground	Trailered Boat Launch	Kayak / Canoe	Marina	Fishing	Hiking	Biking	X-Country Skiing	Playground	Lighthouse	Beach Strolling	Sandy Beach	Stony or Rocky Shore	Dunes	Bluff	Wetland
Frankfort City Boat Launch & Fishing Pier	Frankfort. 9th and Main Street.		●	●					●		●	●		●											
Frankfort Marina Park	Frankfort. Main St. between 6th and 8th.		●	●				●	●				●	●				●							
Luedtke Park	Frankfort. Main Street.		●					●	●															●	
Frankfort North Inner Pier	Frankfort. Use parking at Frankfort Beach, west end of Main Street.		●		●	●								●											
Frankfort Beach	Frankfort. West end of Main St.		●		●		●							●				●	●		●				
Frankfort Breakwater & Light	Frankfort. Use parking at Frankfort Beach, west end of Main St. or on SAC Street.		●		●	●	●							●					●		●				
Frankfort Beach Street End Accesses	Frankfort. End of SAC, Miami and Nippising Streets W of Michigan Ave.		●		●	●	●							●					●		●				
Point Betsie & Lighthouse	5 miles N of Frankfort, follow M-22 and turn W on Pt. Betsie Road.		●						●					●					●	●	●	●	●		
Zetterberg Preserve	5 miles N of Frankfort, follow M-22 and turn W on Pt. Betsie Road.				●										●								●		

Frankfort inhabits the north side of Betsie Lake across from Elberta. The town has revamped itself from its days as a maritime port into a trendy tourist town and a sportfishing haven. To the north, Point Betsie features one of the lakeshore's favorite lighthouses.

FRANKFORT CITY BOAT LAUNCH & FISHING PIER: The Frankfort Boat Ramp provides a deep, high quality ramp for launching trailered boats. Several boats can be launched at a time. Expect a crowd during peak fishing periods. Fee for launching. A new fishing pier has been added near the ramp.

FRANKFORT MARINA PARK: This is a grassy municipal park along Betsie Lake, the harbor for Frankfort and Elberta. Boat slips line the park's waterfront. Modern restrooms, a small playground and picnic facilities are available. Downtown shops are adjacent. Park on Main Street or in the parking lot found at the harbor end of 5th Street.
   Telephone: (231) 352-9051
   GPS: 44°37.883'N; 86°14.133'W (marina), 44°37.817'N; 86°14.183'W (channel)

LUEDTKE PARK: On Main St. is a small, garden park located among the Frankfort storefronts. Luedtke Park overlooks Betsie Lake atop a short bluff. Picnic tables and pretty landscaping make this a pleasant respite. Street parking.

FRANKFORT NORTH INNER PIER: Separated from the North Breakwater by more than a quarter-mile, the 400-foot-long North Inner Pier of Frankfort Harbor provides an additional fishing spot. Park at Frankfort Beach at the west end of Main Street.

FRANKFORT BEACH: The North Breakwater divides this sandy municipal beach providing two choices for the swimmer. The water inside the breakwater will be relatively warm and calm while the Lake Michigan side will be cool and the wave action more vigorous. Access to the Frankfort Breakwater and Pier can be made from the beach area. Downtown shops are within a couple of blocks.
   GPS: 44°37.922'N; 86°14.738'W

FRANKFORT BREAKWATER AND LIGHT: Fishing for steelhead and other species is popular from the breakwater. Sunset views are often spectacular as well. Many stroll out to the Frankfort Light at the end of the structure. SAC Street, discussed in the listing below, provides the most direct access to the North Breakwater.
   GPS: 44°37.922'N; 86°14.738'W

FRANKFORT BEACH STREET END ACCESSES: Three short residential streets, SAC, Miami and Nippising, end with access to Frankfort Beach and the breakwater. Parallel parking exists along most of the area streets but restrictions apply in some places.

Visit the following locations by turning west from M-22 at Pt. Betsie Road.

POINT BETSIE & LIGHTHOUSE: Pt. Betsie Road takes you right to the Lake Michigan shoreline. Picturesque Pt. Betsie Lighthouse guards the point. This is a good beach for strolling, rock gathering and sunset watching. It is known for hazardous currents, so swim during calm conditions only. Parking is limited to the road end turn-around and shoulder but is usually adequate. Lighthouse tours Thursday.-Sunday during season for $2 fee.

ZETTERBERG PRESERVE: A 100-acre Nature Conservancy site donated by the Zetterberg family is located on Pt. Betsie Road about halfway between M-22 and the Pt. Betsie Lighthouse. Look for a small wooden sign on the south side of the road. A trail leads from this point onto the dunes. View of Lake Michigan from its sand dunes. A good location to see dune flora.
   GPS: 44°41.380'N; 86°15.050'W

Platte River Campground

Eldorado Canoe Access

Platte River Mouth Beach

Lake Twp. Park

Fish Collection Weir

Platte R. Picnic Area

Loon Lk. Ramp

Old Indian Trail

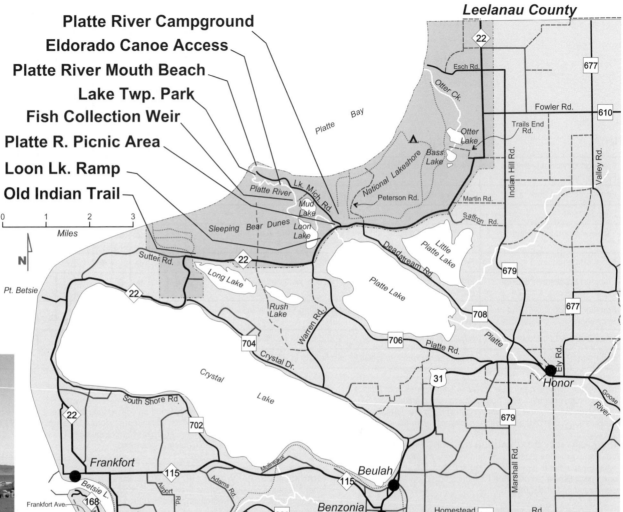

Below left: The Platte River opens to Lake Michigan, a popular summer swimming spot.

Below right: Canoeing, kayaking or tubing the Platte River is a favorite way to reach the beach and dunes.

Benzie County

Platte River

Name	Location	Entrance Fee	Parking	Modern Restrooms	Vault or Portable Toilet	Stair or Path to Shore	Swimming	Picnic Area	Drinking Water	Campground	Trailered Boat Launch	Kayak / Canoe	Marina	Fishing	Hiking	Biking	X-Country Skiing	Playground	Lighthouse	Beach Strolling	Sandy Beach	Stony or Rocky Shore	Dunes	Bluff	Wetland
Sleeping Bear Nat'l Lakeshore	Benzie and Leelanau Counties accessed primarily via M-22.	●	●	●	●	●	●	●	●	●	●	●		●	●	●	●			●	●	●	●	●	●
Old Indian Trail	7 miles NE of Frankfort on M-22 near west end of Sutter Rd.	●	●		●	●	●							●			●			●	●		●		
Loon Lake Ramp	0.25 miles S of Platte River Bridge on M-22.	●	●	●				●	●		●	●		●											
Platte River Picnic Area	Lake Michigan Rd. at M-22.	●	●	●		●	●	●	●			●		●							●	●			
Fish Collection Weir	Lake Michigan Rd., 1 mile NW of M-22.		●		●				●																
Platte River Mouth Beach	End of Lake Michigan Rd. 2.5 miles NW of M-22.	●	●	●			●					●		●						●	●	●	●		
Lake Township Park	End of Lake Michigan Rd. 2.5 miles NW of M-22.	●	●	●			●	●				●		●							●				
El Dorado Canoe Access	Lake Michigan Rd. 2 miles NW of M-22.	●	●		●		●					●		●											
Platte River Campground	Lake Michigan Rd. 0.25 miles NW of M-22, 6 miles from Honor.	●	●	●			●		●	●					●		●								

The southern gateway to the Sleeping Bear Dunes National Lakeshore is filled with public shore, sand and the only natural river outlet on Lake Michigan's east shore.

SLEEPING BEAR DUNES NATIONAL LAKESHORE: Prominent on all maps of the Lake Michigan Coast, the park encompasses large parts of Benzie and Leelanau counties. Other local parks and access points are intermixed within the Sleeping Bear boundaries. National Park listings are denoted by (SBNL) and require an entrance permit. The park's Visitor Center is located in Empire (see p.107).

OLD INDIAN TRAIL (SBNL): The Old Indian Trail system is a series of loops for cross-country skiing. It also is a hiking trail that leads to Lake Michigan at the most south and west portion of Sleeping Bear Dunes National Lakeshore. The shortest distance from the trailhead to the lake is about one mile. Wooded, large dunes and a dune blowout will greet you near the end. The beach is sandy with some small rounded stone. Public beach extends for miles to the east. This area has relatively little use even during the summer.

LOON LAKE RAMP (SBNL): This is boat access to Loon Lake, a good fishing lake. Canoes and kayaks can cross the lake to the Platte River for a 1.5-hour paddle to Lake Michigan. There is a short portage for canoes and kayaks during late summer and early fall when the fish collection weir gate is closed. When the weir gate is open, small fishing boats can navigate the river below Loon Lake to Lake Michigan also. The pilot must be alert for snags and sandbars. Loon Lake and the lower Platte River are good wildlife viewing areas especially in the early morning and late evening.

The following listings are accessed via Lake Michigan Road. From M-22 turn NW near the Platte River Bridge. GPS: 44°42.702'N; 86°07.059'W.

PLATTE RIVER PICNIC AREA (SBNL): A grassy and shaded picnic area located at the M-22 bridge across the Platte River. Swimming is possible in the shallow, sandy river but it is not as nice as at the rivermouth 2.5 miles downstream. A canoe launch provides a starting point for the 1.5 to 2 hour paddle to Lake Michigan. Tables, grills and pavilions. It is a barrier-free area.
   GPS: 44°42.754'N; 86°07.084'W

FISH COLLECTION WEIR: Access to the weir road is normally closed except during fall salmon runs. The Platte River was the trial stream for the introduction of coho salmon into the Great Lakes during the mid-60's. Since the first spawning runs, returning coho have been collected here for artificial fertilization then hatchery rearing before release of the next generation.

PLATTE RIVER MOUTH BEACH (SBNL): The Platte River enters Lake Michigan at the southwest portion of Platte Bay. It is the only large river along Lake Michigan's east shore ending in a natural outlet. Prevailing winds curve outflow of the river to the north forming a long, sand strand between it and the lake. There is a choice of warm river water or cold lake water for swimming. Ride a tube or raft down the last few hundred feet of the river and feel the temperature difference as the fast flow suddenly drops you into the lake. Be careful of deep holes in the river bottom. The river is normally clear enough to see where holes have formed.

Children always find plenty to do here, be it swimming, stone collecting or making castles. Late afternoon winds make kite flying easy. Like other access points in the area, there are miles of beach to walk in each direction. Expect a crowd on warm summer days when parking lots will reach capacity.

There is a canoe landing and pick-up area near the restroom facilities. Lake Michigan Road ends as a boat ramp for small trailered craft. Boat travel into the lake normally will require that you get out and pull the craft across a sandbar formed at the delta. Doing this with heavy boats is not practical. It is a good idea to walk the hundred yards down to the mouth to check it out before your attempt.

Smooth stone mixed into the sand makes ideal nesting sites for the endangered piping plover. The National Park Service closes some of the strand area to use during the summer nesting season, but most of the best beach portions are open.
   GPS: 44°43.848'N; 86°09.344'W

LAKE TOWNSHIP PARK: This is a small parcel of river beach near the mouth of the Platte River. Parking here provides access to adjoining Sleeping Bear Dunes National Lakeshore facilities as well. The rivermouth provides excellent swimming in warmer water. Salmon runs in the fall make this a busy place during September. The township collects a parking fee during prime periods.

EL DORADO CANOE ACCESS (SBNL): Within a few bends of the Platte River's mouth, this small development provides access for canoes, kayaks, tubes and small boats. Fish the bank or wade the stream from here as well.
   GPS: 44°43.631'N; 86°08.628'W

PLATTE RIVER CAMPGROUND (SBNL): The federal campground has 150 sites, modern restrooms and showers. It is close to popular Platte River canoeing and Platte Bay salmon fishing. From it, two trails, each about one mile long, head to Platte Bay. One follows the old Platte Lake-to-Platte Bay rail grade (see p.103). The campground is often full in the summer.
   GPS: 44°42.899'N; 86°07.258'W

Map Labels

Marl Springs
Otter Creek Beach
Bass Lake
Platte Plains Trailheads
Peterson Rd Access
Old Logging RR Trail

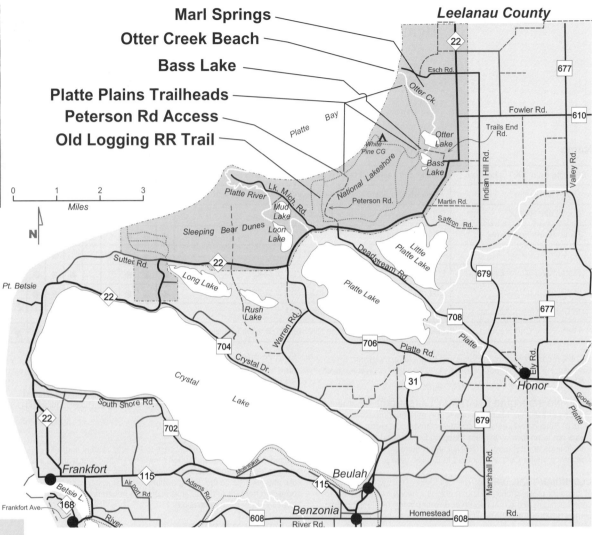

Leelanau County

Esch Rd.
Otter Ck.
Fowler Rd.
Trails End Rd.
Platte Bay
White Pine CG
Otter Lake
Indian Hill Rd.
Valley Rd.
National Lakeshore
Bass Lake
Peterson Rd.
Martin Rd.
Platte River
Lk. Mich. Rd.
Mud Lake
Saffron Rd.
Sleeping Bear Dunes
Loon Lake
Little Platte Lake
Pt. Betsie
Sutter Rd.
Long Lake
Deadstream Rd.
Platte Lake
Rush Lake
Warren Rd.
Crystal Dr.
Platte Rd.
Platte
Crystal Lake
South Shore Rd.
Honor
Goose
Frankfort
Betsie L.
Airport Rd.
Adams Rd.
Molineaux
Beulah
Benzonia
Marshall Rd.
Frankfort Ave.
River
River Rd.
Homestead
Rd.

0 1 2 3
Miles

N

Three scenes from Platte Bay.

Above: Nearing sunset, Platte River Point hooks the bay to the west.

Below left: The bay's sandy shore stretches for miles. Solitude is available, especially during the off-season.

Below right: The Sleeping Bear Dunes backdrop a kayak adventure.

Benzie County

Platte Bay and Otter Creek

Name	Location	Entrance Fee	Parking	Modern Restrooms	Vault or Portable Toilet	Stair or Path to Shore	Swimming	Picnic Area	Drinking Water	Campground	Trailered Boat Launch	Kayak / Canoe	Marina	Fishing	Hiking	Biking	X-Country Skiing	Playground	Lighthouse	Beach Strolling	Sandy Beach	Stony or Rocky Shore	Dunes	Bluff	Wetland
Old Logging Railroad Trail	Primary access via Platte River Campground, Lake Michigan Rd. near M-22.	●			●	●	●							●			●			●	●		●		
Peterson Road	5 miles W of Honor at intersection of M-22 and Deadstream Rd. (CR 708).	●	●		●	●	●					●		●	●	●	●			●	●		●		
Platte Plains Pathway & White Pine Campground	See other listings. Access from Otter Creek, Bass Lake, Peterson Road or Platte River Campground.	●	●		●	●	●			●					●		●			●	●		●		
Bass Lake	6.5 miles S of Empire. From M-22, turn west onto Trails End Road.	●	●		●							●		●	●		●								
Otter Creek Beach	End of Esch Rd. 1.2 miles W of M-22. 4 miles S of Empire.	●	●		●		●					●		●	●					●	●	●	●	●	
Marl Springs	Esch Rd. turn west off M-22. 4.5 miles S of Empire.	●	●												●		●								●

Platte Bay has miles of remote public shore with dunes and great swimming. The access points are interconnected by foot trails.

OLD LOGGING RAILROAD TRAIL (SBNL): The primary access is from the Platte River Campground. It also connects with the Platte Plains Trail System via Peterson Road, listed next. The trail follows the grade of the Platte Lake-to-Platte Bay narrow gauge logging railroad. It once carried lumber from the Platte Lake mill to waiting schooners in the bay.

PETERSON ROAD (SBNL): Peterson is a seasonal road, unplowed in winter, to Platte Bay's broad sandy beach and small dunes. Also, you can access hiking trails (see Platte Plains, next listing) in this area. The road normally has some potholes and can be very dusty but is easily passable by all vehicles. A tenth-mile trail goes to the beach from the road end parking area. The beach is sandy with occasional stones, most rounded for good skipping. Small dunes parallel the shore. Miles of public beach extend each way from this point. Facilities are limited to vault toilets at the parking area. Peterson Road and some connecting two-track lanes are good for all-terrain bicycles. Bicycles are not allowed off designated roads. During the winter, a parking area at M-22 is plowed for skiers.

Peterson Road beach runs east-west protecting it from westerly predominant winds. While there is no steep drop off close to the shore, it quickly reaches depths of several feet deep, so keep a close eye on small children. This is a wonderful sunset spot in the summer. The sun sets just north of the Platte River Point. With the right mix of clouds, the Empire Bluff, seen 4 miles to the northeast, can change to a reddish-purple during the sunset. Move inland from the beach onto the Platte Plains for the nighthawk performance. These birds commonly feed on insects at twilight above the open areas of scrub pine. The male dives, ending each descent in a sudden zoom upwards. The motion makes a throaty, horn-like sound.
     GPS: 44°42.754'N; 86°06.312'W (M-22 / Peterson Rd. turn)

PLATTE PLAINS PATHWAY & WHITE PINE CAMPGROUND: This is an extensive trail system with a back-country campground. The primary trailheads start at the end of Peterson Road, at Bass Lake and from Esch Road at Otter Creek. Each of these areas are listed on this page. Some of the trail is sandy, so do not expect a hard-packed surface. Parts of the trail parallel Platte Bay, offering beautiful views and a true back-country experience. The trail is closed to bikes but much of it would be impassable by bikes anyway. Watch for occasional areas of poison ivy. If you have good endurance, try skis or snowshoes during the winter. Skiers can divert from the pathway to ski up and down the small dunes. If you do not know the area well, take a compass and map. The winds can shift the snow, covering your tracks. Backtracking may not be easy.

Contact the NPS office for camping permits, trail map and access points. Major trailheads have vault toilets as does the White Pine Back-Country Campground.

BASS LAKE (SBNL): Parking is located at Bass Lake which is also near Otter Lake. Both lakes are protected from wind and are good places to paddle and view wildlife. Deer, beaver, otter and loons are potential sights especially in the early morning. You can access the Platte Plains Pathway from here. Platte Bay is a 2-mile hike from the parking lot.
     GPS: 44°44.221'N; 86°03.925'W (parking), 44°43.966'N; 86°03.154'W (M-22 / Trails End Rd. intersection)

OTTER CREEK BEACH (SBNL): The ghost town of Aral sat at the mouth of Otter Creek during the lumber days. Only a couple of pier posts and some foundations remain. Today, it draws those looking for natural, uninterrupted public shore. From the end of Esch Road, you can access miles of beach: either north or south. Development is limited to a vault toilet and a few signs. Beyond that, the natural features of small dunes, high bluffs and sandy beach line Platte Bay. Park along the road shoulder. A long line of parked cars will extend from the lake on sunny, summer days. Early in the day or during the off-season, you can park very close to the lakeshore. Canoeists and kayakers will find it a short carry from the road end to the lake. The small creek enters Lake Michigan just south of the road end. Children love to play in its shallow waters. Wave action regularly changes the shape of the outlet, making it different each time you come. Spring and fall surfcasting can be productive off the creek as well.

Walk the beach to the north for the Empire Bluff. The bluff is steep and climbing to the top from the beach is not advised as it causes erosion. You will find some rock and an increase of stone north of the creek including occasional Petoskey Stones. Empire is about 3.5 miles from Esch Road and there is no development in between. To the south are small sand dunes that extend to Platte River Point, over five shore miles away to the southwest. A hike or beach stroll can take you away to your own "private" beach even on the busiest of days.

A few other characteristics make this spot special. Otter Creek is a prime sunset location. In winter, ice mounds build in the bay making interesting formations and occasionally "blow holes" where waves shoot water up through volcano-like ice formations. The north trailhead for the Platte Plains is also found here.
     GPS: 44°45.780'N; 86°04.472'W

MARL SPRINGS (SBNL): These small, natural springs near Otter Creek are hard to find. Trail maps do not show them, so pretend this is a scavenger hunt and follow these clues. Park at the Platte Plains Trailhead at Esch Road and follow the trail sign to the east. Walk until the trail enters a plantation of red pine. Shortly after leaving the plantation, an open field of grass will appear along the trail's left. After several turns, the grass field will end as the main trail takes a sharp left at a marker post. Here, a barely-worn path heads straight ahead. Follow the path less traveled. The springs lie among cedars near Otter Creek. Their cool water temperature, (low 40's) makes for a refreshing environment on a summer day. Explore a little.

Dune Climbing Tips

The east shore of Lake Michigan has some of the best known sand dunes on the planet. The great sand hills at Silver Lake (Oceana), Warren Dunes (Berrien), Saugatuck (Allegan), Hoffmaster (Muskegon) and the Sleeping Bear (Leelanau) top the list. Here are some tips for the uninitiated planning a day at these sites.

1). Dune climbing is strenuous activity. The slopes are steep, often at the angle of repose. Dry sand has little traction and on a steep uphill, you will slide back almost as far as you step up. Make sure you are physically ready.

2). Avoid using shoes or footwear. They will fill with sand in no time, squeezing your feet and causing constant stops to empty your load.

3). The sand will get very hot on sunny summer days especially at mid-day. Consider morning or evening jaunts.

4). The dunes are dry, shadeless and often windy. Use sun block and have a hat handy. There is no escaping the elements in these mini-deserts. Take water if you are venturing across dunes. You will dehydrate quickly.

5). Kids love to scramble down the dunes. This is normally a safe activity, but they can gain great speed running downhill. Sometimes the feet slow in the sand. You get the picture! Soon their head is moving faster than their feet, ending in a face-plant followed by a slide down the dune. The fun temporarily stops when the crying starts and sand begins spitting from the mouth. Usually the trauma is short lived but the memories last forever!

6). No matter how hard you try, sand will find its way into every nook and crevice. Expect it. A shower or swim later will feel good.

7). Stay on trails and avoid areas where conservation agencies have established erosion control measures. Trampling the dune grasses can easily harm the native plants. Their environment provides enough challenge already. The grasses can also cause painful cuts and punctures to bare feet.

8.) Many experienced dune trekkers like cloudy days following a rain. Moist sand is cool and easier to walk through. The clouds lessen the sun's effect. Alternatively, a sunny morning or evening combines cooler temperatures with a scenic sunrise or sunset while avoiding the heat of afternoon.

9). If you plan to hike in the larger dune areas take a compass, a map and know how to use them. Landmarks are few. Do not expect to follow your footprints back. Shifting sands can cover your tracks in no time.

Clockwise from the top left:
- On a hot, sunny day, beachgoers head to the lake via the trail at Sleeping Bear Point.
- A steep path leads down Saugatuck Dunes.
- Silver Lake Dunes exhibit a seemingly endless desert of sand. The lack of features requires some navigation skills.
- Climbers look like ants on Sleeping Bear's Dune Climb.

Leelanau County

The Leelanau Peninsula, Michigan's "little finger," is small in area but long on shoreline. The western side rides along Lake Michigan proper. Its eastern coast saddles up to Grand Traverse Bay. Several smaller bays and wild islands add more character. The shore alternates between sandy beaches and stretches of rock or stone.

Following M-22 from the county's southwest, the Sleeping Bear Dunes National Lakeshore continues. Its Visitor Center is located in Empire, a small town whose livelihood depends on the park tourists. To its north on Highway M-109 is the park namesake. The Sleeping Bear Dune ranks as the area's biggest attraction. For years, families have ventured to this giant sand pile. Good exercise and fun await as you kick off your shoes and climb. When breathless and near the top, turn around to see turquoise Glen Lake shimmering below. Nearby, drive the paved Pierce Stocking Scenic Drive to the top of the dunes. Pull-off areas provide spectacular views of Lake Michigan, Glen Lake, the dunes and the off-shore islands.

In addition to Empire, M-22 strings together several other trendy small towns. Glen Arbor, Leland, Northport and Suttons Bay each serve travelers in their own way with interesting shops and waterfronts. Orchards are plentiful. Apples and cherries lead the way but raising wine grapes has increased dramatically as the county's vintners garner awards for their quality goods. Try the wine tasting offered at several wineries. Lighthouse Point, at the peninsula's tip, makes a pleasant afternoon stop.

Leland's "Fishtown" harbor is the departure point for those heading to the Manitou Islands. North Manitou Island, now a backpacker wilderness, has remnants of old farmsteads reverting to forest. South Manitou Island has a number of interesting sites including a one of a kind view from its lighthouse tower.

The protective waters of Grand Traverse Bay are home to private yachts and craft. Much of the shore is rocky but sandy beaches can be found in Northport, Omena and Suttons Bay. M-22 follows the bay and the water is rarely out of view. By the time you reach the southeast corner of the Leelanau Peninsula, you will sense nearness to Traverse City, a fast-growing city at the base of the bay.

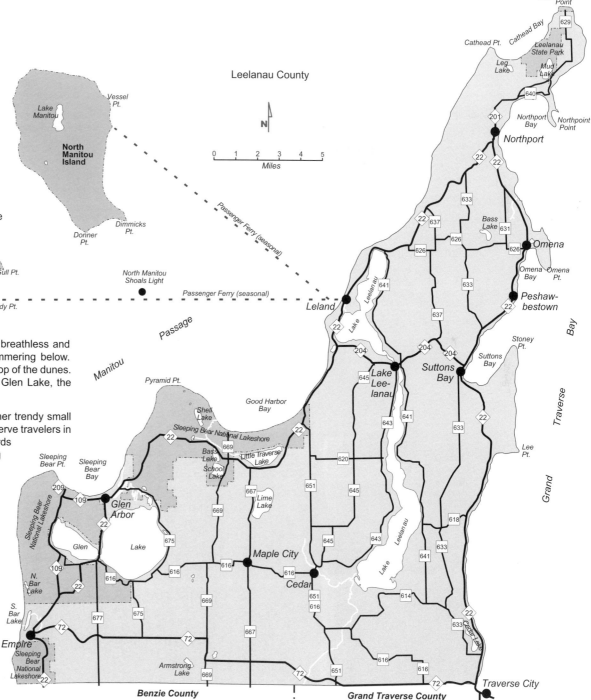

Leelanau County

Above left: Empire Beach and the Sleeping Bear Dunes seen from the Empire Bluff Trail.

Below left: Sleeping Bear Bluffs backdrop Empire Beach.

Opposite page: North Bar Lake empties through a small gap into Lake Michigan.

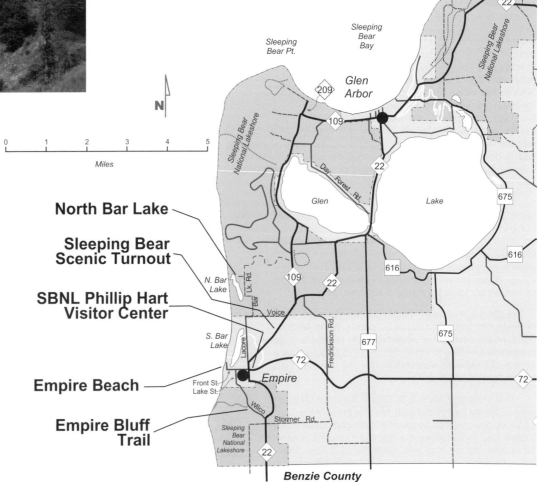

North Bar Lake

Sleeping Bear Scenic Turnout

SBNL Phillip Hart Visitor Center

Empire Beach

Empire Bluff Trail

Leelanau County

Empire and the Bar Lakes

Name	Location	Entrance Fee	Parking	Modern Restrooms	Vault or Portable Toilet	Stair or Path to Shore	Swimming	Picnic Area	Drinking Water	Campground	Trailered Boat Launch	Kayak / Canoe	Marina	Fishing	Hiking	Biking	X-Country Skiing	Playground	Lighthouse	Beach Strolling	Sandy Beach	Stony or Rocky Shore	Dunes	Bluff	Wetland
Empire Bluff Trail (SBNL)	One mile S of Empire. From M-22 turn W on Wilco Rd. 0.5 miles.	●	●		●	●									●		●							●	
Empire Beach	Empire. Lake Michigan Dr.		●	●			●	●				●		●				●			●	●	●		
Phillip Hart Visitor Center (SBNL)	Empire. M-72 just E of M-22.		●	●					●																
Sleeping Bear Scenic Turnout	1 mile NE of Empire on M-22.		●					●																	
North Bar Lake	2.5 miles N of Empire. From M-22, W on Voice Rd 0.5 miles then N on North Bar Rd.	●	●		●	●	●					●		●							●	●	●	●	

The Empire Bluff rises several hundred feet above the coast then gives way to the lowlands near the pleasant town of Empire, a gateway to vacation country.

EMPIRE BLUFF TRAIL: This 3/4-mile trail leads through a beautiful maple and, beech forest to the Empire Bluff. The tall forest overstory creates a large umbrella for much of the way. A brochure explains points of natural and historical interest. The first overlook peers down on Empire Beach and South Bar Lake. The trail ends at an observation platform nearly 400 feet above Lake Michigan. On clear, sunny days, the color of the lake varies from turquoise to deep blue. Platte Point, South Manitou Island and the Sleeping Bear Dunes are all within view. The Empire Bluff is steep and prone to slides. Access to the beach from the trail is not advised. Part of the SBNL, a permit is required. After your hike, drive the beautiful, tree-lined Wilcox Road as it winds its way downhill into Empire Village.
  GPS: 44°47.711'N; 86°03.019'W (trailhead), 44°47.671'N; 86°02.990'W (Wilcox Rd. & M-22 intersection)

EMPIRE BEACH: Empire Beach sits between Lake Michigan and South Bar Lake. Good swimming and picnicking are available at this developed but low-key park. The beach is sandy with a rounded stone mix. A few Petoskey Stones can be found. The base of the Empire Bluff can be reached by walking to the south. There is a small portion of private land between the bluff and park but the landowners permit beach walking. A kayak can be easily carried to the shore for a tour of the bluffs, Platte Bay or paddle north toward the Sleeping Bear Dune area. The park also has a boat launch for small craft on South Bar Lake. Other facilities include a shelter, basketball and beach volleyball courts.
  GPS: 44°49.499'N, 86°02.585'W

PHILLIP HART VISITOR CENTER: The Sleeping Bear Dunes National Lakeshore's Visitor Center has a small interpretive exhibit telling of the area's geology, flora and fauna. Park visitor orientation programs are presented here. Books of local of interest, maps and park permits are sold.
  GPS: 44°48.662'N; 86°03.399'W

SLEEPING BEAR SCENIC TURNOUT: A small, roadside park with a couple of picnic tables sits on the west side of M-22 north of Empire. The park's vantage point overlooks Lake Michigan about a mile away. The Empire Bluff rises in the southwest view. No restroom facilities.
  GPS: 44°49.499'N; 86°02.585'W

NORTH BAR LAKE: North Bar Lake is a thin pond paralleling the Lake Michigan shore. An outlet stream makes its way to Lake Michigan when the level of North Bar Lake is high enough and the winds permit it to break through the ever-building sand bar. The outlet is narrow, shallow and never much longer than a hundred feet. All in all, it is a very pretty setting with development mostly relegated to the parking area.

Long a favorite swimming beach for locals, North Bar Lake has a sharp drop-off and warm water. Lake Michigan's beach is sandy with a rounded stone mix and cold water. There are several private residences near the North Bar site. Despite this, there is a still a feeling of isolation.

The National Park Service has recently developed a parking area roughly 750 feet from North Bar Lake. The walk is fairly level and wide making it a reasonable carry for canoes and kayaks. A very short paddle through North Bar Lake takes you to Lake Michigan. Pedestrian users will walk an additional 1000 feet over the dune to the lakeshore. The NPS has also begun a dune protection program to promote vegetative growth on the small dunes found on the north side of the small lake.
  GPS: 44°50.627'N; 86°03.708'W

Above left: An old lifesaving dory is one of a number of artifacts at the Sleeping Bear Point Coast Guard Station Maritime Museum.

Above right: Hikers along the Dunes Trail above the Sleeping Bear Dune Climb. Glen Lake forms the backdrop.

Below: The Stocking Scenic Drive is open for skiing in the winter. The sand and snow mixes on the dunes. At the Lake Michigan overlook, South Manitou Island lies off the Sleeping Bear Bluff surrounded by ice and snow.

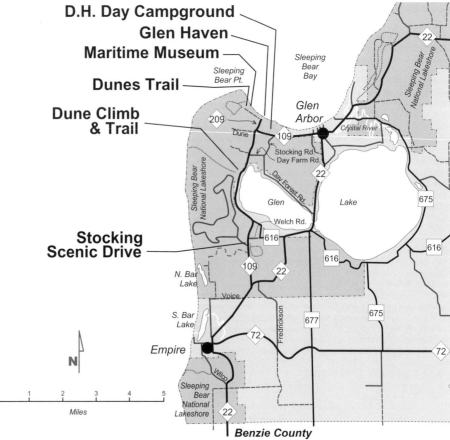

Leelanau County

Sleeping Bear Dunes

Facilities   **Environment**

Name	Location	Entrance Fee	Parking	Modern Restrooms	Vault or Portable Toilet	Stair or Path to Shore	Swimming	Picnic Area	Drinking Water	Campground	Trailered Boat Launch	Kayak / Canoe	Marina	Fishing	Hiking	Biking	X-Country Skiing	Playground	Lighthouse	Beach Strolling	Sandy Beach	Stony or Rocky Shore	Dunes	Bluff	Wetland
Pierce Stocking Scenic Drive	3.5 miles N of Empire on M-109.	●	●		●	●		●							●	●	●						●	●	
Dune Climb and Trailhead	5 miles N of Empire on M-109.	●	●	●		●		●	●						●								●		
Glen Lake Picnic Area Beach	6 miles N of Empire on M-109.	●	●				●	●				●		●							●				
Sleeping Bear Point Trailhead	3 miles W of Glen Arbor. From M-109 turn N on M-209 then W on Sleeping Bear Drive.	●	●			●	●	●							●					●	●	●	●		
Coast Guard Station Maritime Museum	3 miles W of Glen Arbor. From M-109 turn N on M-209 then W on Sleeping Bear Drive.	●	●			●		●												●	●	●			
Glen Haven	2 miles W of Glen Arbor. From M-109 turn N on M-209.	●	●			●		●	●			●								●	●	●			
D.H. Day Campground	1 mile W of Glen Arbor on M-109.	●			●	●		●		●	●	●								●	●	●			

The impressive, perched dunes of the Sleeping Bear define the area. The unique geology makes this a premiere destination. Note: All the listings on this page are part of the Sleeping Bear Dunes National Lakeshore. A park permit is required for use.

PIERCE STOCKING SCENIC DRIVE: One of the most popular activities at the Sleeping Bear Dunes National Lakeshore is touring the Pierce Stocking Scenic Drive. The 7-mile, paved road sits atop part of the Sleeping Bear Dunes. Several overlooks include views of Glen Lake, Lake Michigan, the Sleeping Bear Dunes, and out to the Manitou Islands.

Mr. Stocking developed the original do-it-yourself drive on top of the dunes in the late 1960's. The National Park Service upgraded it after it reverted to the federal government following the formation of the park. On a sunny day, "Dunes Overlook" provides a view of the varying hues of Glen Lake, rated one of the world's most beautiful lakes. You will see why. Likewise, the stop at the Lake Michigan bluff will display the different blues of the big lake as it contrasts with the sheer sand bluffs.

Stocking Drive is one of the best ways for the physically handicapped to experience the lakeshore and the dunes. Several stops offer short hikes as well. Open May through mid-October to vehicular traffic, look for breathtaking views of vivid fall colors at peak color change. It is unplowed and open for cross-country skiing in the winter. Bicycling, especially in early morning before the heavy traffic, is fun for the very well conditioned. Choose a bike geared for steep hills.
    GPS: 44°51.159'N; 86°02.215'W

DUNE CLIMB AND TRAILHEAD: The "Dune Climb" is the number one activity of the Sleeping Bear Dunes National Lakeshore. The tall dune overlooks gorgeous Glen Lake and creeps slowly towards it, grain-by-grain. The climb is a couple of hundred feet up. From the top,

the turquoise water of Glen Lake flashes on sunny days. Sleeping Bear Bay and the Manitou Islands are visible to the north when the weather is clear. Children love speeding down the dune, running, leaping or rolling to the bottom.

The climb area includes a concession building, modern restrooms, interpretive displays, and a short, wheelchair-accessible trail at the north end of the parking lot. The dune climb is also the trailhead for the "Dunes Trail" to Lake Michigan. The 3.5-mile round trip trail is entirely sand. It is an arduous hike requiring common sense, sun block, water and more water. If you are new to dune hiking, read the feature on page 104.
    GPS: 44°52.879'N; 86°02.371'W

GLEN LAKE PICNIC AREA AND BEACH: Located on M-109 just north of the dune climb area, this unit of the SBNL has a picnic area and beach on Glen Lake.
    GPS: 44°53.120'N; 86°02.148'W

Note: The next three listings are found by turning onto M-209 from M-109 at 44°53.939'N; 86°01.810'W

SLEEPING BEAR POINT TRAILHEAD: The trailhead is located just west of the Old Coast Guard Station and Maritime Museum located near Glen Haven. There is a 2.8-mile loop on the dunes and a short hike from it to the shore along Sleeping Bear Bay. The distance from the trailhead to the lake takes only a few minutes. The shore is a mix of sand and round stones. The Manitou Islands and Passage are in full view. Sleeping Bear Point has been the site of several large landslides in recent years as the lake constantly challenges the steep angle of the dune.

COAST GUARD STATION MARITIME MUSEUM: The former Coast Guard Station at Sleeping Bear Point now serves as an interesting museum administered by the National Park Service. The narrow Manitou Passage has long been treacherous to shipping during fog and storm. Imagine braving the rough seas in a small, lifesaving dory boat kept at the ready to pull crew from wrecked ships or icy waters. The museum has samples of the seemingly crude equipment and the stories of those who risked their lives. Begun in 1901, the station closed in 1941 and is now restored to its 1931 appearance.
    GPS: 44° 54.450'N; 86° 02.079'W

GLEN HAVEN: Glen Haven is essentially a ghost town on Sleeping Bear Bay, whose final death blow, ironically, came with the formation of the Sleeping Bear Dunes National Lakeshore. Its history includes fishing, fruit and the once-popular rides across the Sleeping Bear Dunes. The garages and related buildings of the "dune buggies" remain along M-209 now preserved by the park. The specially modified vehicles drew tourists during the 1950's and 60's.

Today, the NPS operates a historic display in the old Leelanau Canning Company building. Picnic tables are found by the lake. The beach is sandy with a round stone mix. Canoes and kayaks can be easily carried to the bay.
    GPS: 44° 54.263'N; 86° 01.624'W

D.H. DAY CAMPGROUND: Day Campground is extremely popular due to its proximity to the Dune Climb and its location on Sleeping Bear Bay. Vault toilets and hand water pumps are the primary facilities for the 88 sites. A camping fee is charged in addition to park entrance fees.
    GPS: 44° 53.777'N; 86° 01.259'W

Left: Stone hunting near Glen Arbor

Right: Glen Arbor's Lake Street Road End has a boat ramp and benches and is close to shopping.

Below: Pyramid Point Trail leads to a tall bluff overlooking the Manitou Passage.

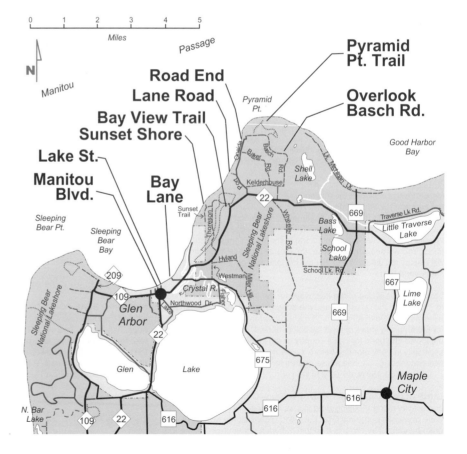

Name	Location	Entrance Fee	Parking	Modern Restrooms	Vault or Portable Toilet	Stair or Path to Shore	Swimming	Picnic Area	Drinking Water	Campground	Trailered Boat Launch	Kayak / Canoe	Marina	Fishing	Hiking	Biking	X-Country Skiing	Playground	Lighthouse	Beach Strolling	Sandy Beach	Stony or Rocky Shore	Dunes	Bluff	Wetland
Manitou Blvd.	Glen Arbor. Turn N on Manitou Blvd.						●				●	●									●	●			
Lake Street Road End	Glen Arbor. Turn N on Lake Street.						●				●	●									●	●			
Bay Lane Beach	Glen Arbor. Turn W from M-22 on Bay Lane across from CR 675.		●				●					●									●	●			
Sunset Shore	4 miles NE of Glen Arbor. From M-22 turn W on Thoreson then W on Sunset Trail, then N at unnamed turnaround.		●			●	●					●								●	●	●			
Bay View Trail (SBNL)	4 miles NE of Glen Arbor. From M-22 turn W on Thoreson Rd.	●	●		●										●		●								
Lane Road	5 miles NE of Glen Arbor. From M-22 turn N on Port Oneida Rd. then W on Lane Rd.		●			●	●					●								●	●	●			
Unnamed Road End	6 miles NE of Glen Arbor. From M-22 turn N on Port Oneida Rd. then W just S of Basch Rd.		●			●	●					●								●	●	●			
Pyramid Point Trail (SBNL)	7 miles NE of Glen Arbor. From M-22 turn N on Port Oneida Rd. then E on Basch Rd.	●	●		●	●									●		●							●	
Overlook - Basch Rd	6 miles NE of Glen Arbor. From M-22 turn N on Basch Rd.		●																					●	

Glen Arbor is a small summer town that draws the resorters of Glen Lake and the transient tourists of the dunes to its eateries and art shops. The Sleeping Bear Dunes National Lakeshore lies on each side of town.

MANITOU BLVD.: This is a road end beach access with no facilities. It is an easy walk from the Glen Arbor shops. The boat ramp can handle small boats. Street parking.
GPS: 44°54.015'N; 85°59.431'W

LAKE STREET ROAD END: Lake Street is another road end in Glen Arbor. Space and parking is limited and the small park is busy on sunny, summer days. A few benches are available. The beach is a sand, stone mix and the area available to swim is small. There is a fee for boat launching. Some of the Glen Arbor shops are adjacent to the beach area and the rest are within short walking distance.
GPS: 44°54.034'N; 85°59.340'W

BAY LANE BEACH: Probably the least busy of Glen Arbor's three road end beaches, this area is small with no facilities. The beach is a sand and stone mix.
GPS: 44°54.298'N; 85°58.808'W

SUNSET SHORE: The undeveloped beach is sand with an occasional boulder in the water. Swimming is good and the beach is less known than most in the area. No facilities exist. Parking is limited to the large turn-around area. It is a difficult beach to find. Thoreson Road is a gravel lane that intersects M-22 at two locations. It is best to

turn at the north intersection, the farthest one from Glen Arbor, as this avoids parts of Thoreson that are poor two-track. After it makes a turn to the south, look for Sunset Trail. Sunset Trail initially heads west, when it begins to turn south look for the dirt trail to the right (north).
GPS: 44°55.858'N; 85°57.882'W

BAY VIEW TRAIL: There is about 9 miles of hiking and skiing trail on the highlands east of Sleeping Bear Bay. The easiest trailhead to find is just off M-22 at its north intersection with Thoreson Road. A half-mile north of the trailhead is a lookout with views of the bay.
GPS: 44°56.067'N; 85°56.950'W

LANE ROAD: Lane Road ends at a turn-around on a small bluff at the lakeshore. The beach is sand with some stone. South Manitou Island sits in view 8 miles to the west. No facilities.
GPS: 44°56.817'N; 85°56.800'W

UNNAMED ROAD END: "Seasonal Road" and "No Camping" signs mark this narrow gravel lane. It ends with primitive parking in tall hardwoods. Additional parking is along the road. You must scale a sharp but short bluff to reach the shore. The beach has a sand and stone mix. Petoskey Stones are common here and swimming is good. No facilities.
GPS: 44°57.485'N; 85°56.276'W

PYRAMID POINT TRAIL: One of the favorite hikes within the Sleeping Bear Lakeshore, Pyramid Point looks directly out to North Manitou Island 6 miles away. In between is the North Manitou Shoal

Light, about four miles off shore. The walk to the point is 0.6 miles. You will end at the top of the 400-foot bluff. On a sunny day, Lake Michigan will show its varying hues. While most make the trip to the point and then back, additional trail loops to the east and then back along Basch Road to the trailhead.

The temptation is to descend the bluff to the beach below. Besides hastening erosion, it is unadvised for other reasons as well. The slope here is at the angle of repose or as steep as gravity will allow the sand and gravel to hold together without sliding down. Traveling down the slope will cause the slope to break away. Stones will start tumbling making it hazardous, especially for anyone below. The hike back up is arduous. During high winds, the beach may be dangerously awash with high waves.
GPS: 44°57.708'N; 85°55.835'W

OVERLOOK - BASCH RD.: The overlook is about one mile from the shore of Good Harbor Bay but provides a nice view of forest, field and Good Harbor Bay beyond. No facilities.
GPS: 85°55.835'N; 85°54.767'W

Left: Across from Shalda Creek, the Leelanau Peninsula continues to the north.

Below left: The old pier pilings near Good Harbor Creek provide the foreground as summer twilight casts Pyramid Point in silhouette.

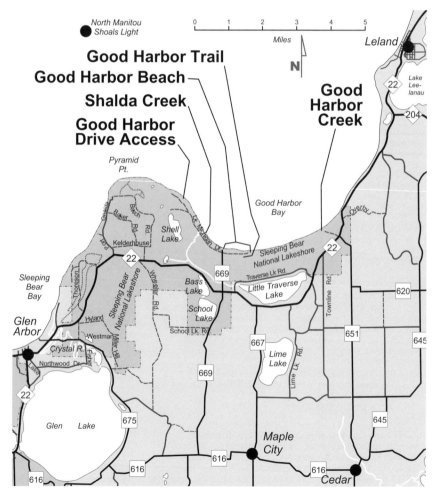

112

Leelanau County

Good Harbor Bay

Name	Location	Entrance Fee	Parking	Modern Restrooms	Vault or Portable Toilet	Stair or Path to Shore	Swimming	Picnic Area	Drinking Water	Campground	Trailered Boat Launch	Kayak / Canoe	Marina	Fishing	Hiking	Biking	X-Country Skiing	Playground	Lighthouse	Beach Strolling	Sandy Beach	Stony or Rocky Shore	Dunes	Bluff	Wetland
Good Harbor Drive Access Points (SBNL)	1 mile N of M-22 to end of CR 669 then 3 miles west.	●	●			●	●					●								●	●	●		●	
Shalda Creek Access (SBNL)	1 mile N of M-22 to end of CR 669 then one mile west.	●	●			●	●							●						●	●	●			
Good Harbor Bay Beach (SBNL)	1 mile N of M-22 at end of CR 669.	●	●		●		●	●				●								●	●		●		
Good Harbor Bay Trailhead (SBNL)	1 mile N of M-22 at end of CR 669 turn right about one mile.	●	●		●							●			●		●			●	●		●		
Good Harbor Creek (SBNL)	At end of Good Harbor Trail Road (CR 651), 5.5 miles S of Leland, 0.5 mile NW of M-22.	●	●		●		●					●		●						●	●		●		

Good Harbor Bay's sandy beach stretches for several miles offering room to take a stroll and find the occasional Petoskey Stone.

Note: To reach the first four listings, turn north at the CR 669 intersection with M-22. GPS: 44°55.308'N; 85°52.391'W

GOOD HARBOR DRIVE ACCESS POINTS: Recently the National Park Service has removed most of the private residences between Pyramid Point and CR 669. Each former driveway has become an access point. The area just east of Pyramid Point offers some shade and generally less use than the beach nearer to CR 669. It is an easy kayak launch to reach the base of Pyramid Point's cliff. No facilities.
  GPS: 44°57.760'N; 85°54.144'W

SHALDA CREEK ACCESS: Shalda Creek is a narrow, shallow stream that flows into Good Harbor Bay. It is a great place for small children who like to float on tubes along its last few feet before merging with Lake Michigan. A few Petoskey Stones lay scattered in the area. Parking is limited to a couple of places along the gravel roadside. Look for the gray sign marking the short path to the beach. Watch for poison ivy along the trail.
  GPS: 44°56.704'N; 85°53.033'W

GOOD HARBOR BAY BEACH: North-facing Good Harbor Bay is mostly owned by the Sleeping Bear Dunes National Lakeshore. Access is plentiful, however, there are still private residences scattered along the shore. The main parking areas for access are at the end of CR 669 as well as at the east end of Lake Michigan Drive, once the site of a state campground. The beach is sandy with a mix of stones. It is also a place for Petoskey Stone hunting. Paddlers can carry their craft to the shore here with relative ease. Pyramid Point, to the west, protects the bay from prevailing westerly winds.
  GPS: 44°56.370'N; 85°52.367'W

GOOD HARBOR BAY TRAILHEAD: A hike and ski trail loops south of the bay from a small parking area found along Lake Michigan Drive. A NPS park permit is required.
  GPS: 44°56.208'N; 85°51.438'W

GOOD HARBOR CREEK: At the end of Good Harbor Trail is a sandy beach with plenty of room to walk. Remnants of the Good Harbor Pier stick out from the water near the road end. The creek enters the lake west of the road end. In the evening, watch the sunset near Pyramid Point, about five miles across the bay. It is an easy place to carry canoes and kayaks to the water.
  GPS: 44°56.801'N; 85°48.685'W

Note: The lands featured on this page are part of the Sleeping Bear Dunes National Lakeshore and an entrance fee is required for their use. Parking at Shalda Creek and the road ends of CR 669 and Good Harbor Trail is along the road shoulder. This is county road right-of-way. To view the bay from the road ends does not require a park pass.

Right: The Leland Breakwater and Leland Beach in the late day sun.

Below: Boats and shanty-style stores line the dock along the rivermouth in Leland's "Fishtown," a tourist favorite.

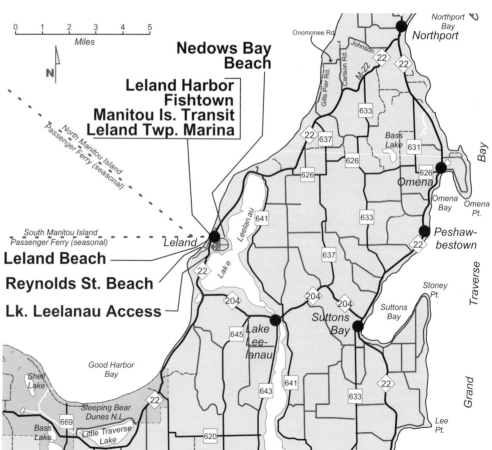

Leelanau County

Leland

Name	Location	Entrance Fee	Parking	Modern Restrooms	Vault or Portable Toilet	Stair or Path to Shore	Swimming	Picnic Area	Drinking Water	Campground	Trailered Boat Launch	Kayak / Canoe	Marina	Fishing	Hiking	Biking	X-Country Skiing	Playground	Lighthouse	Beach Strolling	Sandy Beach	Stony or Rocky Shore	Dunes	Bluff	Wetland
Lake Leelanau Access	S of Leland approx. one mile on west side of M-22.						•					•									•				
Reynolds Street Road End	Leland. On south end of town 3 blocks W of M-22 on Reynolds Street.		•		•		•					•									•				
Leland Beach Cedar Street Road End	Leland, 2 blocks west of M-22 on Cedar Street		•		•	•	•					•									•				
Leland Harbor (Fishtown)	Leland. Two blocks W of M-22 on River St.		•	•				•	•			•		•											
Manitou Island Transit Dock	Leland. At Leland Harbor.		•	•					•																
Leland Township Marina	Leland. At Leland Harbor.	•	•	•				•	•		•		•												
Nedows Bay (Bartholomew Park)	Leland, E 0.5 miles from M-22 on Pearl St.		•				•	•			•	•		•							•				

The quaint tourist town of Leland lies between Lakes Michigan and Leelanau. It has small, independent shops with art, food and vacation fare. The Leland River flows through town falling over its dam at the scenic harbor.

LAKE LEELANAU ACCESS: This is a roadside pull-off south of Leland on M-22 and the shore of Lake Leelanau. There is no development, just a small beach with a warm water alternative to Lake Michigan and a view of Lake Leelanau.
GPS: 45°00.166'N; 85°45.765'W

REYNOLDS STREET ROAD END: A sandy beach access located a few blocks south of Leland Harbor. Park on the shoulder of the road. Great swimming area.
GPS: From M-22 turn W at 45°01.078'N; 85°45.755'W

LELAND BEACH CEDAR STREET ROAD END: A pure sandy beach that is easy to miss. Cedar Street is 1/2-block south of the Leland River Bridge in the middle of town. The parking area is relatively small and unpaved. A small "rules" sign marks the beach parking lot. During the summer months, a portable toilet sits in the lot. You cannot see the lake from the parking lot because of the trees and vegetation. A short, narrow trail travels from the lot to the beach.

Note: Parking is at a premium at the Leland Harbor area during prime, summer days. This affects the next three listings. Nearby parking is metered or has a short duration restriction.

LELAND HARBOR (FISHTOWN): This is the location of Leland's marina and the dock for the passenger ferry to North and South Manitou Islands. "Fishtown" shops line the docks of the Leland River. Picturesque and a favorite spot of summer tourists, stop here to purchase fresh or smoked fish, a souvenir or perhaps an artisan's product.

MANITOU ISLAND TRANSIT DOCK: Passenger ferry service from Leland to either South or North Manitou Island originates at the Leland Harbor dock. Both islands are part of the Sleeping Bear Dunes National Lakeshore. For more information, see the sections about the islands following this page.
Telephone: (231) 256-9061
Web: www.leelanau.com/manitou/

LELAND TOWNSHIP MARINA: Within the protective Leland Harbor, the marina contains 48 transient slips and an excellent boat launch. Fee for both mooring and launching boats. Picnic area with pavilion, grills and tables.
Telephone: (231) 256-9132
GPS: 45°01.433'N; 85°45.850'W

NEDOWS BAY (BARTHOLOMEW PARK): A small public beach on Lake Leelanau that provides a warm water alternative to Lake Michigan.
GPS: 45°01.391'N; 85°44.972'W

Above left: Remnants of South Manitou's maritime past abound. The *Francisco Morazan* found the island shoals in a November 1960 storm, its rusted hull sits in easy view off the south shore.

Below left: The South Manitou Lighthouse towers 100 feet above the sand providing a view of the island and shimmering waters (top right).

Opposite page: A freighter glides around the North Manitou Shoals Light on its way southbound through the Manitou Passage. Ferry service to the island passes within a few hundred feet of the light.

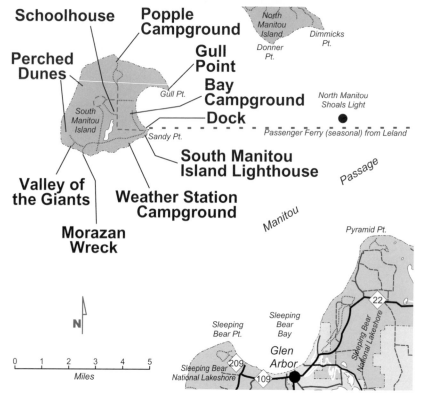

Schoolhouse

Popple Campground

North Manitou Island

Dimmicks Pt.

Donner Pt.

Gull Point

Perched Dunes

Gull Pt.

Bay Campground

North Manitou Shoals Light

South Manitou Island

Dock

Sandy Pt.

Passenger Ferry (seasonal) from Leland

South Manitou Island Lighthouse

Passage

Valley of the Giants

Weather Station Campground

Manitou

Morazan Wreck

Pyramid Pt.

Sleeping Bear Pt.

Sleeping Bear Bay

Sleeping Bear National Lakeshore

22

N

Glen Arbor

0 1 2 3 4 5
Miles

Sleeping Bear National Lakeshore

209

109

Name	Location	Entrance Fee	Parking	Modern Restrooms	Vault or Portable Toilet	Stair or Path to Shore	Swimming	Picnic Area	Drinking Water	Campground	Trailered Boat Launch	Kayak / Canoe	Marina	Fishing	Hiking	Biking	X-Country Skiing	Playground	Lighthouse	Beach Strolling	Sandy Beach	Stony or Rocky Shore	Dunes	Bluff	Wetland
		Facilities																			**Environment**				
South Manitou Island	Passenger ferry from Leland	●		●	●	●	●	●	●	●		●		●	●				●	●	●	●	●	●	●

SOUTH MANITOU ISLAND: The entire island is part of the Sleeping Bear Dunes National Lakeshore and is open for exploration. The island lies about 7 miles northwest from the Sleeping Bear Point on the mainland. The Manitou Passage rests between the two and contributes much to the maritime past of the island. Shallows of the passage put ships in peril during storms and fog. The bay on the island's east shore provides good shelter for ships during gales. Few other protective coves are available on Lake Michigan. The South Manitou Island Light, located on the southeast corner, once provided guidance. Today, you can climb its tower for a great view. Shipwrecks litter the area near shore. One, the Liberian freighter Morazan, is largely intact and visible from shore. The waters surrounding the island are part of the Manitou Passage State Underwater Preserve. Several shipwrecks are marked with buoys. A large gull colony, giant white cedars, large perched sand dunes and the remnants of past inhabitation are other interesting points on the island.

Most visitors travel to South Manitou by the Manitou Island Transit Company passenger ferry from Leland. The craft sails once daily during the summer season. The trip takes about 1.5 hours each way. The boat is comfortable with both open deck and inside seating. The staff helps travelers plan their stay. Island maps, snacks and drinks are sold aboard. During the voyage, the ferry passes close to the North Manitou Shoal Lighthouse, a solitary monument planted in the middle of the Manitou Passage to guide ships. Passengers staying for the day have 5 hours to tramp the beaches, woods and dunes before the return to Leland. Pack a lunch and water bottle, no food is available.

Personal craft can travel to South Manitou as well. The pilot should be well aware of the weather and boat regulations. The NPS allows 20 minutes to dock for unloading. Private boats must self-anchor. The most protected area is within the bay on the east side. Leland and Frankfort are the closest mainland harbors. A shallow boat ramp exists at the end of Lake Street in Glen Arbor which is nearly 8 miles of open water to the island. Kayakers can make arrangements with Manitou Island Transit to ferry their kayaks to the island. Kayakers have been known to make the open water voyage. Only the very experienced and weather-knowledgeable should entertain the notion.

A number of trails and old two-track roads criss-cross South Manitou. Lake level has been low recently, so the shoreline is wide enough to allow one to circumnavigate the island by foot via the beach. Manitou Island Transit has open-air vehicles, formerly used in Glen Haven for the dunemobile rides, which tour old community sites of the island for a fee. The tour guides are well informed, with personal connections to the island's heritage. Camping is available for a fee at three primitive campgrounds. They are located at the north, south and east sides of the island. Gear must be packed in. Drinking water is available at several points including the boat dock area and the Weather Station Campground.

The island shore is a mix of stone and sand. Swimming spots abound. Water does not warm until July when it will still feel cool to most. Away from the lighthouse and campgrounds, you will see only an occasional beach walker. This is especially true after the boat departs to Leland with the day's passengers. National park pass required for the visit.
Telephone: (231) 326-5134
Web: www.nps.gov/slbe/SMI_page.htm

TRANSPORTATION: Manitou Island Transit, Leland (reservations highly recommended). Adults - $25, Under 12 years old - $14 (round-trip)
Telephone: (231) 256-9061
Web: www.leelanau.com/manitou/

ISLAND DOCK: The arrival point for island ferry service, the Visitor Center, restroom, potable water and the meeting place for island tours are near the dock.
GPS: 45°00.750'N; 86°05.500'W

SOUTH MANITOU ISLAND LIGHTHOUSE: The 100-foot tower, which rises from the southeast portion of the island, guided ships from 1871 to 1958. During the summer, the rangers lead climbs up its tall circular staircase. At the top, an outside platform provides spectacular views of the island, Manitou Passage and the Sleeping Bear Dunes across the way.

WRECK OF THE *FRANCISCO MORAZAN*: The Liberian freighter *Morazan* ran aground during a storm in November 1960 and lays at the south end of the island. Much of the ship still looms above the water. A trail on the south side of the island leads to a bluff overlooking the wreck.

VALLEY OF THE GIANTS: A bit west of the Morazan's resting place is a grove of old growth cedar trees. Estimated to be 500 years old and deemed some of the largest white cedar, age and weather have started to take their toll on the giants.

PERCHED SAND DUNES: The west side bluff consists of 400-foot-high perched dunes. A perched dune consists of a glacial moraine (hill) in which the winds have piled sand on its top. From the dock, you must hike across the width of the island to reach the dunes. The view from the top includes the entire island, North Manitou Island to the northeast and the mainland dunes to the southeast.

Note: An avid hiker can visit the dunes, cedars, Morazan wreck and lighthouse during the Manitou Transit 5-hour layover but will have little time to spare.

SCHOOLHOUSE AND COMMUNITY SITE: South Manitou served as a way station for ships during the late 1800's and early 1900's. Hundreds passed by each day. Island forests provided wood to fuel early steamers. Farms also existed. Buildings and foundations from this period sit at the center of the island. Visit the cemetery and old schoolhouse and learn the island's history.

GULL POINT: The northeast corner houses a large colony of ring billed and herring gulls. The area is closed, but sit near the point and listen to the racket, especially during the mating season.

CAMPGROUNDS: Camping, for a nightly fee of $5, is allowed only at Manitou Island's three campgrounds. Each has primitive sites only and each requires campers to backpack in their equipment and supplies.
• *Weather Station Campground* has a water pump at the campground and is located about one mile from the dock and lighthouse.
• *Popple Campground* is located about 5 miles from the dock at the north side of the island and faces toward North Manitou Island.
• *Bay Campground* is located one mile north of the dock on the island's protected bay. On quiet nights, you will hear the chug of freighters passing through the passage.

Left: Rangers meet a ferry load of backpackers at the Village Dock.

Right: Farm building remnants provide insights into the island's past.

Bottom left: The view from the bluff at Johnson Place includes South Manitou Island.

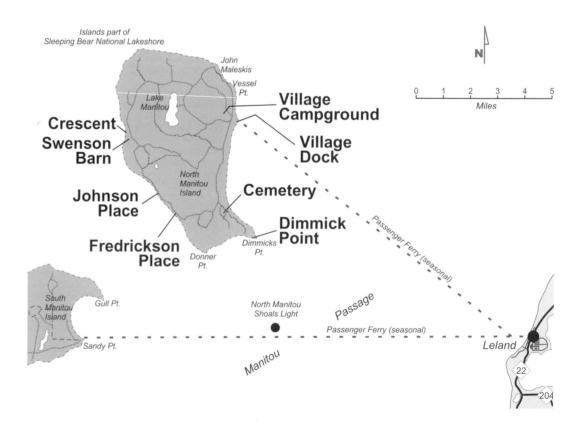

118

Leelanau County

North Manitou Island

Name	Location	Entrance Fee	Parking	Modern Restrooms	Vault or Portable Toilet	Stair or Path to Shore	Swimming	Picnic Area	Drinking Water	Campground	Trailered Boat Launch	Kayak / Canoe	Marina	Fishing	Hiking	Biking	X-Country Skiing	Playground	Lighthouse	Beach Strolling	Sandy Beach	Stony or Rocky Shore	Dunes	Bluff	Wetland
		Facilities																		**Environment**					
North Manitou Island	Passenger ferry from Leland	●			●	●	●	●	●	●		●		●	●					●	●	●	●	●	●

NORTH MANITOU ISLAND: Another island of the Sleeping Bear Dunes National Lakeshore lies north of South Manitou. North Manitou is nearly 4 times larger than South Manitou but without as many notable points of interest. Except for the Village Dock area and its campground, the island is managed as wilderness. Do not think "Village Area" means shops and restaurants. The name derives from its past, not the present. A few buildings still exist but with nothing for you to buy. Once on the island, you are on your own.

The island sits some 10 miles west of Leland and was private for much of its history. The NPS acquired the property through condemnation in the 1980's. Island landmarks carry the names of past occupants. Barns, a cemetery, school ruins, cottages and orchards mark the land as once inhabited, not the wilderness that today's rules imply. Still, North Manitou has tall hardwood forests inland, nice beaches and beautiful views. Its remoteness and wilderness policy limit its use. Sleeping Bear Lakeshore is among the busiest national parks, yet at North Manitou it all slows down.

Manitou Island Transit Company runs a passenger ferry out of Leland from May to November. During the main summer season, the craft sails once daily. Off-season, the boat goes every few days. A reservation is necessary on most days. The trip takes just over an hour one way. After unloading, the boat departs immediately back to Leland. This is a backpacker's trip. A one-day tour is not available like the one to South Manitou Island.

Personal craft can travel to North Manitou as well. The pilot should be well aware of the weather and boat regulations. The NPS allows 20 minute unloading at the Village Dock located on the east side. Private boats must self-anchor. While the east side is the most protected, the North Manitou coast does not offer the same degree of protection as South Manitou's east shore. Leland is the closest harbor and has a boat ramp. Manitou Island Transit will ferry kayaks to the island with proper notice. Kayakers have been known to make the voyage. Only the very experienced and weather-knowledgeable should entertain the notion.

Trails and old two-track roads circle and cross North Manitou. The lake level has been low recently and much of the shoreline can be hiked. No designated campsites exist except at the Village Campground, about one mile from the dock. Get drinking water near the ranger station at the dock area. Water from other sources should be treated. Fires are not allowed except at the Village Campground. You will need a stove to cook in the back-country. Prepare to properly dispose of your human waste and pack out your trash. Camp fee is $5 per night. A National Park pass is required for the visit.
Telephone: (231) 326-5134
Web: www.nps.gov/slbe/SMI_page.htm

TRANSPORTATION: Manitou Island Transit, Leland (reservations highly recommended). Adults -$25, Under 13 - $14 for round-trip ticket
Telephone: (231) 256-9061
Web: www.leelanau.com/manitou/

Brief descriptions of what the shoreline offers follow.

EAST SHORE - *from Vessel Point south to Dimmick's Point*. A trail travels north-south, parallel to much of the east coast. Generally, it is on a slight rise, about 15 feet above the lake level. South of the boat dock, the beach is easily walked, providing an option to the trail. The shore is sand and stone, with many places to swim. The southeast portion has many open, unshaded areas. North of the dock to Vessel Point, the beach is not as easy to walk and the lake view is sometimes obscured from the trail.

VILLAGE DOCK AND RANGER STATION: At the dock area is a 27-acre parcel outside the wilderness area. It has the only potable water source, ranger station and working dock. Ferry service arrives and departs from here.
GPS: 45°07.287'N; 85°58.519'W

VILLAGE CAMPGROUND: Eight campsites within a mile of the dock provide a rustic camp for those uninterested in wilderness camping. From here, its is reasonable to visit any part of the island via day hikes. Fires are allowed in designated pits at this site only.

CEMETERY: The old island cemetery sits in an overgrown open area suffering from neglect. The NPS has erected a list of those buried.

DIMMICK'S POINT: The point area has large stones. North of the point, the beach becomes sandier. Area closed during Piping Plover nesting period, May 1 to August 15.

WEST SHORE - *Donner Point to Crescent:* A trail follows some of the shoreline. Unlike the eastern part of the island, bluffs dominate most of the west shore. An exception is near the Crescent Dock ruins where the land slopes gently from the island's higher, inland center. Good camping close to Lake Michigan exists from Donner Point north past Johnson Place.

FREDRICKSON PLACE: Located near the southwest. The highland area ranges from grassy and open to hardwood cover. The beach is sand with some small stone and excellent for swimming.
GPS: 45°04.201'N; 86°01.060'W

JOHNSON PLACE: The beach is sandy at this location where the bluff is high but easy to traverse.
GPS: 45°05.056'N; 86°02.140'W

UNNAMED POINT: The south portion of the west shore travels roughly southeast-northwest. The northern portion roughly north-south. A knob or point forms at the junction between Johnson Place and Crescent. A rocky shore is found at the southerly part of this juncture. Swans, gulls and ducks congregate. Just to the north of the knob, sand returns and swimming is good. A high bluff lines the shore in this area so the best access is walking the beach from Crescent or Johnson Place.

CRESCENT DOCK AND SWENSON BARN AREA: A lowland here makes for good access to the shore. Some places are low enough to form wetland. The blackberry and rose hip crops are plentiful in late August. The deteriorating Swenson Barn presents a photo opportunity. From here the island's center trail heads east back toward the dock.

NORTH SHORE - *Crescent to near Vessel Point:* North of Crescent, the bluff and dunes increase. Much of it is too steep to hike up or down. To prevent erosion, do not make the attempt. The steep bluffs continue along the north nearly to Vessel Point. A couple of trails make forays to the north from the "Old Grade" but no trail parallels the bluff. The steep drop limits camping opportunities in this area because a water source is not readily available. Southeast from "John Maleski's," the high bluff begins to recede from the shoreline, a trail parallels the beach and camping possibilities increase.

Right: Daughter follows dad during a stone hunt at Christmas Cove.

Below right: Grand Traverse Lighthouse at Leelanau State Park.

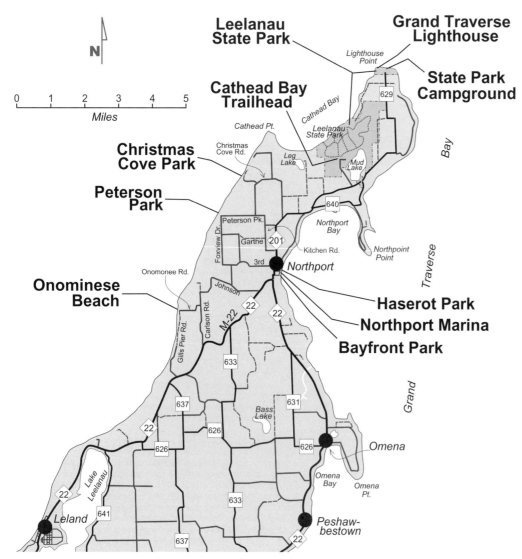

Leelanau State Park

Grand Traverse Lighthouse

Cathead Bay Trailhead

State Park Campground

Lighthouse Point

629

Cathead Bay

Cathead Pt.

Leelanau State Park

Christmas Cove Park

Christmas Cove Rd.

Leg Lake

Mud Lake

Bay

Peterson Park

640

Northport Bay

Peterson Pk.

Foxview Dr.

Garthe 201

Northpoint Point

Traverse

Kitchen Rd.

3rd

Northport

Onominese Beach

Onomonee Rd.

Johnson

Carlson Rd.

Gills Pier Rd.

M-22

22

22

Haserot Park

Northport Marina

Bayfront Park

633

Grand

637

631

Bass Lake

626

22

626

626

Omena

641

22

Lake Leelanau

Leland

633

Omena Bay

Omena Pt.

637

22

Peshaw-bestown

N

0 1 2 3 4 5
Miles

Leelanau County

Northport and the Northern Tip

Name	Location	Entrance Fee	Parking	Modern Restrooms	Vault or Portable Toilet	Stair or Path to Shore	Swimming	Picnic Area	Drinking Water	Campground	Trailered Boat Launch	Kayak / Canoe	Marina	Fishing	Hiking	Biking	X-Country Skiing	Playground	Lighthouse	Beach Strolling	Sandy Beach	Stony or Rocky Shore	Dunes	Bluff	Wetland
Onominese Beach	N of Leland 7 miles. Turn N from M-22 on Gills Pier Rd then W at Onominese Rd.		●			●						●									●	●			
Peterson Park	NW of Northport 3 miles on Peterson Park Rd.		●		●	●	●	●	●									●				●		●	
Christmas Cove Park	N or Northport 3 miles on Christmas Cove Rd.		●		●		●	●				●										●			
Leelanau State Park	6 miles N of Northport via CR 629.	●	●	●	●	●	●	●	●	●				●	●		●	●	●	●	●	●	●		
Cathead Bay Trail	N of Northport 4 miles. CR 629 (Woolsey Rd.) then N on Densmore Rd.	●	●		●	●	●								●			●		●	●		●		
Lighthouse Park	End of CR 629, 6.5 miles N of Northport.	●	●		●	●	●	●	●	●								●	●	●		●			
Haserot Park	Northport. Rose and 2nd St. one-block E of M-201.		●		●			●	●	●			●									●			
Northport - G. Marsten Dame Marina	Northport. Nagonaba (1st St.) and Bay St. one block E of M-102.	●	●	●				●	●		●	●	●	●											
Bayfront Park	Northport. Main and Bay St., one-block east of M-201.		●		●			●	●			●						●			●				

The Lake Michigan side of Leelanau's northern tip has tall bluffs or dunes along much of the shore. The east side sits on Grand Traverse Bay with protective coves and often, rocky shore. Northport is enough off-the-beaten track to have a quiet side, especially in the off-season.

ONOMINESE BEACH: Located at the end of Onominese Road, the undeveloped beach area is sand with stone bottom. A small point extends into the lake. Sunset watching might be the best use of this road end. The hill on Onominese Road provides a nice view of Lake Michigan as well.

PETERSON PARK: Follow M-201 north from Northport. Turn left on Peterson Park Road. The park sits on a tall bluff and has a picnic area with pavilion and a playground. A long staircase leads to the shore. The shore is stony and Petoskey Stones are common. It is swimmable but not sandy. Normally, you will not find a big crowd here and the atmosphere is pleasantly laid-back.
GPS: 45°09.121'N; 85°38.758'W

CHRISTMAS COVE PARK: Follow M-201 north from Northport. Turn left on Peterson Park Road, right on Scott Road, then left on Christmas Cove Road. The shore is rocky and known for excellent Petoskey Stone hunting. A short way into the water, the stony bottom turns mostly to sand and swimming is good.
GPS: 45°10.147'N; 85°37.947'W

LEELANAU STATE PARK: The park is located at the northern tip of the peninsula county. Motor vehicles need a Michigan State Park Vehicle Permit to enter. There are two separate units. Find beach, trails and a beautiful hardwood forest at the naturally kept Cathead

Bay portion. The lighthouse and campground are at the Lighthouse Point unit.

CATHEAD BAY TRAIL: This part of Leelanau State Park is undeveloped except for the trail system and facilities at the trailhead. The area is well wooded inland from the dunes that border the bay. The trail has several loops. Access the beach via the south loop. The shortest trail distance to the beach is about one mile. The beach is sandy and small dunes add to the atmosphere. This is a nice spot for those who do not mind a walk and want an undeveloped beach away from most of the crowd. Another trail spur goes to a dune overlook. This portion of the trail is hilly with a stairway near the end and offers a view out to South Fox Island.
GPS: 45°10.379'N; 85°34.472'W

LIGHTHOUSE PARK: At the very tip of the "little finger" of the Michigan mitten, the developed portion of Leelanau State Park is punctuated with the Grand Traverse Lighthouse. The lighthouse dates back to 1858. The Grand Traverse Lighthouse Foundation offers tours of it and their museum for a small fee. Hours vary, but are normally during the daytime in the summer and on some fall weekends. Interesting stone sculptures, the product of a past lightkeeper, decorate the lighthouse grounds.

The shore is mostly stone and rock. Swimming is not great here. Birding and other activities predominate. A rustic campground is located along the shore. A large picnic and play area is also available.
Telephone: (231) 386-5422
GPS: 45°12.525'N; 85.32°728'W

The following three sites are adjacent to one another along the Northport Village waterfront. Walking distance between them is relatively short. Northport shops are within walking distance as well.

HASEROT PARK: This grassy park borders the harbor and bay. A footbridge over Northport Creek connects it with the marina and Bayfront Park to the south. Picnic tables and benches are plentiful.

NORTHPORT - G. MARSTEN DAME MARINA: The Northport Marina is sandwiched between Bayfront and Harbor Parks on Northport Bay. It has a good boat launch and 115 marina slips.
Telephone: (231) 386-5411
GPS: 45°07.800'N; 85°36.633'W

BAYFRONT PARK: Bayfront has a sandy beach on Northport Bay as well as a playground, volleyball and picnic areas.
GPS: 45°07.680'N; 85°36.898'W

OMENA BEACH

Left: The small park and beach at Omena has great swimming and a scenic view.

Right: Locally-owned, trendy shops draw tourists to Suttons Bay.

Below right: The large marina on Suttons Bay gives the town a boating flavor.

Opposite page: A rock marks the simple 45th Parallel Park along M-22.

Omena Beach

Greene Park

45th Parallel Park

Marina Park & Beach

South Shore Park

Steimel Park

Leelanau County

Omena and Suttons Bay

Name	Location	Entrance Fee	Parking	Modern Restrooms	Vault or Portable Toilet	Stair or Path to Shore	Swimming	Picnic Area	Drinking Water	Campground	Trailered Boat Launch	Kayak / Canoe	Marina	Fishing	Hiking	Biking	X-Country Skiing	Playground	Lighthouse	Beach Strolling	Sandy Beach	Stony or Rocky Shore	Dunes	Bluff	Wetland
Omena Park	Omena. Just E of M-22 on Omena Pt. Rd.		●		●		●					●						●			●				
Graham Greene Park:	M-22, 0.75 miles N of Peshawbestown.		●		●	●						●										●			
45th Parallel Park	2 miles N of Suttons Bay on M-22.		●				●	●														●			
Marina Park Beach & Marina	Suttons Bay, one block E of M-22, turn at Adams St.	●	●	●	●		●	●	●		●	●	●	●				●			●				
South Shore Park	Stony Point Rd., one mile S of downtown Suttons Bay.		●	●				●										●			●	●			
Vic Steimel Park	Stony Point Rd, 3.5 miles NE of Suttons Bay.		●			●		●				●										●			

Suttons Bay and Omena lie along protective bays within the Grand Traverse Bay. Sailboats and pleasure craft frequent the area during the summer months.

OMENA PARK: Well protected, Omena Bay is formed by a prominent point. The park is small with approximately 50 feet of beachfront. Parking is found across the Omena Point Road from the bay. Facilities include tables, grills and a large swing set. A vault toilet is at the parking lot. The beach is sandy with small, rounded stone. Canoes or kayaks are easily portaged from the parking lot to the bay for launch.
   GPS: 45°03.364'N; 85°35.161'W

GRAHAM GREENE PARK: Greene Park is hard to find because the road is not marked and the turn not obvious. About half-mile north of Peshawbestown on M-22 is Putnam Road, which spurs to the west. An unmarked gravel road to the north of the M-22 and Putnam intersection heads east to the park. Look for it near a curve on M-22. The park is wooded and has a path and short stairway down to its beach. The beach is sandy but low water has exposed much of the rock bottom making swimming poor during recent low water periods. Swimmers might want water sandals or shoes here.
   GPS: 45°02.110'N; 85°35.915'W

45TH PARALLEL PARK: Taking its name for its location on the parallel halfway between the equator and North Pole, this is a roadside park on Grand Traverse Bay. There is a marker on a boulder, picnic table, stony beach and view of the tip of Old Mission Peninsula. Swimming is possible but not the best.
   GPS: 45°02.110'N; 85°35.915'W

MARINA PARK BEACH & MARINA: The small town of Suttons Bay lures tourists with its shops and galleries but its allure began with its location on the water. A block from the main shopping area lies a municipal park on Suttons Bay. This park has about 250 feet of sandy beach and an adjacent marina. The marina includes three long docking areas with a boardwalk trail that connects these to the rest of the park. It has 155 slips of which 22 are for transient use. The boardwalk bridge crosses a wetland where a T-shaped pier provides a place to sit and view the bay. The swimming area has designation buoys and lifeguards. Picnic tables and grills are available through out. Large shade trees give the user a choice of shade or sun in the picnic areas. There are three entrances with parking areas. The two south parking areas are intended for boaters with slips. There are portable toilets near the beach and modern restrooms one-block up the hill between the park and town. The boat ramp has a fee for use. Several festival events use the park in the summer.
   Telephone: (231) 271-6703
   GPS: 44°58.533'N; 85°38.717'W

SOUTH SHORE PARK: This park can be accessed using Beach Street from M-22. The 200-foot sandy swimming beach is located on Suttons Bay. The restrooms are large enough to change in. The covered picnic area is within 50 feet of the bay and a few feet from the parking area.

VIC STEIMEL PARK: Located at aptly-named Stony Point, the parking area is well shaded and there is a short path to the lake. The boat launch is very shallow. During low water periods it is usable by canoes and kayaks at best. The park does provide a great view of West Grand Traverse Bay and is a nice stop for those bicycling the peninsula.

Right: Greilickville Harbor is busy even in the fall as seen here.

Below right: The two roadside parks closest to Traverse City have new viewing platforms, tables and stairways to the shore.

Opposite page: Hendryx Park has a view and tables. Bicyclists find it a quiet stop off the main road.

Hendryx Park

W. Gd. Traverse Bay Boat Launch

Roadside Park

Roadside Park

Roadside Park

Greilickville - Elmwood Twp. Harbor

Elmwood Twp. Beach

Grand Traverse County

Leelanau County

South End of West Grand Traverse Bay

Name	Location	Entrance Fee	Parking	Modern Restrooms	Vault or Portable Toilet	Stair or Path to Shore	Swimming	Picnic Area	Drinking Water	Campground	Trailered Boat Launch	Kayak / Canoe	Marina	Fishing	Hiking	Biking	X-Country Skiing	Playground	Lighthouse	Beach Strolling	Sandy Beach	Stony or Rocky Shore	Dunes	Bluff	Wetland
Hendryx Park	Lee Point Rd., 0.75 miles east of M-22.		●		●		●	●				●									●	●			
West Grand Traverse Bay Boat Ramp	M-22 at Hilltop Rd., 5 miles S of Suttons Bay.		●		●						●	●									●				
Roadside Park	M-22, 5.5 S of Sutton's Bay.		●					●														●		●	
Roadside Park Scenic Overlook	M-22, one-mile S of Crain Hill Rd. or 4 miles N of Greilickville.		●			●		●														●		●	
Roadside Park	On M-22, 2.5 miles N of M-72 near Greilickville		●			●		●														●		●	
Greilickville - Elmwood Township Harbor	M-22, 0.5 mi. north of M-72	●	●	●									●												
Elmwood Township Beach (West Bay Park)	M-22, 0.5 mi. north of M-72		●	●			●	●				●						●			●				

M-22 parallels close to the bay along the stretch between Suttons Bay and Traverse City. The shore is mostly private, but the water is always in view making this a scenic drive.

HENDRYX PARK: With about 50 feet of shore, Hendryx provides a view of Marion (Power) Island and the Bowers Harbor area across the way on the Old Mission Peninsula. It has a table and a portable toilet but swimming is marginal. The beach is sandy but the lake bottom is rocky.

WEST GRAND TRAVERSE BAY BOAT RAMP: This paved launch has good depth. An channel is dredged when needed. The parking area is large.
GPS: 44°54.373'N; 85°37.859'W

ROADSIDE PARK: Low lake levels and shoreline growth make access poor to the stony shore. A gravel pull-off, picnic table and wastebasket are the lone improvements. A small road sign marks its approach.

ROADSIDE PARK SCENIC OVERLOOK: The roadside park has tables and an overlook of Grand Traverse Bay which are easily accessible for those in wheelchairs. A short stairway leads to the mostly stony shore. This stretch of M-22 is busy most of the year. Road noise may be annoying up on the small bluff.
GPS: 44°49.773'N; 85°39.024'W

ROADSIDE PARK: Nearly a twin to the previous listing, the listed characteristics are the same in every way.
GPS: 44°48.254'N; 85°38.248'W

GREILICKVILLE - ELMWOOD TOWNSHIP HARBOR: The marina and boat ramp provide boat access to West Grand Traverse Bay.

Greilickville is a landmark found just north of Traverse City's west end. Elmwood Township Beach borders to the south.
Telephone: (231) 946-5463
GPS: 44°47.283'N; 85°38.000'W

ELMWOOD TOWNSHIP BEACH (WEST BAY PARK): Elmwood Township Beach adjoins the public Geilickville-Elmwood Township Marina. Play equipment and tables can be found in this grassy, partially-shaded park. Recent low lake levels have not been kind to the beach, which is partially sand with some muck. Modern restrooms can be found at the marina, a short walk north.
GPS: 44°47.238'N; 85°38.256'W

A Leelanau Day Tour

There are many pleasant drives along the coast but none quite like the loop around the Leelanau Peninsula. You can make the trip in a long, but manageable day, using as little as two highways. The shore is always close at hand, except along the M-72 portion between Empire and Traverse City. Lake Michigan bounds the route on the western side of the peninsula with Grand Traverse Bay on the east. The small, coastal towns of Empire, Glen Arbor, Leland, Northport and Suttons Bay each provide an art gallery or two, small shops and casual dining. Orchards and vineyards still make up much of the rural landscape. The scenery intensifies on sunny days, when the local waters turn vivid shades of turquoise. It goes up a few notches during the bloom of cherry and apple orchards and during the fall, when the hardwood hills turn to orange and red.

Traverse City, in Grand Traverse County, has the most hotel rooms in the vicinity, so it seems the logical place to begin a tour. Highway M-22 starts at the county line in the northwest corner of the city. Head north in the morning on M-22 along West Grand Traverse Bay toward Suttons Bay. The sun rises over Old Mission Peninsula on the bay's opposite side, softening dawn's chill. By mid-morning several inviting galleries in Suttons Bay open. After browsing the shops, take a stroll at the marina and listen to the chime of hardware clanging against the masts of the sailboats.

Farther north, try your luck in the casino at the Native American community of Peshawbestown. Northport has more neat shops. Tour the Grand Traverse Lighthouse at the tip of the "little finger" and climb its tower. It is a great place for a picnic. Search for Petoskey Stones at Christmas Cove or Peterson Park.

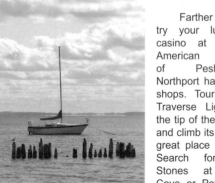

By afternoon you pull into Leland, a busy, but small, summer town. Wander through Leland's "Fishtown" section, along the Leland River at its harbor.

As the day heats up, look to Good Harbor Bay for a quiet beach, then pick up a light dinner in Glen Arbor and take a quick tour of the shops. If you arrive earlier, the historical exhibits at Glen Haven should be open. Check out the old Coast Guard Life Saving Station and take a hike over the dune at Sleeping Bear Point. The Pierce Stocking Scenic Drive atop the Sleeping Bear Dunes is great anytime but particularly in the evening when the west sun sparkles on the water below. Finish your day in the Empire area watching the sun set at North Bar Lake, Empire Beach or on the Empire Bluff. An evening snack in town readies you for the short drive back to Traverse City on M-72.

Clockwise from left to right:

- A lone sailboat floats on Grand Traverse Bay.
- End the day with a hike out to Empire Bluff for the sunset.
- Pierce Stocking Drive has breathtaking views of the dunes and lakes.

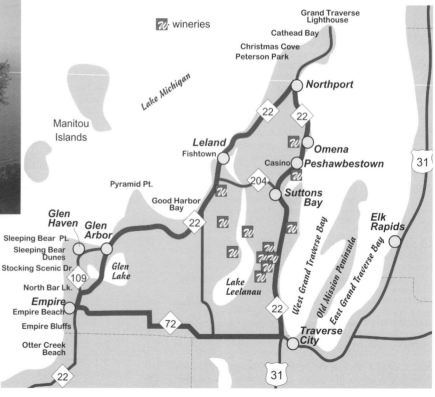

Grand Traverse County

No city on the coast owes more to its location than Traverse City. Growing fast as a desirable destination for travel, business meetings and a place to live, "TC" stretches across the base of Grand Traverse Bay. To its north, the long and narrow Old Mission Peninsula slices the bay in two. The city's core lies along the West Arm of the bay where much of the waterfront is in public hands. At the bottom of the East Arm, hotels and motels line US-31, satisfying the tourists' demand for accommodations. The National Cherry Festival, held in early July, celebrates the region's heritage as a premier producer of that crop. The festival ranks as one of the largest in the country. Its week-and-a-half run features top performers, almost daily parades and of course, a cherry pie eating contest.

Old Mission Peninsula contains most of the county's coastline. It is a high ridge between the two arms of the bay. Highway M-37 runs along the crest, affording views of the deep blue bays with orchards and vineyards in the forefront. Peninsula Drive closely follows the West Arm. A number of low-traffic roads skirt along the East Arm. The peninsula has many vistas and the views heighten when the fall colors turn or the orchards bloom. Old Mission Point Park, sitting at the tip, looks out towards the bay's opening. It features an old lighthouse, shoreline nooks and wooded trails. If you have a boat or kayak, try the excursion to Marion Island, off Bowers Harbor

The Traverse Area Recreation Trail (TART) traverses the city east to west. In-line skaters, joggers, walkers and bicyclists share the asphalt promenade. The trail's west portion ties together the West End Beach and Clinch Park on the waterfront. Each park provides excellent swimming and relaxation in a small city atmosphere. Clinch Park is the town's centerpiece. The park's small zoo, beach, museum and newly renovated marina connect to the downtown business district via a pedestrian tunnel under Grandview Parkway (US-31). Interesting eateries, galleries, recreational goods stores and specialty shops make up most of the downtown. Traverse City lodging can be pricey during the peak periods. Camping at Traverse City State Park is a bargain. The park has a fine beach on the East Arm.

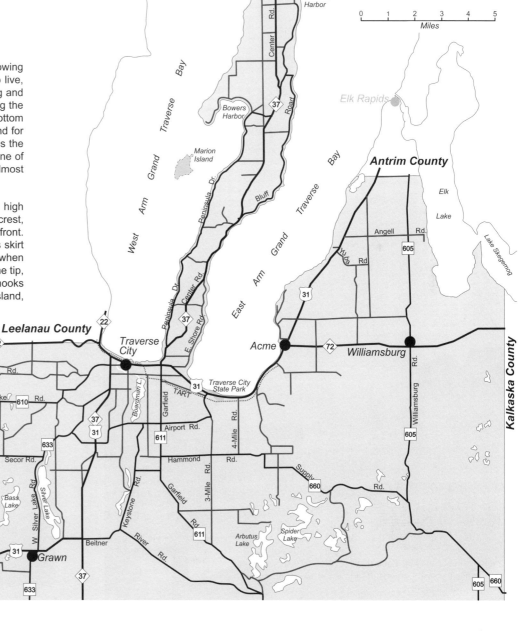

Grand Traverse County North Portion

Below left: The newly revamped marina forms part of Clinch Park's recreational complex.

Below right: The lifeguard station at Bryant Park sits lonely in the early morning.

Opposite page: Downtown Traverse City lies a block behind the beach at Clinch Park.

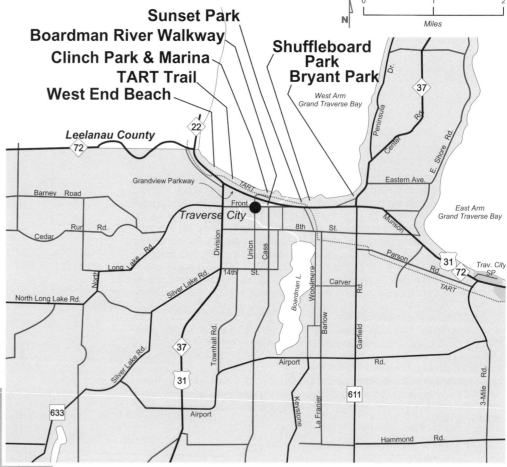

Sunset Park
Boardman River Walkway
Clinch Park & Marina
TART Trail
West End Beach

Shuffleboard Park
Bryant Park

West Arm Grand Traverse Bay

East Arm Grand Traverse Bay

Leelanau County

Grandview Parkway

Barney Road

Traverse City

Cedar   Run   Rd.

Long Lake Rd.

North Long Lake Rd.

North

Silver Lake Rd.

Silver Lake Rd.

Division

14th

Union St.

Cass

Front

8th   St.

Boardman L.

Woodmere

Barlow

Carver

Garfield

Rd.

Munson

Parson   Rd.

Eastern Ave.

Peninsula

Center   Rd.

E. Shore Rd.

Townhall Rd.

Airport

Keystone

La Franier

Hammond   Rd.

3-Mile   Rd.

Airport

Trav. City SP

TART

Name	Location	Entrance Fee	Parking	Modern Restrooms	Vault or Portable Toilet	Stair or Path to Shore	Swimming	Picnic Area	Drinking Water	Campground	Trailered Boat Launch	Kayak / Canoe	Marina	Fishing	Hiking	Biking	X-Country Skiing	Playground	Lighthouse	Beach Strolling	Sandy Beach	Stony or Rocky Shore	Dunes	Bluff	Wetland
TART (Trail)	Traverse City. See below.		●	●					●						●	●									
West End Beach	Traverse City. Grandview Parkway (M-22).		●	●			●	●	●			●			●	●				●	●				
Clinch Park	Traverse City. Union Street and Grandview Parkway (US-31).		●	●			●	●	●		●	●	●	●	●	●		●			●				
Duncan Clinch Marina	Traverse City. In Clinch Park, Grandview Parkway (US-31).		●	●			●	●	●		●	●	●	●											
Boardman River Walkway	Traverse City. Just S of Grandview Parkway (US-31) E of Union St. to the rivermouth.		●	●								●		●											
Sunset Park	Traverse City. Grandview Parkway (US-31) at Hope St.		●				●	●				●						●			●				
Shuffleboard Park	Traverse City. Grandview Parkway (US-31) at Barlow St.		●	●			●	●	●												●				
Bryant Park	Traverse City. Peninsula Dr. just W of Garfield Rd. (M-37).		●	●			●	●	●			●						●			●				

The downtown of fast-growing Traverse City lies one block from West Grand Traverse Bay. Much of the shore is a city park offering most any activity you might choose.

TART: The Traverse Area Recreation Trail is an asphalt pathway that travels west-to-east across Traverse City. A west terminus of the TART is at the West End Beach parking lot discussed below. From here you can bike, walk or skate the asphalt east along the west bayfront to other parts of the city. Along the way, you pass West End's numerous beach volleyball courts and Clinch Park marina, zoo and beach. The central and east portions of the trail follow an old rail grade passing through residential areas .

WEST END BEACH: West End Beach sits on a half-mile-long sliver of land between Grandview Parkway (M-72) and the West Arm. A small parking lot is available just west of Division Street, the north-south portion of US-31. The primary swimming area and the restroom are near the parking lot. Grassy areas along the beach make a refreshing spot to sit and enjoy the bay. Beach volleyball is found to the east.
GPS: 44°46.166'N; 85°38.084'W

CLINCH PARK: Clinch Park forms the nucleus of Traverse City's West Bay waterfront. The complex includes a newly enlarged marina, a small zoo with native animals, a museum, boat launch and the beach. The TART, an asphalt recreation trail, conveys bicyclists, walkers and skaters along the bayfront. The "Open Space" on the west end of the park, hosts special events particularly during the city's week-and-a-half-long National Cherry Festival in July. Enter the limited on-site parking area by turning north from Grandview Parkway (US-31) at Union Street. These metered spaces fill during nice summer days. Additional metered parking can be found between the park and downtown Traverse City, south of US-31. A pedestrian tunnel under US-31 leads from the parking lot at Cass Street to the park. This is an easy walk. The zoo, museum, and boat launch have fees. There is no fee for the beach or trail. Fish from the marina's barrier-free breakwater or along the open space. Expect brown trout or steelhead in the spring, bass, perch or catfish in the summer and salmon in the fall.
GPS: 44°45.933'N; 85°37.443'W

DUNCAN CLINCH MARINA: Recently renovated, Traverse City's public marina hosts both seasonal and transient moorings. The marina has boat fuel. The Clinch Park Zoo lies a hundred feet from the docks. Downtown shops sit about two blocks away.
GPS: 44°46.083'N; 85°37.333'W
Telephone: (231) 922-4906

BOARDMAN RIVER WALKWAY: The Boardman River flows through the city emptying into the West Arm on the east side of Clinch Park. A boardwalk follows the riverbank along the stretch between the downtown shopping area and Grandview Parkway (US-31). Metered parking is adjacent to much of it. Fishing can be productive at times. Restrooms are available at Clinch Park by taking the underpass at Cass Street.

SUNSET PARK: This small park with picnic tables, playground and swimming is located between the Holiday Inn and the Great Lakes Maritime Academy. It is a short, flat carry for kayak access to the bay.

SHUFFLEBOARD PARK: A shady city park featuring shuffleboard courts and a senior center lies along US-31 east of the Great Lakes Maritime Academy. Swimming is also available.

BRYANT PARK: Located at the southeast corner of the West Arm, Bryant is a city park with a 200-foot sandy beach. The tree-covered area behind the beach has play equipment, tables and grills. A lifeguard is on duty during prime times.
GPS: 44.45.934'N; 85.35.743'W

Above: Art students interpret the scene at Old Mission Point. The lighthouse sits at the peninsula's tip.

Below: Old Mission Point Park features a bit of local history as well as woods, shore and trails.

Opposite page: Trillium decorate the woodlots in spring.

THE HESSLER LOG HOME
IN 1854-1856 THIS LOG HOME WAS BUILT
IN THE SOUTHERN PART OF THE
OLD MISSION PENINSULA BY EARLY SETTLERS,
MARY & JOSEPH HESSLER. THE HUGE
LOGS CUT FROM PINE TREES WERE HAND HEWN
AND STACKED ON TOP OF EACH OTHER
TO FORM THE WALLS, WHILE MODIFIED
DOVE-TAILED JOINTS HELD THE CORNERS SNUGLY
TOGETHER WITHOUT NAILS OR FASTENERS.
THE CABIN WAS MOVED TO THIS PARK, REPAIRED,
AND FURNISHED DURING 1992-1997 TO ASSIST THE
PUBLIC IN UNDERSTANDING HOW OUR PIONEER
FAMILIES LIVED AND UTILIZED THE UNTAMED LAND.

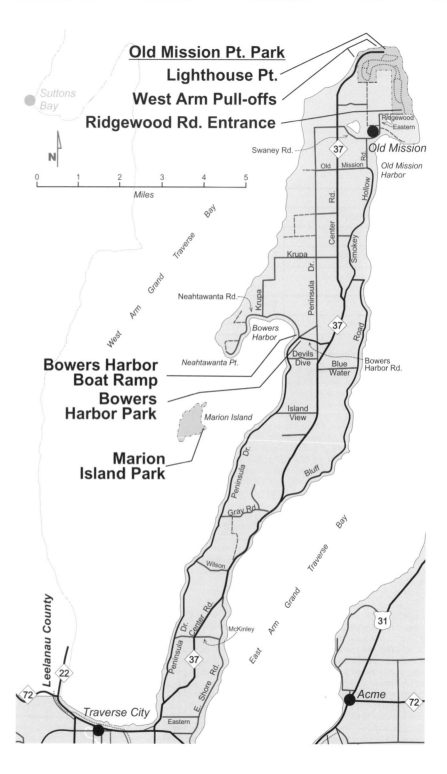

Old Mission Pt. Park
Lighthouse Pt.
West Arm Pull-offs
Ridgewood Rd. Entrance

Bowers Harbor
Boat Ramp
Bowers
Harbor Park

Marion
Island Park

Name	Location	Entrance Fee	Parking	Modern Restrooms	Vault or Portable Toilet	Stair or Path to Shore	Swimming	Picnic Area	Drinking Water	Campground	Trailered Boat Launch	Kayak / Canoe	Marina	Fishing	Hiking	Biking	X-Country Skiing	Playground	Lighthouse	Beach Strolling	Sandy Beach	Stony or Rocky Shore	Dunes	Bluff	Wetland
Marion Island Park	West Arm Grand Traverse Bay, 3 miles SW of Bowers Harbor Boat Ramp.						●	●		●		●		●	●						●				
Bowers Harbor Park	Bowers Harbor Rd., just E of Peninsula Drive.		●		●			●	●									●							
Bowers Harbor Boat Ramp	Neah-Ta-Wanta Road just W of Peninsula Drive.	●	●		●						●	●													
Old Mission Point Park	End of Center Road (M-37).		●		●	●	●	●	●			●			●	●	●	●	●	●	●	●			
West Arm Pull-offs	Old Mission Point Park. Along Center Road (M-37).		●				●					●									●	●	●		
Lighthouse Point	Old Mission Point Park. At end of Center Road (M-37).		●		●	●			●						●	●	●	●	●	●	●	●			
Ridgewood Road Entrance	Old Mission Point Park. From Center Rd. (M-37), E on Swaney Rd. to Forest Rd., N on Eastern Rd., then E on Ridgewood Rd.		●		●										●	●	●								

Peninsula Drive follows close to the shore for half its journey up the peninsula. Private residences reduce possible access but do not hamper a slow, winding drive with great views.

MARION ISLAND PARK: Marion, also known as Power Island, is the only major island in Grand Traverse Bay. The entire isle is a largely undeveloped, forested, public park administered by the county and accessible only by boat. The closest public access site is the boat launch at Bowers Harbor approximately 3 miles away. A public dock with nearby picnic tables is available at the island. The park has hiking trails through its 200-acre wooded interior. Primitive camping is allowed. No ferry service is available.
Telephone: (616) 922-4818
GPS: 44.51.920'N; 85.34.270'W

BOWERS HARBOR PARK: A developed township park a short way from the bay at the Bowers Harbor area, it includes soccer and baseball fields. It also has volleyball and tennis courts. There are shaded picnic grounds with grills, walking trail, restrooms and a large playground. A welcome stop for the bicyclist.

BOWERS HARBOR BOAT RAMP: Operated by the Michigan DNR, the Bowers Harbor launch has ample parking, vault toilets and a few benches along the shore. Bowers Harbor and the adjoining West Arm have good fishing for trout and smallmouth bass. Marion (Power) Island lies about 3 miles from the launch or about 1.3 miles south of Neah-Ta-Wanta Point. This is a good launch point for kayaks, canoes or boats headed for the island park.
GPS: 44.53.722'N; 85.31.388'W

Note: Many of the east-west roads north of Bowers Harbor end at the West Arm of the bay. These are designated water pumping points for the fire department and "no parking" signs are prominent. While they are public land, parking problems at these road ends prevented their inclusion in this book. Bicyclists, however, can take advantage of these stops. They are stony with little frontage and provide a view of the bay at best.

OLD MISSION POINT PARK: In recent years, the Peninsula Park Commission was formed to protect the northern tip of Old Mission Peninsula. The park is referred to as Old Mission Point or Lighthouse Point Park. The following listings are part of the park.

WEST ARM PULL-OFFS: Near the park's main entrance on M-37 and just west and south of Lighthouse Point are 4 pull-offs along sandy, wooded stretches of the northern West Arm. These undeveloped parts of Lighthouse Park lead to one of the better swimming spots on the peninsula. The two closest pull-offs to the lighthouse area have very short "two-track" roads that lead to crude parking. Each of these have been "developed" by use over time. Normally, there is enough ground clearance and the soil is packed well enough for even sedans to travel off the highway. The two located farthest to the southwest are one or two car pull-offs along the highway shoulder. A short path through the woods leads to the beach. Each can accommodate only a couple of cars which means the site might be taken on a nice summer day. It also means you have a reasonably private spot if you are the one that gets there first. Recent low water levels have exposed rock and made the swimming less desirable than in the past.
GPS: 44.59.389'N; 85.29.269'W to 44.59.838'N; 85.29.936'W

LIGHTHOUSE POINT: The Old Mission Point Lighthouse sits on the north tip of the Peninsula close to the 45th Parallel. From here, one looks out to the opening of Grand Traverse Bay with the Leelanau Peninsula on the left and the mainland on the right. The old lighthouse graces the park. It is viewable from outside the white picket fence. Scattered playground equipment can be found at the beachfront. Plaques provide information about the site. Drinking water is available and the vault toilets are the modern-type, free of most odor. There are grills and tables as well. The lighthouse area has no swimming due to shallow water and large boulders. Hike to the west from the lighthouse and the beach and swimming gets better. This park has shoreline to stroll. Mountain bikers, hikers, skiers and kayakers will also find this a great place.
GPS: 44.59.421'N; 85.28.823'W

RIDGEWOOD ROAD ENTRANCE: Harder to find, Ridgewood Road Trailhead provides a quiet access to Old Mission Point Park. Trails in this section cross old farm land and require a hike, bike or ski for views of the distance bay. Parking lot and vault toilet available.
GPS: 44.58.147'N; 366'W

Above: The "Old Mission" provides a quick glimpse of area history.

Below: A sailboat moored in East Grand Traverse Bay near Archie Park.

Opposite page: One of Old Mission Peninsula's scenic views. If you seek a pleasant drive or bicycle route, this is it. The many cherry and apple orchards are spectacular when they bloom.

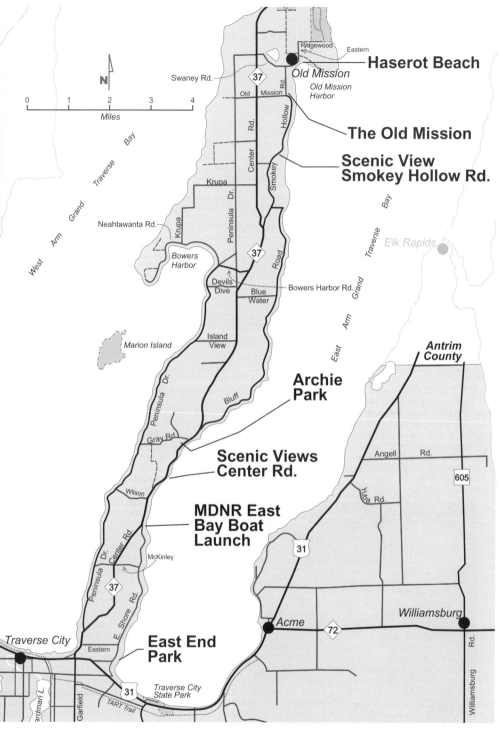

Name	Location	Entrance Fee	Parking	Modern Restrooms	Vault or Portable Toilet	Stair or Path to Shore	Swimming	Picnic Area	Drinking Water	Campground	Trailered Boat Launch	Kayak / Canoe	Marina	Fishing	Hiking	Biking	X-Country Skiing	Playground	Lighthouse	Beach Strolling	Sandy Beach	Stony or Rocky Shore	Dunes	Bluff	Wetland
Haserot Beach	0.2 miles E of Old Mission. From M-37, W on Swaney Rd. to Forest Ave.		●		●		●	●	●		●	●						●			●				
The Old Mission	Old Mission. Old Mission Rd., 0.5 mi. E of M-37		●																						
Scenic View (Smokey Hollow Rd.)	Smokey Hollow Rd. near Ladd Rd.																								
Scenic View (Center Rd.)	M-37 (Center Rd.) from Bluff Drive S to East Shore Rd.																								
Archie Park	M-37 (Center Rd.) at Gray Rd.		●		●	●		●	●									●				●			
DNR East Bay Boat Ramp	M-37 (Center Rd.) at East Shore Rd. 3.5 miles N of Traverse City.	●	●		●						●	●													
East Bay Park	Traverse City. 3 blocks N of US-31, East Bay Blvd and Shawnee St.		●	●			●	●	●			●						●			●				

A number of low-traffic paved roads take you along the East Arm with terrific views of the orchards and bay. The farther north, the more laid-back life is on the peninsula.

HASEROT BEACH: A nice township park located on Old Mission Harbor near the northern end of the East Arm, its sandy beach is the best on the peninsula and includes a buoy-designated swim area. Grills are available along with picnic tables and a water faucet. The boat ramp is shallow. A basketball court, playground and some information signs about local history round out the park. Kayaks have access to the protected bay. If the weather permits, try paddling the four-mile (one-way) trip up to Old Mission Point.
GPS: 44.57.687'N; 85.29.113'W

THE OLD MISSION: A replica of the log mission building of the early white settlement era, it contains a short history of the natives, missionaries and the area in general. Self-guided.
GPS: 44.57.319'N; 85.29.402'W

SCENIC VIEW (SMOKEY HOLLOW RD.): There is a high overlook of the East Arm from Smokey Hollow Road as it descends towards the Old Mission Area.

SCENIC VIEW (CENTER RD.): Center Road (M-37) runs near the east shore at some points along its 18-mile journey up the Old Mission Peninsula. For most of its length, it sits high on the ridgeline at the center of the peninsula. The view often includes scenes of both the West and East Arms of Grand Traverse Bay. On a sunny day, the bay waters display a blue to turquoise hue. Cherry orchards bloom in spring and display the red fruit in early July. Apples follow with summer blooms and fall fruit. The vineyards yield their crop for fall wine making. While development of the peninsula has increased, Center Road still displays many quiet, rural scenes.

ARCHIE PARK: Most of the park lies on the opposite side of M-37 from East Bay. Picnic tables, a grill and portable toilet facilities adjoin the parking area. All are well shaded. A stairway located across the highway leads to the shore. The dramatic housing increase on the peninsula has led to more and faster traffic, so be careful crossing the road. The public shoreline is small, rocky and not very good for swimming. The park is a handy stop for bicyclists. It is named for the ghost town of Archie which lives only in history.

DNR EAST BAY BOAT RAMP: This is the best boat launching facility on the peninsula side of the East Arm. The launch area is dredged during periods of low water making it usable by large boats almost all the time. A short dock is available to assist with loading. The parking area may fill during peak fishing periods, .
GPS: 44.48.588'N; 85.33.681'W

EAST BAY PARK: The park sits in a quiet, city neighborhood at the southeast corner of East Grand Traverse Bay. The beach is sandy and the swimming area shallow. There are modern bathrooms, tables and grills. The boat launch accommodates only small craft. During low water, launching even those will be difficult. Parking is plentiful.
GPS: 44.45.734'N; 85.34.578'W

Below left: Deepwater Point Natural Area features woods, a stony shore and usually some solitude.

Below right: Traverse City State Park has a long sandy beach on East Grand Traverse Bay.

Opposite page: The forest edges right up to the shore at Sayler Park.

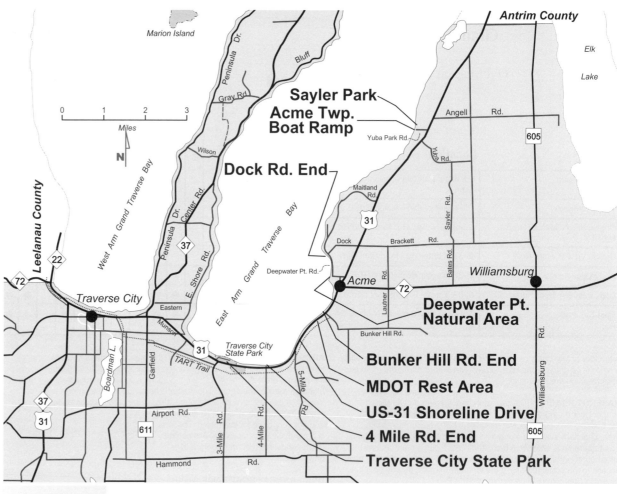

Grand Traverse County

Traverse City East, Acme and North

Name	Location	Entrance Fee	Parking	Modern Restrooms	Vault or Portable Toilet	Stair or Path to Shore	Swimming	Picnic Area	Drinking Water	Campground	Trailered Boat Launch	Kayak / Canoe	Marina	Fishing	Hiking	Biking	X-Country Skiing	Playground	Lighthouse	Beach Strolling	Sandy Beach	Stony or Rocky Shore	Dunes	Bluff	Wetland
Traverse City State Park	East of Traverse City. US-31 between 3 and 4 Mile Roads.	●	●	●			●	●	●	●								●			●				
4-Mile Road End	East of Traverse City. End of 4 Mile Road, one block N of US-31										●										●				
US-31 Shoreline Drive	US-31 between Traverse City and Acme.																								
MDOT Highway Rest Area	US-31, one mile S of Acme just S of Bunker Hill Rd.		●		●		●	●	●			●									●	●			
Bunker Hill Road End	W of US-31 at Bunker Hill Rd.		●								●	●									●	●			
Deepwater Point Natural Area	Acme, W of US-31 0.2 miles on Shore Rd.		●			●															●	●			
Dock Road End	1 mile N of Acme, W on Dock Road.										●	●									●	●			
Acme Township Road End Ramp	6 miles S of Elk Rapids at Yuba. W of US-31 at end of Yuba Park Rd.										●	●									●	●			
Sayler Park	6 miles S of Elk Rapids at Yuba. W of US-31 end of Yuba Park Rd.	●	●				●	●	●									●			●	●			

Hotels, motels and resorts line the East Arm of Grand Traverse Bay along US-31, ready to cater to tourists.

TRAVERSE CITY STATE PARK: Traverse City State Park lies at the south edge of East Grand Traverse Bay. It has several hundred feet of excellent sandy beach as well as a picnic area and change room. The parking area is large. Motor vehicles require the Michigan State Park permit.

A pedestrian overpass connects it with a large camping area on the other side of busy US-31. The park is a popular, economical place to stay. Camping reservations are advised in the summer months. The city has grown around the park, making it a 45-acre oasis. The

Traverse Area Recreational Trail (TART) is located nearby but does not pass through the park directly.
    GPS: 44°44.952'N; 85°33.532'W (Beach Entrance), 44°44.894'N; 85°33.237'W (Campground)

4 MILE ROAD END: During periods of higher lake levels, 4 Mile Road was a popular boat launch for access to the bay. The water levels during the early 2000's made it nearly useless. The parking is limited and the growth of the hotel business on each side has made the area less accommodating for casual visits.

US-31 SHORELINE DRIVE: Just south of Acme, US-31 parallels the shoreline of East Grand Traverse Bay with open views of the water. This highway stretch is busy with no advisable place to pull off. The highway rest area at the north end of this section is the best choice for parking.

MDOT HIGHWAY REST AREA: The Michigan Department of Transportation maintains a rest area on East Grand Traverse Bay between Acme and Traverse City. It has a sandy beach with some stone and shallow water. There is a large parking lot, tables, grills, water pump and a vault toilet. The view is pleasant, but during busy summer travel periods, it can be hard to exit from the park to the north.
    GPS: 44°45.786'N; 85°30.606'W

BUNKER HILL ROAD END: This location is used primarily for launching boats. The highway rest area, listed above, is a better choice for other activities.
    GPS: 44°45.910'N; 85°30.399'W

DEEPWATER POINT NATURAL AREA: An Acme Township Park, Deepwater Point is a wooded area with a primitive beach along East Grand Traverse Bay. There is a small parking area at the intersection of Shore and Deepwater Roads. From there, reach the shore by a short walk via paths through the woods. Best characterized as an uncrowded natural area offering a view of the lower bay, few would find the area good for swimming due to vegetation and rocks at the shoreline.
    GPS: 44°46.615'N; 85°30.182'W (park), 44°46.618'N; 85°29.839'W (turn at M-22)

DOCK ROAD END: Acme Township maintains a road end on East Grand Traverse Bay at the end of Dock Road. Primarily used as a boat launch, it is shallow with a mix of sand and stone. The road end is accessible via Shore and Deep Water Roads as well.
    GPS: 44°47.066'N; 85°30.393'W (location), 44°47.227'N; 85°29.430'W (turn at M-22)

Reach the next two listings from US-31 by turning west at Yuba Park Rd. (GPS: 44°49.553'N; 85°27.401'W) near the old townsite of Yuba.

ACME TOWNSHIP ROAD END RAMP: This is a shallow boat launch with a cement pad. It is at the end of the road leading to Sayler Park. There are no facilities at the launch but the park next door has them.

SAYLER PARK: Acme Township maintains Sayler Park along East Grand Traverse Bay. The facility sits among tall red pine and includes a large picnic area with 3 shelters and many tables and grills. The 300-foot beach is kept primitive and consists of sand and small stones. Volleyball courts, horseshoe pits and play equipment are available as well. The modern restroom is new.

Orchards and Vineyards

The eastern Lake Michigan shore has an ideal climate for growing many fruits. The cool lake moderates the air temperature of the early growing season, minimizing the likelihood of destructive frosts. In the fall, the reverse occurs as the relatively warm lake prevents early freezing temperatures that can ruin some crops. Cherries, apples, blueberries, grapes, peaches and plums, respectively, are the top-growing crops of the region. Berrien, Van Buren, Leelanau and Oceana counties have the most acreage in fruit crops. About 5 percent of Leelanau County is cultivated for orchards and vineyards.

The coast has two major grape regions making it the fourth largest grape producing state in the nation.

In the south, Berrien and Van Buren have a long history of growing the fruit. Most vines are native Concord or Niagara grapes used in juice making, but there are 10 vintners growing and fermenting in this area as well. The Leelanau and Old Mission Peninsulas, near Traverse City, began developing as a wine region in the 1970's. Here, almost all the grapes are used for wine. Presently, 18 vintners exist but the number continues to climb. The primary Michigan wine grapes include Europe's Riesling, Pinot Noir and Chardonnay. Most of the newer Michigan grape plantings use these and other vinifera varieties. French-American hybrids produce a bit more than a third of Michigan wine.

Development pressure has reduced the amount of orchard land, particularly in the fast-growing Grand Traverse region. Increased land values raise property taxes and provide a tempting incentive for fruit growers to sell their orchards for vacation home sites. Recent programs to ease the burden on the farmers and to preserve farmland may slow the trend.

Wander off the main roads past the pleasant rows of fruit trees. Fruit stands in front of many of the farmhouses sell fresh produce during the harvest season, often via a self-serve honor system. Grab a bag of peaches or a pint of cherries, throw your money in the pot then find the nearest beach or park to have a bite and rediscover the simple joys of summer.

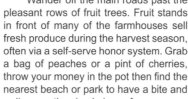

Clockwise from the left:
- The fall harvest of apples.
- A mixed field with an orchard behind a row of wine grapes
- The summer harvest of cherries earned the Grand Traverse region the title of "Cherry Capital" and resulted in one of the country's largest festivals each July.

Antrim County

Antrim County borders the east side of Grand Traverse Bay, extending north to the point where the bay opens to Lake Michigan proper. The shoreline alternates between sand and rock with private entities owning much of it. US-31 threads its way north between the bay and a couple of long, thin inland lakes. The rural atmosphere returns as you head north from busy Traverse City. The drive is pretty. Orchards and fruit stands mark farms along the way.

Elk Rapids is the major commerce center. Just far enough away from Traverse City to have its own character, the pleasant downtown has small shops. Several parks and the marina provide great access to the town shore. Elk Rapids County Park offers a nicely wooded view of the bay. The beach and swimming gets better at Veterans Park which occupies the bayfront south of the marina. Another worthwhile beach lies tucked away behind the hydroelectric dam to the north of the marina. The dam area and the short stretch of river downstream offer excellent fishing as well.

The county has three natural areas. The Nature Conservancy plays a role at the Wilcox-Palmer-Shah Nature Preserve where the site has been kept completely natural. The Torch Bay Nature Preserve resulted when local interests rescued this block of land from development. It has a self-instructional interpretative area, some short trails plus a shoreline wetland. In the far north of the county, the off-the-beaten-track location of the Antrim Creek Natural Area generally guarantees low use. With a long shore and wooded trails, it is a great place to relax and hunt for stones.

Antrim is the only county on Lake Michigan's east shore without a state or federal park. Although small in comparison, Barnes County Park is the closest in terms of facilities. Here you will find a small beach, a forested campground and a location close to scenic Torch Lake.

US-31 continues as the primary route connecting the bayside communities. While lake views are infrequent along this highway, the scenery is pleasantly rural and the lake shore is never far away.

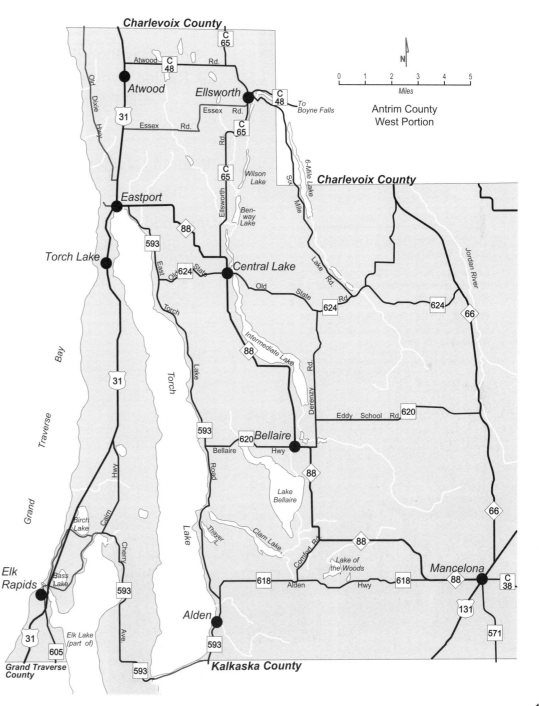

Antrim County
West Portion

Above: The Elk Rapids hydroelectric dam, a short way from Grand Traverse Bay, is a popular fishing spot.

Below left: Elk Rapids Marina has a number of services including an excellent boat ramp and a picnic spot.

Below right: Old Mission Peninsula, in the background, lies a few miles west of Elk Rapids County Park.

Opposite page: A short path leads from the parking lot at the Hydroelectric Park to the sandy beach.

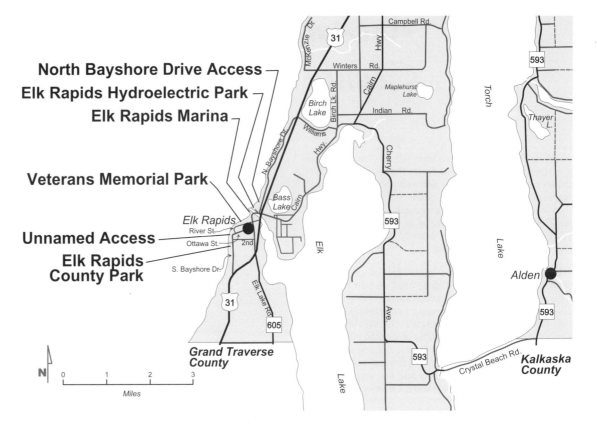

North Bayshore Drive Access
Elk Rapids Hydroelectric Park
Elk Rapids Marina

Veterans Memorial Park

Unnamed Access
Elk Rapids County Park

Elk Rapids

Name	Location	Entrance Fee	Parking	Modern Restrooms	Vault or Portable Toilet	Stair or Path to Shore	Swimming	Picnic Area	Drinking Water	Campground	Trailered Boat Launch	Kayak / Canoe	Marina	Fishing	Hiking	Biking	X-Country Skiing	Playground	Lighthouse	Beach Strolling	Sandy Beach	Stony or Rocky Shore	Dunes	Bluff	Wetland
Elk Rapids County Park	South of downtown Elk Rapids on Bayshore Road.		●	●		●	●	●	●			●						●			●	●			
Unnamed Public Access	Elk Rapids. Ottawa Street and Bayshore Rd.					●	●					●									●	●			
Veteran's Memorial Park	Elk Rapids, downtown 2 blocks W of US-31 on River Street.		●	●			●	●	●					●				●			●				
Elk Rapids-Edward C. Grace Memorial Marina	Elk Rapids, downtown. From US-31, W on River St. then N on Cedar St.		●	●				●			●	●	●												
Elk Rapids Hydroelectric Park	Elk Rapids. From US-31 turn W on Dexter St. at traffic light, then 2 blocks to Dam St.		●		●	●	●					●		●							●				
North Bayshore Drive Access	Elk Rapids. From Dexter St. turn N on Bayshore Drive. Bayshore intersection is just W of US-31 at traffic light.		●				●					●									●				

Elk Rapids is a small, summer port town with a fine selection of parks on East Grand Traverse Bay.

ELK RAPIDS COUNTY PARK: Antrim County's Elk Rapids Park is large and wooded with natural underbrush. The shore is about 600 feet long. The upland beach is sandy, but the lake bottom is stony. It has a modern restroom with a changing area. Picnic tables and grills are scattered throughout the area. The wooded nature allows some seclusion at each picnic site. The park has a covered picnic pavilion as well.
 GPS: 44°53.329'N; 85°25.341'W

UNNAMED PUBLIC ACCESS: Bayshore Road curves and becomes Ottawa Street just north of Elk Rapids County Park. To the west is a short path to a 50-foot section of public beach. A small sign marks the access. No formal parking exists although there is room for a few cars to pull off the side of the road. The beach is sand with some stone and the water drops off relatively fast. There are no facilities or improvements. Good swimming.
 GPS: 44°53.651'N; 85°25.339'W

VETERAN'S MEMORIAL PARK: The public owns much shore in Elk Rapids. Veteran's Park, south of the harbor, occupies a big stretch. The developed park includes tennis and basketball courts, picnic tables, grills, play equipment and benches. The beach is sandy with few stones. Parking is plentiful. Parts of the park are shaded. Sidewalks lead to the downtown business district; an easy walk.
 GPS: Parking and access from 44°53.826'N; 85°25.274'W to 44°53.858'N; 85°24.987'W

ELK RAPIDS-EDWARD C. GRACE MEMORIAL MARINA: The marina park is a block from the downtown shopping district. Besides having boat slips, the development includes a wheelchair-accessible picnic area near the harbor entrance. Equipped with picnic tables, grills and covered areas for rain or sun protection, this spot provides a great view of the bay, the harbor and Veteran's Park Beach. The ramp provides a deep launch for boats. The marina has some parking, primarily for cars with boat trailers. A municipal parking lot is located next to it on Cedar Street. A short boardwalk lines the river entering the harbor area. Modern public restrooms are located across from the Cedar Street lot. The public library is located here as well. Fee charged for boat launching or boat slips.
 Telephone: (231) 264-8174
 GPS: 44°54.150'N; 85°25.067'W

ELK RAPIDS HYDROELECTRIC PARK: With a large, dirt parking lot, the dam area does not look like much, but it has some great recreation opportunities. Fish along the Elk River from the dam walkway or the platforms lining the north harbor area found just downstream. At the far end of the parking area, a path through the small dunes leads to a large, sugar-sand beach. From here, watch the boats enter and leave the town's harbor or put in a kayak for a jaunt by the marina and the other Elk Rapids parks to the south.
 GPS: 44°54.054'N; 85°24.722'W

NORTH BAYSHORE DRIVE ACCESS: Marked by a small "Public Access" sign, the North Bayshore Drive site has a sandy beach and plenty of parking. The public beach is about 50 feet long. There are no facilities. A lone, large shade tree with some grass provides relief from the sun if needed.
 GPS: 44°54.282'N; 85°24.551'W

Above and below: Wilcox-Palmer-Shah Nature Preserve provides a great example of the Nature Conservancy effort. A number of lakeshore parcels have made their way into the program in recent years.

Opposite page: O'Dell Road ends at Grand Traverse Bay providing a view or a kayak launch but limited recreational possibilities.

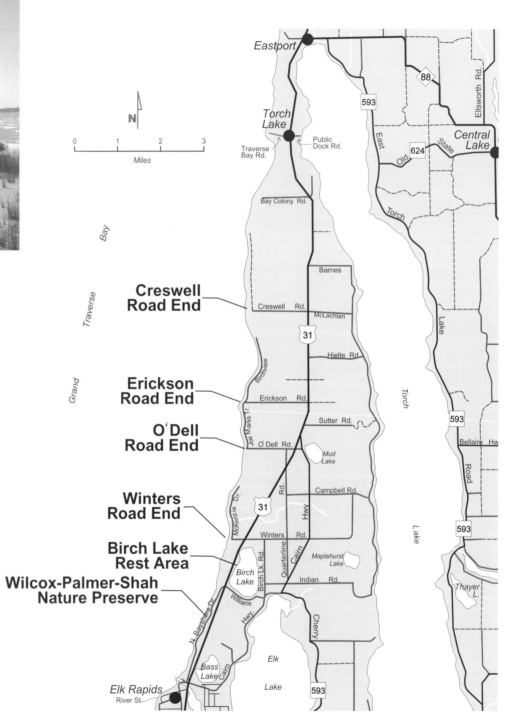

Between Elk Rapids and Torch Lake

Name	Location	Entrance Fee	Parking	Modern Restrooms	Vault or Portable Toilet	Stair or Path to Shore	Swimming	Picnic Area	Drinking Water	Campground	Trailered Boat Launch	Kayak / Canoe	Marina	Fishing	Hiking	Biking	X-Country Skiing	Playground	Lighthouse	Beach Strolling	Sandy Beach	Stony or Rocky Shore	Dunes	Bluff	Wetland
Wilcox-Palmer-Shah Nature Preserve	North Bayshore Drive, 2 miles N of Elk Rapids.					●														●	●	●			
MDOT Birch Lake Rest Area	3 miles N of Elk Rapids on US-31 between Williams and Winter Roads.	●			●		●	●	●			●									●				●
Winters Road End Access	3.5 miles N of Elk Rapids. From US-31, W 0.3 miles on Winters Rd.						●					●									●	●			
O'Dell Road End	5.5 miles N of Elk Rapids. From US-31, one mile W on O'Dell Rd.											●									●	●			
Erickson Road End	6.5 miles N of Elk Rapids. From US-31, 1.3 miles W on Erickson Rd.																				●	●			
Creswell Road End	4 miles SW of Torch Lake. From US-31, 1.5 miles W on Creswell Rd.											●									●	●			

Private homes stretch along most of the shore north of Elk Rapids making for few access opportunities. As such, the road ends are offered up for those looking for a glimpse of the lake.

WILCOX-PALMER-SHAH NATURE PRESERVE: The Wilcox-Palmer-Shah Nature Preserve is privately owned land held by the Grand Traverse Regional Land Conservancy. About 40 acres in size with more than 1/2-mile of shoreline, its plant species include the threatened Pitcher's Thistle and Lake Huron Tansy.

The Preserve is a fine example of what can be accomplished through the Nature Conservancy. W-P-S evolved from an initial land gift of the Wilcox family and additional lands garnered by their Palmer and Shah descendants. The name is derived from the three families involved. Continued public use depends upon people adhering to the rules described on the sign. Fires, pets, camping, motorized vehicles and hunting are prohibited. Stay on marked trails or on the beach below the high-water mark (non-vegetated portion). Enjoy the solitude of this wonderful gift!

Note: Bayshore Drive runs north and south between US-31 and the shore. Access it in Elk Rapids where it nearly intersects US-31 west of the traffic light or 2.5 miles north of Elk Rapids by turning west near the US-31 and Williams Road intersection south of the highway rest area. Find the small, pull-off area, suitable for parking a couple cars, along Bayshore Drive at the north end of the preserve. A wooden sign marks this place. A short, sandy trail heads to the shoreline.
GPS: 44°55.229'N; 85°24.053'W

MDOT BIRCH LAKE REST AREA: A highway rest area, maintained by the Michigan Department of Transportation, sits along US-31 on Birch Lake. The facilities include a vault toilet, picnic tables, grills and a hand water pump. The tables sit in the shade along the lake. A small area with sandy bottom is a possible swimming spot.
GPS: 44°56.548'N; 85°23.184'W

WINTERS ROAD END ACCESS: A sandy beach with a sand and rock lake bottom. Limited access and parking
GPS: 45°56.788'N; 85°23.382'W

O'DELL ROAD END: A small road end with a boat ramp and limited parking. The ramp has been high and dry during recent low lake levels.
GPS: 44°58.548'N; 85°22,863'W

ERICKSON ROAD END: Another road end access with little room. Most of the shore in this area is private and undergoing development. The shore is poor sand with a stony lake bottom.
GPS: 44°59.437'N; 85°22.942'W

CRESWELL ROAD END: The shore here is sandy with a rocky lake bottom. The road end provides little space. It looks out towards the Lighthouse Point on Old Mission Peninsula.
GPS: 45°01.200'N; 85°22.863'W

Below: At Torch Lake Nature Preserve, a barrier-free observation platform overlooks a shoreline wetland. Grand Traverse Bay lies just beyond.

Opposite page: The viewing platform along the trail at Antrim Creek Natural Area looks out at the lake. An interesting plaque shows the area as the native peoples saw it.

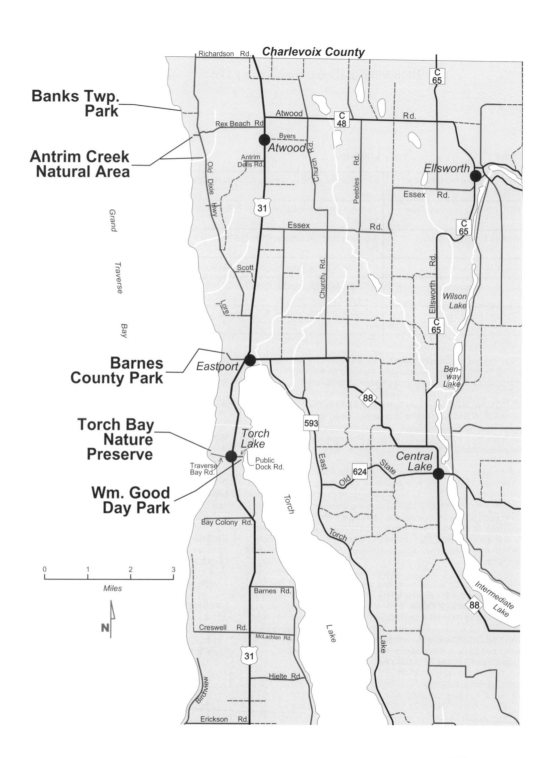

142

Antrim County

Torch Lake to Charlevoix County Line

Facilities | **Environment**

Name	Location	Entrance Fee	Parking	Modern Restrooms	Vault or Portable Toilet	Stair or Path to Shore	Swimming	Picnic Area	Drinking Water	Campground	Trailered Boat Launch	Kayak / Canoe	Marina	Fishing	Hiking	Biking	X-Country Skiing	Playground	Lighthouse	Beach Strolling	Sandy Beach	Stony or Rocky Shore	Dunes	Bluff	Wetland
William Good Day Park	Torch Lake. End of Public Dock Rd. E one block from US-31.	●	●				●	●	●		●	●		●				●			●				
Torch Bay Nature Preserve	Torch Lake. End of Traverse Bay Rd. W one block from US-31.		●			●	●					●			●						●	●			●
Barnes County Park	Eastpoint, 0.5 miles W of US-31 at intersection with M-88.	●	●	●		●	●	●	●	●								●			●	●		●	
Antrim Creek Natural Area	2 miles W of Atwood on Old Dixie Hwy at Rex Beach Rd.		●		●							●			●					●	●	●	●		
Banks Township Park	2 miles S of Norwood. Lakeshore Drive W of Old Dixie Hwy.		●		●	●	●	●				●									●	●		●	

While private homes dominate the lakeshore of northern Antrim County, several local government parks provide good access for the public.

WILLIAM GOOD DAY PARK: A short distance from Lake Michigan, the township park provides a variety of facilities on the very long Torch Lake. There is a designated swimming area of mostly sand bottom with some stone. The boat ramp is very good. A fee of $5 is charged for launching. A cement pier juts into the lake near the ramp. Much of the park is grassy. The playground is small. Volleyball and basketball courts are available. The picnic area has tables, grills and two shelters with modern restrooms.
  GPS: 45°04.461'N; 85°21.377'W

TORCH BAY NATURE PRESERVE: As you drive slowly through the townsite of Torch Lake, a small sign will alert you to the preserve. It is easy to miss, as Traverse Bay Road is poorly marked. The preserve has about 720 feet of frontage on Grand Traverse Bay and a quarter-mile of forested dune and wetland back from the lakefront. Hiking trails meander through the woods. A barrier-free trail leads to a coastal pond overlook. Interpretive displays give information about the flora, fauna and geology.

The shore is stony with some sand. Petoskey Stones can be found. A primitive boat launch is available for canoes and kayaks. Swimming is possible but it is not the best due to the stones. William Good Day Park, located nearby and listed above, has restrooms and other facilities.
  GPS: 45°04.527'N; 85°21.686'W

BARNES COUNTY PARK: This large county park is based on camping. The wooded campground attracts many regular visitors making Barnes a busy place during the prime of summer. A camping fee is charged. The park includes a picnic shelter and restrooms and a variety of recreational playfields. The beach is sandy with some rocks.
  GPS: 45°06.403'N; 85°21.162'W (Turn at US-31 intersection)

ANTRIM CREEK NATURAL AREA: Antrim Creek is newly developed and worth the effort to find. Find its entrance along Old Dixie Highway, a county road that runs roughly parallel to and about 1 to 1.5 miles west of US-31. One way to reach it is to turn west on Rex Beach Road near the town of Atwood. There are two parking areas for the park. The primary one is at the end of the western portion of Rex Beach Road. The second is along Old Dixie Road and is a trailhead for the park at its southeast corner.

The park has 156 acres and one mile of shore. Most of it is stony with some sand. Petoskey Stone hunts are popular. Small dunes line a portion of the waterfront. Cedar, fir and hardwoods forest the park. Development is minimal and mostly confined to the main parking area. Kayak access is good. Hiking trails wander through the forest. An interesting map, located at a barrier-free viewing platform, shows the native Anishinaabe names of the Antrim County area and the location of the special places of these earlier inhabitants.
  GPS: 45°10.834'N; 85°22.534'W (Main entrance), 45°10.390'N; 85°22.350'W (Old Dixie Road trailhead)

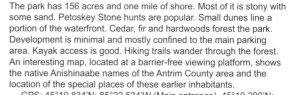

BANKS TOWNSHIP PARK: Banks Township has a pretty park that is hard to find. The park lies at the end of a gravel road, 0.3 miles west of Old Dixie Highway between Richardson and Rex Beach Roads. Few maps show it. No sign marks it. The road leading towards it does not have a street sign either. To make it worse, one commonly available commercial map shows it in the wrong place! A couple of residences are near, but its hidden nature makes it a quiet place on most days.

The grassy picnic area sits on top of a small bluff overlooking the lake. Large trees shade the grills and tables. A short stairway leads to the beach where Grand Traverse Bay opens to the Lake Michigan. The 200-foot beach is sandy with some stone. It would not be difficult to carry a kayak to the water as the stairway is short.
  GPS: 45°11.276'N; 85°22.968'W (park), 45°11.273'N; 85°22.565'W (Dixie Hwy. intersection)

Beaver Island

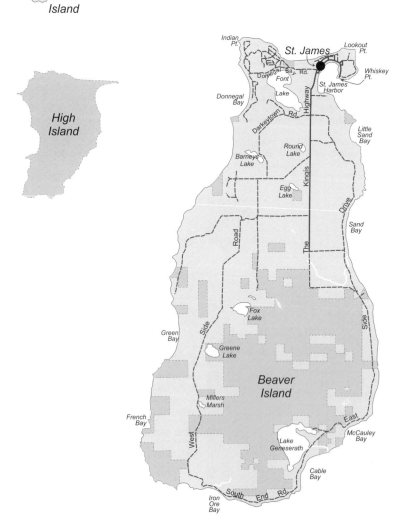

Beaver Island forms the largest land mass in the group of isles known as the Beaver Island Archipelago. The grouping goes as far south as the Manitou Islands in Leelanau County and includes the Fox Islands that lay in between. Several islands, such as Garden, High and Hog, lay just off shore from Beaver. Large parts of these are in public ownership, but Beaver and North and South Manitou Islands (see Leelanau County, (pp. 116-120) are the only ones with regular transit to their shores. Beaver Island has the only remaining town - St. James. The Manitous are a part of Sleeping Bear Dunes National Lakeshore.

Native Americans have used Beaver Island for several thousand years. By the mid-1600's, colonial settlement of America pushed the Odawa (Ottawa) tribe west. A portion made their way to the island. The local waters provided plentiful fishing grounds. Whites migrated to the island in the early 1800's to trap, trade and support passing steamers with fuel wood. A community of traders grew at Whiskey Point on the north of the island's harbor.

In New York State, during the 1830's, a young lawyer named James Strang met the Mormon leader Joseph Smith. He asked Strang to begin a branch of the religion in Wisconsin. Smith was killed during this period and following his death, Strang challenged Brigham Young for leadership of the Mormons. Most followed Young, but a number went with Strang on a journey to Illinois, then Wisconsin and finally, in 1848, to Beaver Island. His island colony grew strong enough to elect him to the Michigan legislature. Strang's flock took on the gentiles at Whiskey Point, effectively driving non-Mormons off the island. He then crowned himself king. Legal attempts to oust him failed. In 1856, two men assassinated King James and later mainland mobs drove the Mormons off the island.

The rich fishing grounds of the area next attracted Irish fishermen. Soon the island had a decided Irish flavor that exists to some extent today. Once a prolific fish producer, the area stocks began to decline in the late 1800's as fishing methods improved. Lumber production came and went. The economy could not be sustained and eventually small settlements on the nearby islands began to disappear. Today, Beaver Island draws vacationers looking for solitude and beauty. St. James, the lone remaining island town, caters to both tourists and summer residents. During the winter, the few year-round inhabitants enjoy a peaceful isolation.

The Mormon print shop, preserved in St. James, produced the newspaper during the time of King Strang.

Charlevoix County

The southwest coastline of Charlevoix County starts at the top of Grand Traverse Bay. It concludes at its northeast by forming the south shore of Little Traverse Bay. In between, the mainland's shoulder faces northwest toward Beaver Island, the former Mormon kingdom. You can take your pick of environments. The area has a small but lively city, Lake Michigan shore, inland waters and isolated island life. Charlevoix County combines all these elements.

The City of Charlevoix anchors the center. The vigorous summer town stretches from Lake Michigan along the Pine River Channel to Round Lake, which serves as its harbor. Round Lake, in turn, opens into Lake Charlevoix, extending for miles inland. The city has a number of interesting shops and galleries facing a waterfront park across from its marina. A short walk down the channel walkway leads to the city beach. Congestion peaks in town during July and August. Don't fight the traffic. Park, walk and stay a while.

Fisherman's Island State Park lies to the southwest of the city. Shoreline camping, natural beach and beautiful forest await here. It is the largest coastline park between Sleeping Bear Dunes National Lakeshore and Wilderness State Park near the Straits of Mackinac. The south part of the park is isolated, hard to find, and has minimal use. Mt. McSauba Recreation Area sits just north of the city. Its beach is free, undeveloped, sandy and has a dune backdrop.

Highway US-31 follows close to the shore along Little Traverse Bay, offering beautiful scenery. The Little Traverse Wheelway, which connects Charlevoix with the Emmet County towns of Petoskey and Harbor Springs, shares the same corridor as US-31 through the county. Bicyclists can join the route for their own scenic "drive" at many of the lake access points listed on the next few pages.

For much the year, ferry service connects Charlevoix with Beaver Island, 40 miles from the mainland. Beaver has a single, small town, few permanent residents and an interesting history. The island presents a wonderful get-away for those with the time to absorb it. You should plan a couple of nights minimum. Flights are also available from Charlevoix. It is expensive to ferry your car there and most of the roads are gravel. This makes it a great mountain bike spot, especially in the off-season when traffic is minimal.

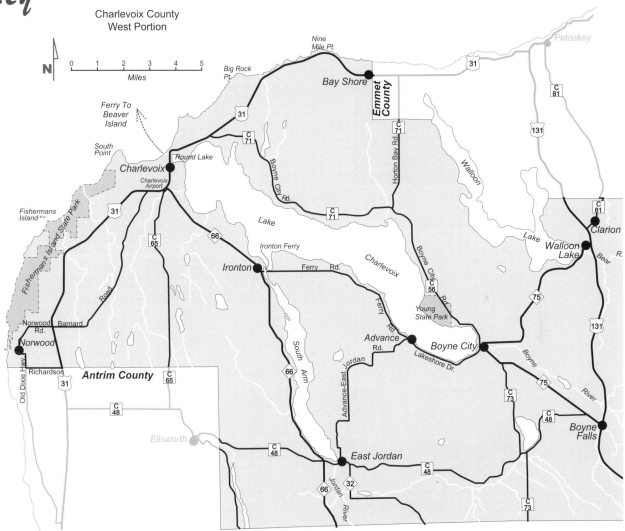

Charlevoix County
West Portion

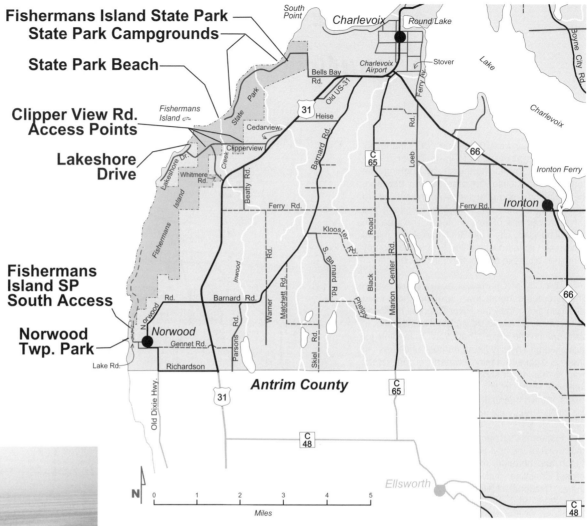

Fishermans Island State Park
State Park Campgrounds

State Park Beach

Clipper View Rd.
Access Points

Lakeshore
Drive

Fishermans
Island SP
South Access

Norwood
Twp. Park

South Point

Charlevoix Round Lake

Lake

Boyne City Rd.

Stover

Charlevoix Airport

Bells Bay Rd.

Charlevoix

Fishermans Island

State Park

Creek

Old US-31

31 Heise

Cedarview

Clipperview

Lakeshore Dr.

Whitmere Rd.

Fishermans Island

Barnard Rd.

Ferry Av.

C 65

Loeb Rd.

66

Ironton Ferry

Ferry Rd.

Ferry Rd. Ironton

Klooster Rd.

66

Beatty Rd.

Inwood

Norwood Rd.

Barnard Rd.

Warner Rd.

Matchett Rd.

S. Barnard Rd.

Road

Black

Marion Center Rd.

Phelps

Norwood

Gennet Rd.

Parsons Rd.

Skiel Rd.

Lake Rd.

Richardson

Old Dixie Hwy.

Antrim County

31

C 65

C 48

Ellsworth

C 48

N   0   1   2   3   4   5

Miles

Above left: Its out-of-the-way location makes Norwood Township Park a quiet choice.

Left: Beachcombers search for stones at Fisherman's Island State Park.

Charlevoix County

Norwood and Fisherman's Island State Park

Facilities   **Environment**

Name	Location	Entrance Fee	Parking	Modern Restrooms	Vault or Portable Toilet	Stair or Path to Shore	Swimming	Picnic Area	Drinking Water	Campground	Trailered Boat Launch	Kayak / Canoe	Marina	Fishing	Hiking	Biking	X-Country Skiing	Playground	Lighthouse	Beach Strolling	Sandy Beach	Stony or Rocky Shore	Dunes	Bluff	Wetland
Norwood Township Park	Norwood. Lake Rd. 2 miles W of US-31. See site listing below.		●		●	●	●	●				●									●	●			
Fisherman's Island State Park	4.5 miles SW of Charlevoix. Take Bells Bay Rd. W from US-31.	●	●		●	●	●	●	●	●		●		●	●	●	●			●	●	●			
Fisherman's Island State Park South Access	Norwood. Lake Rd. 2 miles W of US-31. See Norwood Twp. Park.	●	●		●	●	●	●				●		●	●	●	●			●	●	●			
Lakeshore Drive Road End	6.5 miles SW of Charlevoix. Take Clipper View Rd. W from US-31 then N on Lakeshore.							●	●						●					●	●	●			
Clipper View Rd. Access Points	6 miles SW of Charlevoix. Take Clipper View Rd. W from US-31.							●	●						●					●	●	●			
State Park Campgrounds	Fisherman's Island State Park.	●	●		●			●		●	●									●	●	●			
State Park Beach	Fisherman's Island State Park.	●	●		●	●	●	●	●					●	●					●	●	●			

Isolated, public shore greets you from Norwood nearly to the City of Charlevoix. The lake bottom alternates from rock to sand to a mix of each.

NORWOOD TOWNSHIP PARK: The Norwood Township Park is enough off-the-beaten-track that most users are local residents. Since the area's population is small, it is normal peaceful. Finding it is a bit difficult though. Travel US-31 until reaching the Charlevoix-Antrim County line. Richardson Road heads west for a little more than a mile. It ends at Old Dixie Highway. Turn right until Old Dixie ends at Gennet Road. Turn left onto Gennet and travel straight until the road curves right at the bluff overlooking Lake Michigan. In a block, the street turns right, heading back toward the Norwood townsite. At that point, take a left down the hill on the gravel road to the lake. The road swings to the right and the park is on the left.

The park has picnic grounds in a grassy area near the street. Picnic tables, grills and portable toilets are available. A short path takes you to a sand and rock beach.
GPS: 45°13.064'N; 85°23.268'W (turn at Norwood).

FISHERMAN'S ISLAND STATE PARK: Fisherman's Island State Park was named for a small island off the coast. The lake levels have dropped and the island is now a peninsula. The park was once state forest land until its rustic, Bell's Bay Campground became very popular, prompting the formalization into a state park during the 70's. With nearly 2700 acres of land and miles of Lake Michigan beach, Fisherman's Island Park is a gem. The shoreline is generally sandy in its northern half. Stones and rocks will be found at the water line and on the lake bottom. There is good swimming along much of its shore. The southern portion near Norwood is rockier. Three small streams flow through the park. Hunting is permitted in season except near the campgrounds and buildings. There are hiking trails. Cross-country skiing is popular, though no trails are groomed. There are many places to carry a kayak or canoe to the shore for launching.
Telephone: (231) 547-6641
Web: www.michigan.gov/dnr

FISHERMAN'S ISLAND STATE PARK SOUTH ACCESS: The south end of Fisherman's Island State Park is difficult to find. Follow the directions to Norwood Township Park, listed above, and then continue past it to the north. After passing a couple of driveways, you will be on park property. High ground clearance will be required to negotiate the two-track road. Potholes are large and often filled with water after rains. Another choice is to park at the Norwood Township Park and ride a mountain bike to the area. Canoeists and kayakers may wish to carry their craft to the Norwood Township Park beach and paddle up to the state park. Hikers or skiers can access the area via the two-track as well.

The lane goes in about 2 miles ending at Whiskey Creek. Cedars line most of the lake on the way in. The shore is a sand-stone mix near the south end. It then changes to stone and rock until near the creek, where it is becomes a sand-stone mix again. Use of this area is minimal and unmarked hiking trails can be found.

LAKESHORE DRIVE ROAD END: On Lakeshore Drive is a small private development of lake homes nestled about midway along the Fisherman's Island State Park shore. At the north end of the subdivision a path leads through the fence into the park. The island is a short walk from here. This is an undeveloped portion of the park. Parking is limited to the shoulder.
GPS: 45°16.770'N; 85°21.404'W

CLIPPER VIEW RD. ACCESS POINTS: Along Clipper View Road there are three trailheads leading into Fisherman's Island State Park. Parking is primitive and limited to one or two cars at best. Hunters probably use this access the most. A hike from these points to the shore is a mile or less, coming out near the actual Fisherman's Island. Along the paths are small dunes with typical dune vegetation and forest.
GPS: 45°16.692'N; 85°20.858'W

The primary access to Fisherman's Island State Park, its campgrounds and beach are reached via the north entrance listed below. From US-31, turn west on Bell's Bay Road located at 45°18.056'N; 85°17.242'W.

STATE PARK CAMPGROUNDS: There are two campgrounds with a total of 81 campsites. Both are rustic, meaning vault toilets and no electricity. Some of the sites are on the lakeshore. Most campsites are well spaced for privacy. Make campsite reservations through the DNR parks reservation system at 1-800-44PARKS.
GPS: 45°18.483'N; 85°18.623'W

STATE PARK BEACH: About 3 miles into the park at Inwood Creek is a mile-long swimming area. The beach area's minimal development consists of vault toilets and picnic tables. A short path over small dunes leads to the shore. One path has a footbridge across the creek. Fisherman's Island is a short walk down the beach. It is now a peninsula and can be accessed by foot. During nesting season, some of its shore may be closed for the endangered Piping Plover. Kayakers can make the voyage to the "island" easily.
GPS: 45°17.129'N; 85°20.608'W

Right: The Charlevoix Light marks the Pine River Channel at Michigan Beach. The sand welcomes a number of beachgoers on sunny days.

Below: During the boating season, the Pine River Channel Drawbridge in Charlevoix opens on the half-hour. Traffic on US-31 can back up a long way. Keep this in mind when traveling through town.

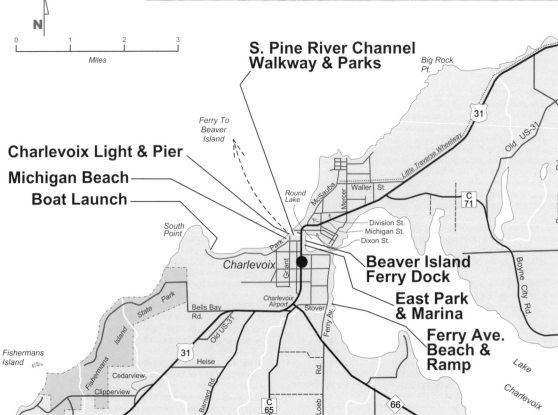

Charlevoix County

City of Charlevoix, South

Name	Location	Entrance Fee	Parking	Modern Restrooms	Vault or Portable Toilet	Stair or Path to Shore	Swimming	Picnic Area	Drinking Water	Campground	Trailered Boat Launch	Kayak / Canoe	Marina	Fishing	Hiking	Biking	X-Country Skiing	Playground	Lighthouse	Beach Strolling	Sandy Beach	Stony or Rocky Shore	Dunes	Bluff	Wetland
Ferry Avenue Beach & Ramp	Charlevoix. Ferry Ave. near Stover E of M-66.	●	●				●	●	●		●	●						●			●				
East Park	Charlevoix. US-31 between Mason and Clinton Streets downtown.	●	●						●				●												
Charlevoix City Marina	Charlevoix at East Park.		●						●				●												
Beaver Island Ferry	Charlevoix. From US-31, turn E just S of drawbridge.		●						●																
Boat Launch	Charlevoix. Lakeshore Dr. 2 mi. W of the Charlevoix Breakwater.	●									●	●												●	
Michigan Beach	Charlevoix. From US-31, W on Clinton 2 blocks then N on Grant.	●	●				●	●	●					●	●			●	●	●	●			●	
Charlevoix Breakwater & Light	Charlevoix at Michigan Beach.								●					●					●						
South Pine River Channel Walkway & Parks	Charlevoix between Park Street and the Channel.	●				●								●	●					●					

Charlevoix features water of all kinds. Round Lake, Lake Charlevoix, the Pine River Channel and Lake Michigan all contribute to its upscale, marine atmosphere. Intermixed are the town's galleries and shops.

FERRY AVENUE BEACH AND RAMP: This pleasantly shaded, grassy park and sandy beach are on Lake Charlevoix. It features a gently sloping lake bottom and warm water that make it popular with younger children. Nearby is a top-notch boat launch that can accommodate large trailered boats. From here, you can travel to Round Lake and through the Pine River Channel to Lake Michigan. Fee for boat launching.
  GPS: 45°18.127'N; 85°14.936'W (boat ramp entrance)

EAST PARK: During the summer, Round Lake serves as a boat basin between the larger Lakes Charlevoix and Michigan. It is also the waterfront for downtown Charlevoix. East Park doubles as a marina and gathering place for the town. Summer festivals and art fairs use the park. A bandshell houses events as well. Downtown Charlevoix can be very busy during July and August. At times, East Park can be an escape from the congestion on the street. At other times, its events are the source of the chaos. Parking capacity near the park is not adequate during peak tourist periods. Often it is best to park at other points and walk to this area.
  GPS: 45°19.031'N; 85°15.529'W

CHARLEVOIX CITY MARINA: The marina on Round Lake is a short distance from the Pine River Channel to Lake Michigan. There are 72 slips of which 60 are for transient mooring.
  Telephone: (231) 547-3272
  GPS: 45°19.000'N; 85°15.383'W (marina); 45°19.283'N; 85°15.967'W (channel)

BEAVER ISLAND FERRY: Beaver Island, the largest of Lake Michigan's islands, lies about 32 miles from Charlevoix. Today, the island community is composed of isolated summer cottages, the small town of St. James, much public forest and a colorful history (see p.144). The Beaver Island Boat Company provides regular car and passenger service to Beaver Island from their dock on Round Lake, near the drawbridge. Service varies with the time of year and travel time depends on the boat. There are two to three departures and arrivals per day during peak summer periods. During the spring and fall, sailings are reduced to one per day. Travel time is about 2.5 hours. Reservations are advised during peak periods, especially for vehicle transport.
  Telephone: toll free (888) 446-4095 or locally (231) 547-2311
  Web: www.bibco.com
  GPS: 45°19.084'N; 85°15.520'W

BOAT LAUNCH: A poorly maintained boat ramp is located near the end of Lakeshore Drive near the cement plant. Lakeshore Drive spurs off Park Avenue at the hospital. Small boats, canoes and kayaks might find this suitable for launch. Larger craft will need to launch at Ferry Avenue Beach and navigate the channel to Lake Michigan.

MICHIGAN BEACH: Just south of the Pine River Channel lies sandy Michigan Beach Park. While the beach is the focus, the park offers a variety of things to do. On the bluff, above the beach, is a wooded area with short trails and picnic grounds. Park along Park Avenue for easy access to the bluff area.

At the east end of the park is the main beach area. Paved parking can be found by entering the park near the north end of Grant Street. Modern restrooms, a picnic shelter, play equipment and shuffleboard courts are some of the facilities. Lifeguards are on duty at scheduled hours. A concession is opened during the summer. Charlevoix's

breakwater and light are in view from the beach. Use the park's lot to access the breakwater and the adjoining Pine River Channel Walkway listed below. Downtown shops are a short walk using Park Avenue or along the Pine River Channel. The town bustles during the height of summer tourist season. If you want to shop, try walking from here to town to avoid downtown traffic hassles.

CHARLEVOIX BREAKWATER AND LIGHT: Charlevoix's short pier and navigation light are the center of the town's south channel park development. Parking is found at Michigan Beach Park off Grant Street. To the east, one can walk on the Pine River Channel Walkway to the drawbridge then on to downtown.

SOUTH PINE RIVER CHANNEL WALKWAY & PARKS: The paved walkway along the south side of the Pine River Channel has a pleasant mix of sights and sounds. Pleasure craft ply the short channel from Round Lake out to Lake Michigan. Fishing is common. During the summer, the drawbridge on US-31 rises twice an hour to allow boats to pass. Stroll between the bridge area and the south breakwater light. The walk is lighted making it a great evening destination on warm, summer nights.

Two small parks are located between the walkway and Park Avenue. At 103 Park Avenue is a park with benches and some historic information about the area. The Charlevoix Historic Society is next door. Near 213 Park Avenue is Hoffmann Park (unmarked). A trail leads to benches with a lookout over the channel. A stairway takes you to the channel walkway below.

The best parking for the walkway is at Michigan Beach listed above. Restrooms are located at East Park, the ferry dock and Michigan Beach.

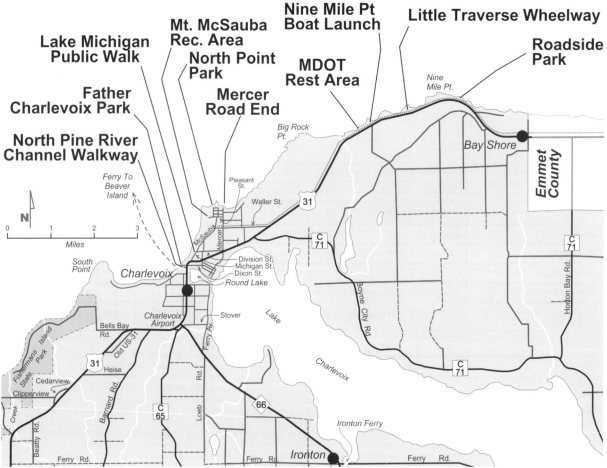

Lake Michigan Public Walk

Mt. McSauba Rec. Area

North Point Park

Nine Mile Pt Boat Launch

Little Traverse Wheelway

Roadside Park

Father Charlevoix Park

MDOT Rest Area

Mercer Road End

North Pine River Channel Walkway

Above left: A steel staircase heads to the shore at Father Charlevoix Park at the end of Dixon Street.

Left: The nuclear plant at Big Rock Point seen from the MDOT Rest Area. The plant, the country's first for commercial service, has been decommissioned.

Right: Mt. McScuba Recreation Area has dunes and beach.

Name	Location	Entrance Fee	Parking	Modern Restrooms	Vault or Portable Toilet	Stair or Path to Shore	Swimming	Picnic Area	Drinking Water	Campground	Trailered Boat Launch	Kayak / Canoe	Marina	Fishing	Hiking	Biking	X-Country Skiing	Playground	Lighthouse	Beach Strolling	Sandy Beach	Stony or Rocky Shore	Dunes	Bluff	Wetland
North Pine River Channel Walkway & North Breakwater	Charlevoix at end of Pine River Road one block N of US-31 drawbridge.		●			●	●	●						●							●	●			
Father Charlevoix Park	Charlevoix. End of West Dixon Street one block W of US-31.		●			●	●														●	●			
Lake Michigan Public Walk	Charlevoix, along Michigan Street.		●			●	●														●	●			
Little Traverse Wheelway	Charlevoix to Petoskey and Harbor Springs in Emmet County.		●												●	●									
Mt. McSauba Recreation Area	Charlevoix. From US-31, N on Mercer then W to end of Pleasant.		●			●	●								●		●			●	●	●	●		
North Point Park	Charlevoix. Bay St., 3 blocks N of Pleasant St just N of Mt. McSauba Recreation Area		●			●						●								●		●			
Mercer Road End	Charlevoix. From US-31, N on Mercer St. to end.		●																			●			
MDOT Roadside Park	US-31, 5 miles NE of Charlevoix.		●		●			●	●			●		●								●			
Nine-Mile Point Boat Launch	US-31, 9 miles W of Petoskey.		●								●	●										●			
Roadside Park	US-31, 8 miles W of Petoskey.		●			●		●						●								●		●	

Charlevoix continues, leading to the dunes of Mt. McSauba then to the rocky shore of southern Little Traverse Bay.

NORTH PINE RIVER CHANNEL WALKWAY AND NORTH BREAKWATER: The Pine River Channel flows between Round Lake and Lake Michigan in the town of Charlevoix. Narrow walkway parks line both sides of the 1/4-mile-long channel. Reach the north channel park by turning west on Pine River Road at the *Weathervane Terrace Inn*. This is just north of the drawbridge on US-31. Find the parking lot shortly past the restaurant. Passing boats can be viewed from the channel area or walk down the steps and out on the north breakwater. A small beach area is available.
GPS: 45°19.168'N; 85°15.525'W

FATHER CHARLEVOIX PARK: Dixon Street is the second road north of Charlevoix's drawbridge. Parking is limited to the streetside. At the end of the road is a small, grassy area that overlooks the lake and Charlevoix Breakwater. A boulder with a brass plate commemorates the voyage of Jesuit priest Pierre Francois-Xavier de Charlevoix who passed by in 1721. A metal stairway leads to the beach near the north breakwater. The small park has benches and is a beautiful spot for enjoying the sunset.
GPS: 45°19.244'N; 85°15.609'W

LAKE MICHIGAN PUBLIC WALK: A small, paved parking lot with a sign marks this park located in a residential neighborhood on Michigan Street. Michigan Street heads northeast where US-31 curves sharply east just north of the drawbridge in town. The park sits high above the water on a bluff. A path leads down to the sandy shore.
GPS: 45°19.547'N; 85°15.214'W

LITTLE TRAVERSE WHEELWAY: The Little Traverse Wheelway is an asphalt bicycle and pedestrian path connecting Charlevoix to Petoskey and Harbor Springs in Emmet County. The Charlevoix County section parallels US-31 and the Lake Michigan coast. Charlevoix's trail starts on Mt. McSauba Road, at the west end of Division Street. The following listings, except North Point and Mercer Road End, are along the route as well and have parking available.

MT. McSAUBA RECREATION AREA: Mt. McSauba provides a small dune hill for skiing in the winter and its parking lot acts as the trailhead for the path to the area's dunes and sandy beach. Combined with the adjoining North Point Park, there is a mile or more of beach. Some stones and rock will be found in the water and at the beach edge. The view includes the Charlevoix Breakwater and a steady stream of pleasure boats traveling to the channel between Lake Michigan and Round Lake. The cement plant west of town can be seen about 2.5 miles away. Park at the west end of Pleasant Street for beach access.
GPS: 45°20.198'N; 85°14.742'W

NORTH POINT PARK: An undeveloped preserve managed by Charlevoix Township, the park sits on a rocky point. North Point adjoins the Mt. McSauba Recreation Area creating a long stretch of shoreline for strolling and rock hunting. No facilities exist. Parking is limited to the road end or the small, streetside parking area near the west end of Cedar Street. Mt. McSauba has additional parking and better swimming. Watch for poison ivy along trails.
GPS: 45°20.388'N; 85°14.735'W

MERCER ROAD END: Mercer Road ends at the lake with a paved turnaround. There are no facilities at this rocky shore, just a view.
GPS: 45°20.344'N; 85°14.431'W

MDOT ROADSIDE PARK: A rather large park for a rest area, it features both wooded and grassy picnic areas. There is a nice view of Lake Michigan and part of the adjoining Little Traverse Bay. The shore is stony and the water here is shallow. Launching a canoe or kayak will require some wading but it is an easy carry from the parking lot. Big Rock Nuclear Plant, which is being dismantled, sits just to the west along the shore. The Little Traverse Wheelway runs along this section of highway.
GPS: 45°21.781'N; 85°10.408'W

NINE-MILE POINT BOAT LAUNCH: The MDNR boat launch is unusable for trailered boats due to current low lake levels. It is still a good put-in spot for kayaks.
GPS: 45°21.850'N; 85°10.210'W

ROADSIDE PARK: East of Nine-Mile Point, this unassuming park sits on a small bluff. Aside from picnic tables and grills, there are no facilities. A short, wooden stairway leads to the shore where rockhounds can hunt for Petoskey Stones. The Little Traverse Wheelway passes the park.
GPS: 45°22.274'N; 85°07.748'W

Below left: The high bluff at St. James Township Park looks out toward the islands to the north.

Far right: Gull Harbor Natural Area's rocky shore attracts shore birds.

Bottom: Jewell Gillespie Park provides plenty of sand and play equipment for the children. The small park is found at the south end of St. James.

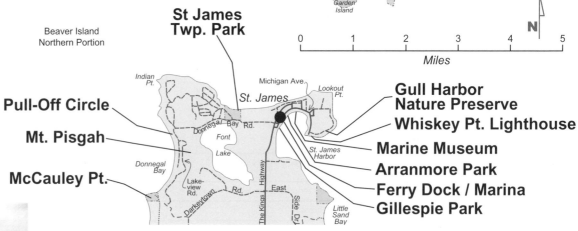

Beaver Island Northern Portion

St James Twp. Park

Gull Harbor Nature Preserve

Whiskey Pt. Lighthouse

Marine Museum

Arranmore Park

Ferry Dock / Marina

Gillespie Park

Pull-Off Circle

Mt. Pisgah

McCauley Pt.

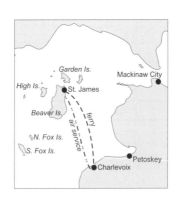

Charlevoix County

Beaver Island - North End and St. James

Name	Location	Entrance Fee	Parking	Modern Restrooms	Vault or Portable Toilet	Stair or Path to Shore	Swimming	Picnic Area	Drinking Water	Campground	Trailered Boat Launch	Kayak / Canoe	Marina	Fishing	Hiking	Biking	X-Country Skiing	Playground	Lighthouse	Beach Strolling	Sandy Beach	Stony or Rocky Shore	Dunes	Bluff	Wetland
Jewell F. Gillespie Park	St. James. South end of Michigan Ave.		●				●					●						●			●				
Ferry Dock	St. James. Michigan Ave. Downtown.		●	●																					
St. James Township - Beaver Island Marina	St. James. Michigan Ave. at Ferry Dock.		●	●					●				●												
Arranmore Park	St. James. On Michigan Ave., one block N of Ferry Dock.		●										●												
Marine Museum	St. James. Michigan Ave. on north side of harbor.		●																						
Whiskey Point (Beaver Island) Lighthouse	St. James. Follow Michigan Ave. around north side of harbor until it ends.		●						●										●			●			
Gull Harbor Nature Preserve	East of Whiskey Pt. on Gull Harbor Dr.		●												●	●				●		●			●
St. James Township Park	1 mile W of St. James on Donnegal Bay Rd.		●		●	●	●	●	●							●					●	●		●	
Pull-off Circle, Donnegal Bay	2.5 miles W of St. James. Donnegal Bay Rd. to Indian Woods Rd.		●			●																●	●		
Mt. Pisgah	2.5 miles W of St. James. Donnegal Bay Rd. to Lakeview Rd.		●												●								●		
McCauley Point	3.5 miles W of St. James. Donnegal Bay Rd. to Lakeview Rd.					●									●							●			

St. James, Beaver Island's only town, has a cozy harbor and a definite maritime feel. To its west lie dunes and the island's highest points. (See page 154 for a map of the entire island).

JEWELL F. GILLESPIE PARK: This small park on St. James Harbor has a sandy beach and plenty of play equipment. It has a view of the harbor and the lighthouse across the way.
GPS: 45°44.843'N; 85°31.261'W

FERRY DOCK: The main dock is the arrival and departure location for the ferry service between Beaver Island and Charlevoix. See page 149 for ferry information.
GPS: 45°44.843'N; 85°30.839'W

ST. JAMES TOWNSHIP - BEAVER ISLAND MARINA: The public marina, locally known as the "yacht dock," is next to the ferry dock. Thirty-four transient slips.
Telephone: (231) 448-2252
GPS: 45°44.850'N; 85°31.000'W

ARRANMORE PARK: Arranmore is a small, grassy, open space on the harbor a block north of the ferry dock. It provides unobstructed views of the harbor. Street parking.
GPS: 45°45.017'N; 85°30.839'W

MARINE MUSEUM: This small museum, housed in an old fish net shed, contains memorabilia from the days when St. James Harbor bustled with fishing fleets and commercial activity. Features include shipwreck stories, tales of rescue, shipbuilding and information about the islands of the Beaver Archipelago. Operated by the Beaver Island Historical Society.

WHISKEY POINT (BEAVER ISLAND) LIGHTHOUSE: The Beaver Island Light and a stone wall memorial to Beaver Islanders who died on the Great Lakes stand at the north entrance to the harbor near the old Coast Guard Station. The name Whiskey Point resulted from a popular item of purchase at the location's early trading post. The lighthouse was built in 1856. The memorial plaque reflects some of the island's social history. The surnames are often repeated and many are of Irish origin representing generations of the island's few families. The shore at this point is stony and not good for swimming.
GPS: 45°44.545'N; 85°30.562'W

GULL HARBOR NATURE PRESERVE: The preserve sits just outside the harbor opening east of Whiskey Point. It is a short drive or bicycle ride from St. James. The road turns to gravel past the lighthouse and soon enters the preserve. This is the only portion of Beaver Island that has exposed bedrock and the shore is stone and rock. Wildflowers, birds and small mammals are the primary inhabitants. Away from the shore is a cedar swamp. A short hiking trail is also here.
GPS: 45°44.907'N; 85°30.076'W

ST. JAMES TOWNSHIP PARK: One of two designated public campgrounds on the island, the park sits high upon a bluff overlooking several islands to the north. The shore is a mix of sand and gravel. The lake bottom is shallow and some wading is required to get to deepwater. Picnic tables are available. Facilities are rustic. Fee for camping.
GPS: 45°44.907'N; 85°32.284'W

PULL-OFF CIRCLE, DONNEGAL BAY: Among the St. James subdivided lands is a pull-off near the end of Donnegal Bay Road. A short path leads over a very small dune to the shore. The shore here is sandy with long grass and is littered with boulders and stone.
GPS: 45°45.107'N; 85°33.992'W

MT. PISGAH: Located in the Port St. James Association, Mt. Pisgah is a high dune with an elevation of 730 feet, 150 feet above Lake Michigan's level. The trail up is mostly through loose dune sand. This is a fine place for sunset views. Parking is limited; there is room for two cars to park in a primitively kept space. The Association has graciously allowed public-use in the past. Please respect their rules.
GPS: 45°44.303'N; 85°33.547'W

McCAULEY POINT: The State of Michigan owns much of the McCauley Point area. Access is difficult. A sign at the south end of the Port St. James Association guides you to the general location. A wooded path leads from the road to the point through part of the Association. Check to see about current policy for public use of the trail. The shore here is stony with some sand and is less than ideal for swimming. High Island lies offshore 4 miles to the west. There is not a good place to park.
GPS: 45°43.711'N; 85°34.127'W

Above: Beaver Head Lighthouse, at the south end of the island.

Below: One of the island's most pleasant places is Little Sand Bay Nature Preserve.

Opposite page: A few larger boulders outcrop from the sand and dunes of Cable Bay.

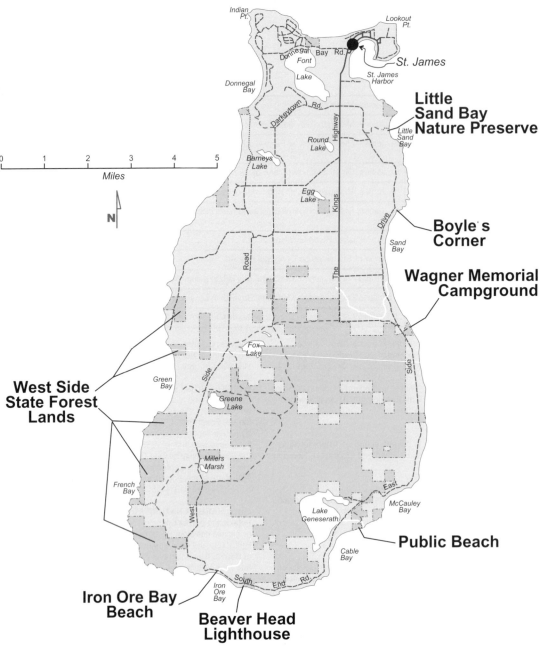

Little Sand Bay Nature Preserve

Boyle's Corner

Wagner Memorial Campground

West Side State Forest Lands

Public Beach

Iron Ore Bay Beach

Beaver Head Lighthouse

Beaver Island South of St. James

Name	Location	Entrance Fee	Parking	Modern Restrooms	Vault or Portable Toilet	Stair or Path to Shore	Swimming	Picnic Area	Drinking Water	Campground	Trailered Boat Launch	Kayak / Canoe	Marina	Fishing	Hiking	Biking	X-Country Skiing	Playground	Lighthouse	Beach Strolling	Sandy Beach	Stony or Rocky Shore	Dunes	Bluff	Wetland
Little Sand Bay Nature Preserve	2 miles S of St. James. East Side Drive. Look for sign just past Welke Airport.		●			●	●							●	●					●	●	●			●
Boyle's Corner	4 miles S of St. James. Access from East Side Drive.						●														●	●			
Wagner Memorial Campground	7 miles S of St. James on East Side Drive.		●		●		●	●	●	●	●	●		●	●	●					●	●			
Public Beach at Cable's Bay	10 miles S of St. James. Look for sign on East Side Drive.		●			●	●	●						●	●					●	●	●	●		
Beaver Head Lighthouse	South end of Beaver Island.		●			●	●							●	●	●			●		●	●		●	
Iron Ore Bay Beach	0.7 miles W of Beaver Head Lighthouse.		●		●							●		●							●				
West Side State Forest Lands	Southwest Beaver Island.					●	●							●	●	●				●	●	●	●	●	

Heading south from St. James, the east shore features a few cottages and a slow pace. The Island's best beaches are along Little Sand, Cable and Iron Ore Bays.

LITTLE SAND BAY NATURE PRESERVE: A project of the Little Traverse Conservancy, the preserve has a 1000-foot trail leading through a cedar swamp to 1300 feet of undeveloped lakeshore. A small, spring-fed creek winds through the trees on its way to the lake. The beach is sand with some stone and an occasional boulder. The preserve encompasses 60 acres, including some upland hardwoods. It is an easy, 3-mile bicycle ride from St. James. The bay's shape isolates the preserve from the rest of the shoreline.
 GPS: 45°43.056'N; 85°30.706'W (turnoff at East Side Dr.),
 45°43.077'N; 85°30.413'W (parking area)

BOYLE'S CORNER: Boyle's Corner is a road end with several seasonal residences and a small creek. The beach is mostly sand with some stone concentrated in one area. There are no facilities.
 GPS: 45°41.665'N; 85°29.998'W

WAGNER MEMORIAL CAMPGROUND: This rustic campground and park has a beach made of sand with a mix of small stone. Swimming is good here. There is a picnic area. Hand-carried watercraft can be easily launched at this site. A manual water pump is available. A mix of jack pine and oak trees forest the area. Much state forest lands lies to the west of the campground across from East Side Drive. From here, many miles of trail can take the hiker to Lake Geneserath or the Beaver Head Lighthouse, well to the island's south. There is a fee for camping. *Note: older maps refer to this site as a state forest campground.*
 GPS: 45°39.454'N; 85°29.692'W

PUBLIC BEACH AT CABLE'S BAY: From East Side Drive, look for a blue, wooden sign marking the turn to the parking area. The access road is a 0.2-mile-long two-track in decent condition. It ends at a turn-around with a small, wooded picnic area. A wooden footbridge across Cable's Creek begins a 0.25-mile trail through the woods and over small dunes to the beach. The shore varies from fine sand to a sand and rock mix. This pleasant beach requires some effort to reach and never has a crowd.
 GPS: 45°35.934'N; 85°31.318'W (turnoff at East Side Dr.),
 45°35.577'N; 85°31.184'W (beach)

BEAVER HEAD LIGHTHOUSE: The restored 150-year-old Beaver Head Lighthouse is owned by the Charlevoix School District. The light tower is open to the public. Inquire locally for the schedule. The house sits on a bluff, looking towards the south. The Fox Islands are visible on clear days. A stairway leads to the beach below. The shore beach is sand but the lake bottom is rocky. While some spots might be swimmable, a better choice is Iron Ore Bay a short distance to the west.

The Beaver Island Nature Trail system has a trailhead here. There is a 1.5 mile lighthouse loop and the more ambitious trails to Lake Geneserath (4.5 miles) and to the Wagner Memorial Campground (9.5 miles).
 GPS: 45°34.541'N; 85°34.384'W

IRON ORE BAY BEACH: A long way from St. James, mostly via gravel roads, is the island's best swimming beach. Its name does not befit this beach of pure sand. The name resulted from the nearby wreck of an iron ore ship. Following the disaster, rust-colored water would drift into the bay. A curious piece of rusted equipment still sits on the beach. The public shore is not large but it is a quiet place to relax. A few summer residences lie on either side, but the distance from St. James means that it is seldom crowded. A small stream bisects the beach, its outlet periodically shifts location depending upon winds and wave action. On site are a couple of picnic tables and a vault toilet.
 GPS: 45°34.768'N; 85°35.051'W

WEST SIDE STATE FOREST LANDS: The west side of Beaver Island has several blocks of state forest land. For the most part, these lands are managed naturally and the primary use is hunting. Access can be difficult for a couple of reasons. In some places, no public access road or easement exists across adjoining private land. In others, a good road into the shore area does not exist. Accessing the shore in this area is a challenge left for the serious hiker with a compass and a map. Maps of this area are poor, often showing old two-tracks that have long been obliterated by fallen trees. The maps can provide a start for the trekker or bicyclist. Be wary, most map information is old and time has made them unreliable.

Petoskey Stones

During the Devonian Period, some 350 million years ago, what is now Michigan existed under the sea in a warm climate near the earth's equator. Coral colonized in the shallow sea. In time, calcite and other minerals fossilized the coral remains, forming a rock representation of their likeness. What is now the Little Traverse Bay area, contained this limestone formation and during the Pleistocene Period, about 2 million years ago, glaciers wrestled away stone from the bedrock and distributed it to a wider area. One type of coral fossil, the Petoskey Stone, derived its named from the Little Traverse Bay town of Petoskey, itself an adaptation of an early resident's name, Odawa Indian Chief Petosegay.

Today, along the Lake Michigan shore from Benzie to Emmet Counties, rockhounds collect Petoskey Stones. Each year ice and waves free a new crop of stone from hiding. Wave action tumbles the stones, rounding and smoothing them in the beach sand. Dry stones are difficult to spot, looking like many of the other gray beach stones. The coral design stands out in the water, making them easier to find. A few hunters cut and polish their stones. Most people are happy just to find a good quality Petoskey to take home. Many local jewelry and gift stores sell polished Petoskey Stones should you strike out.

From the top, left to right:
- Bucket in hand, a couple search a Leelanau County shore, for stones.
- This youngster's collection of fossilized coral includes a Petoskey in the lower left of her hands along with several colony coral specimens.
- The hexagonal design makes for instant recognition of the Petoskey Stone which is much easier to spot if wet (left) than when dry (right).

Because calcite is relatively soft, hand polishing of the stone is practical. Use a progression of wet sand paper from 220 to 600 grit followed by a polishing powder. Make sure that any deep grooves have been removed before going to the next step and rinse in clean water regularly as you sand. If you are too impatient to polish, put your stones and some water in a clear glass jar. The coral design will jump out.

A number of other fossil types lie in the same rock formations along these shores. Two examples are Favosites, a honeycomb colony coral and Halysites, a coral arranged in chains . Brachiopod, Bryozoan and Crinoid fossils also exist in the area. A visit to the educational center at Thorne-Swift Nature Preserve (see p.163) near Harbor Springs in Emmet County provides a quick overview of the region's fossils.

Emmet County

On its north end, Emmet County borders the Straits of Mackinac, which divides Michigan's two peninsulas. Its strategic location attracted early interest from European explorers and traders. Today, you can still feel the historic confluence of the native and white cultures at places like Mackinaw City or Middle Village.

In more modern times, the summer climate became the area's draw. Before air-conditioning, cool breezes attracted the well-to-do from Chicago and places south. Trains brought many visitors into Petoskey. Steamers brought travelers to the dock at Harbor Springs. Cottage communities with stately summer homes grew in and around each of these towns. Take a drive along the waterfront on the east side of Harbor Springs or visit Bayview on the northeast side of Petoskey to get a glimpse of the historic summer neighborhoods.

Petoskey has a vibrant downtown with several blocks of specialty shops, bistros and galleries. A pedestrian tunnel connects the shopping area with Bayfront Park, one of the nicest public developments along the coast. Here, you can fish, boat, walk, picnic or visit the town's museum.

North of Petoskey, US-31 takes an inland route towards Mackinaw City while M-119 begins its shoreline journey to Harbor Springs and then on to Cross Village. Along M-119, Petoskey State Park offers a big, sandy beach and small dunes. Its campground affords inexpensive lodging for this area but it fills fast and reservations are needed in the summer. Zorn Park in Harbor Springs has a good old-fashioned swimming beach with a diving platform.

North of Harbor Springs, M-119 turns into a tree-covered, narrow scenic road. Thorn-Swift Preserve has beautiful scenery plus it offers an educational look at coastal dunes and wetlands. Farther north, find the wonderful, free beaches at Middle Village, Readmond Township Park or along Sturgeon Bay.

Wilderness State Park commands the northwest portion of the county. Its 8200 acres encompass woods, wetlands, islands and many miles of shore, plus nearly every recreational pursuit imaginable. To its east lies the tip of the mitt, Mackinaw City and the Mackinac Bridge, the gateway to the Upper Peninsula.

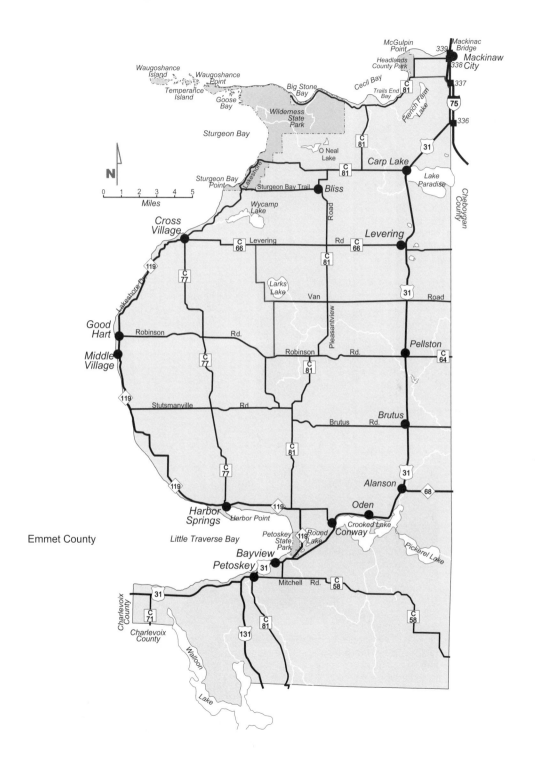

Emmet County

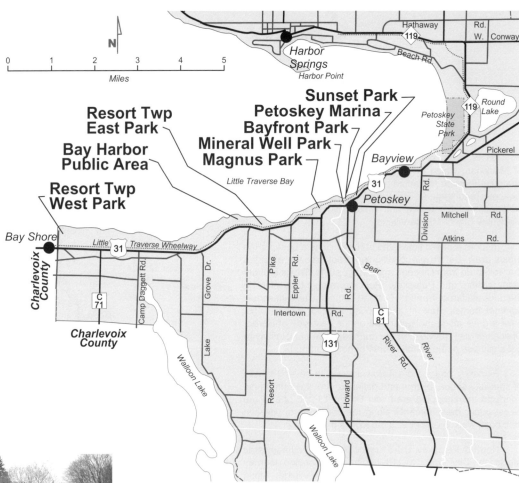

Sunset Park
Petoskey Marina
Bayfront Park
Mineral Well Park
Magnus Park

Resort Twp
East Park

Bay Harbor
Public Area

Resort Twp
West Park

Above left: The Petoskey Harbor Light peeks through the posts of Bayview Park's clock tower.

Left: Bear River tumbles through Mineral Springs and Bayfront Parks at the end of its journey to Little Traverse Bay.

Opposite page: Little Traverse Bay from the bluff at Sunset Park.

Emmet County

Bay Harbor and Petoskey

Name	Location	Entrance Fee	Parking	Modern Restrooms	Vault or Portable Toilet	Stair or Path to Shore	Swimming	Picnic Area	Drinking Water	Campground	Trailered Boat Launch	Kayak / Canoe	Marina	Fishing	Hiking	Biking	X-Country Skiing	Playground	Lighthouse	Beach Strolling	Sandy Beach	Stony or Rocky Shore	Dunes	Bluff	Wetland
Resort Township West Park	Bay Shore. Townline Road just N of US-31.		●		●	●		●								●						●			
Bay Harbor Public Area	Bay Harbor. 3.5 miles W of Petoskey on US-31.		●	●																					
Resort Township East Park	Bay Harbor. 3 miles W of Petoskey on US-31 W of Resort Pike.		●	●				●	●			●			●	●						●		●	
Magnus Park	Petoskey. West end of W Lake St.		●	●				●	●	●		●						●				●			
Mineral Well Park	Petoskey. E Lake St. one block W of US-31.		●	●				●	●					●	●	●									
Bayfront Park	Petoskey. E Lake St. one block W of US-31.		●	●			●	●	●		●	●	●	●	●	●					●	●		●	
Petoskey Marina	Petoskey, in Bayfront Park.		●	●				●	●		●		●												
Sunset Park	Petoskey. US-31 near Lewis St.		●			●		●																	●	

A string of elegant resort communities, anchored by Petoskey, line the southern shore of Little Traverse Bay. Visit the modern at Bay Harbor and finish by traveling through more traditional Bayview. For the coast user, Petoskey's combined waterfront parks are the highlight.

RESORT TOWNSHIP WEST PARK: West Park is tucked between the Bay Harbor development on its east and Bay Shore residences to its west. Find the parking lot and vault toilet off Townline Rd. near US-31. From here, a long trail leads through the woods and a field to the shore. A picnic shelter (no grills) is at the lake. There is about 100 feet of stone and rock shore making for poor swimming or sunbathing.
GPS: 45°21.564'N; 85°05.776'W

BAY HARBOR PUBLIC AREA: Bay Harbor was created in the 1990's on the site of an abandoned cement plant and quarry. It is an upscale resort and housing complex, located along several miles of lakefront. Much of it is a gated community. The public portion includes a small shopping area, hotel and viewing platform.

RESORT TOWNSHIP EAST PARK: East Park is a new park developed in unison with the reclamation of the old cement plant and quarry. The entrance is found off US-31 just west of Resort Pike Road. The park's pavilion sits on a high bluff looking north onto Little Traverse Bay. Several stairways lead down to the shore. Asphalt pathways head into the hardwood forest from the shore area. The lower drive leads to benches and a short path along the rocky shoreline. The rock and stone limit swimming. The Little Traverse Wheelway connects to the park, making this a good trailhead for bicyclists (see p.159, 161).
GPS: 45°22.015'N; 85°00.040'W

MAGNUS PARK: Magnus Park, operated by the City of Petoskey, is located on Little Traverse Bay in the shadows of the city's hospital. The campground composes most of the park. There is a fee for camping. Picnic and play areas are available. The shore is stone and rock making it poor for swimming.
GPS: 45°22.433'N; 84°58.345'W

MINERAL WELL PARK: Mineral Well Park lies along the Bear River's last run before emptying into Little Traverse Bay. The stream gradient is steep during the last mile and the bottom is rocky, causing the river to churn through most of this stretch. The small dam at Lake Street temporarily pools the water, then it spills over and through a final rapids into Petoskey's harbor at adjoining Bayfront Park. Fishing for salmon and trout is popular during spring and fall runs.

A columned pavilion covers the mineral well. Trails head upstream from this developed area, following the stream through woods and wildflowers. Use of the paths is minimal. Normally you will see only an occasional walker, jogger or bicyclist. A modern public restroom is found at the rear (harbor side) of the fire station near the footbridge.

BAYFRONT PARK: Bayfront Park received a face-lift in the 1990's making it the cornerstone of the Petoskey waterfront. Vehicles enter via Lake Street. Pedestrians can enter from Petoskey's downtown "Gas Light" shopping district through a tunnel underneath US-31, by stairway from Sunset

Park or by the walkway and bridge from Mineral Well Park. Bicyclists can ride through it on the Little Traverse Wheelway.

The park incorporates many elements. The town's museum is in the stylishly remodeled, old train station. The marina and harbor boat ramp are here. A softball field often hosts tournaments. Access the harbor's breakwater from the park's west end. Additional vehicle access and parking are found by the breakwater as well. A small, sandy swimming area is located near the breakwater entrance, but there are better places on the bay to swim. In-line skating, fishing, walking, jogging and picnicking are other common pursuits in this pretty city park. There is a fee for using the boat ramp.
GPS: 45°22.553'N; 84°57.612'W

PETOSKEY MARINA: Located in Bayfront Park, the public marina provides seasonal and transient boat mooring for pleasure craft. Viewing yachts is popular with tourists at this park.
Telephone: (231) 347-6691
GPS: 45°22.867'N; 84°57.667'W

SUNSET PARK: Sunset Park sits atop the bluff overlooking Little Traverse Bay, just east of downtown. A gazebo, picnic tables and benches provide a nice viewing area in the grassy park. Telescopes give close-up views of Harbor Springs and other points of interest across the bay. An interpretive display tells of the area's geology, once a coral reef (see p.156). A tall, wooden staircase leads down to Bayfront Park.
GPS: 45°22.756'N; 84°57.104'W

Bluff St. Overlook
Zorn Park Beach
Harbor Springs Marina
Ford Park Launch
Zoll St. Beach
Petoskey State Park
Spring Lake Park
Little Traverse Wheelway Shelter

Above: The shoreline is in view along much of the Little Traverse Wheelway. A shelter, found near Bayview, overlooks Little Traverse Bay.

Below left: Zorn Beach in Harbor Springs has a diving platform at its sandy, harbor location.

Below right: Petoskey State Park's beach draws large crowds but has plenty of space.

Emmet County

Petoskey State Park and Harbor Springs

Facilities | **Environment**

Name	Location	Entrance Fee	Parking	Modern Restrooms	Vault or Portable Toilet	Stair or Path to Shore	Swimming	Picnic Area	Drinking Water	Campground	Trailered Boat Launch	Kayak / Canoe	Marina	Fishing	Hiking	Biking	X-Country Skiing	Playground	Lighthouse	Beach Strolling	Sandy Beach	Stony or Rocky Shore	Dunes	Bluff	Wetland
Little Traverse Wheelway Shelter	Petoskey. 2 blocks N of US-31 on Rice St. to Shire Ave.		●													●						●			
Spring Lake Park	2 miles W of Petoskey. M-119 just N of US-31.		●	●				●	●						●	●	●								●
Petoskey State Park	3 miles NE of Petoskey. M-119, 1.5 miles N of US-31.	●	●	●			●	●	●	●		●			●	●	●			●	●		●		
Zoll Street Beach	Harbor Springs. Zorn St. at Beach St.		●				●	●				●									●				
Ford Park Launch	Harbor Springs. E Bay St.		●	●				●	●		●	●													
Harbor Springs Marina	Harbor Springs. 250 E Bay St.		●	●				●	●			●	●												
Zorn Park Beach	Harbor Springs. W Bay St.		●	●			●	●	●												●				
Bluff Street Overlook	Harbor Springs. From M-119, N on State St. then E on Bluff St.																							●	

Small dunes and a sandy shore characterize Petoskey State Park. The small town of Harbor Springs has a distinctive, summer resort atmosphere.

LITTLE TRAVERSE WHEELWAY SHELTER: The Little Traverse Wheelway is a bike path system around Little Traverse Bay. The total distance is about 28 miles traveling from Charlevoix through Petoskey to Harbor Springs. Parts of the trail are on US-31 and M-119 road shoulder, but much of the route is along its own, separate, asphalt lane. At this location, it follows an abandoned rail route and a gazebo overlooks the bay. The shore is rocky and weedy here making it a favorite place for waterfowl such as duck and heron. The shelter is tucked behind Glen's Market, located along US-31 a block or so west of the traffic signal at M-119. There is plenty of parking here making it a good place to start a day's ride.
GPS: 45°25.512'N; 84°55.127'W

SPRING LAKE PARK: Spring Lake sits less than 0.5 mile from Little Traverse Bay, yet it is part of the Lake Huron watershed. The lake is the headwaters for the Inland Waterway, a system of lakes and streams that flow to Cheboygan some 30 miles by crow flight to the northeast. The Odawas, a native tribe to the area, used the route for travel between Lakes Michigan and Huron. Later, French traders canoed it to trade with the Odawas. The township park has a short, interpretive nature walk around the Spring Lake wetland. The modern bathrooms and picnic gazebo are new and nicely done. The North Country Trail cuts through the park on its long path from New York State to North Dakota. The Little Traverse Wheelway can be accessed across M-119. Part of the park area is barrier-free.
GPS: 45°23.610'N; 84°54.396'W

PETOSKEY STATE PARK: Petoskey State Park has a popular campground and a sandy beach with concession and changehouse. Attendance is high on sunny, summer days but the spacious beach area handles it well. The park sits on the east end of Little Traverse Bay. It gets the full force of the prevailing west wind which builds and funnels waves to the park's shore. This makes for fun swimming during the summer months. Warmer surface water normally gets pushed to the beach by the wind as well. Usually the water here is a bit warmer than at a typical northern Lake Michigan beach. A few stones are intermixed with the sand. The Little Traverse Wheelway connects the park with Petoskey and Harbor Springs. The small campground fills fast. Make reservations for summer dates well in advance.
Telephone: (231) 347-2311
Web: www.michigan.gov/dnr
GPS: 45°24.495'N; 84°54.138'W

ZOLL STREET BEACH: This is a small park used for swimming and as a launch for hand-carried craft. It sits on a normally calm, smaller bay on the north side of Little Traverse Bay. The beach is only about 50 feet wide but it is a good place to relax and view the boat traffic around the Harbor Springs harbor. Parking is limited and will often fill during prime times. Just to the east along Beach Drive are two, long blocks of Victorian-style summer homes.
GPS: 45°24.495'N; 84°58.667'W

FORD PARK LAUNCH: Ford Park has a picnic area in addition to a boat ramp. Benches can be found by the waterfront. The Harbor Springs Historical Society maintains a small museum on site. Parking is available for cars with boat trailers.
GPS: 45°25.796'N; 84°58.977'W

HARBOR SPRINGS MARINA: The Harbor Springs Marina is primarily a docking facility for boats but it has public restrooms, a telephone and flower gardens. City tennis courts border its west side. A 2-hour dock is available for short-duration boat visits to the town. There is a fee for overnight mooring.
Telephone: (231) 526-5355
GPS: 45°25.633'N; 84°59.250'W

ZORN PARK BEACH: Zorn Park has a sandy beach with a large raft used for diving. Lifeguards work the prime season. Yachts and pretty homes surround the park. A grassy area across Bay Street has picnic tables and an artesian well. The stone restroom building has an outdoor shower. Downtown shopping is about a block away.
GPS: 45°25.736'N; 84°59.388'W

BLUFF STREET OVERLOOK: Much of the Harbor Springs residential area is on the bluff overlooking the harbor. Bluff Street parallels the edge of this embankment. From the downtown area, follow M-119 as it begins to head north towards Cross Village. M-119 climbs up the bluff. Near the top, turn north on State Street then take a quick right onto Bluff Street. A wooden observation platform provides an awesome overlook of the town, the harbor and Little Traverse Bay. Parking is limited to that available on side streets.

Above: A few boulders add to the scenery at Readmond Township Beach but do not detract from great swimming.

Below: An old church and cemetery sit in front of the beach at Middle Village.

Opposite page: A dune interpretation overlook south of the beach at Thorne-Swift Nature Preserve.

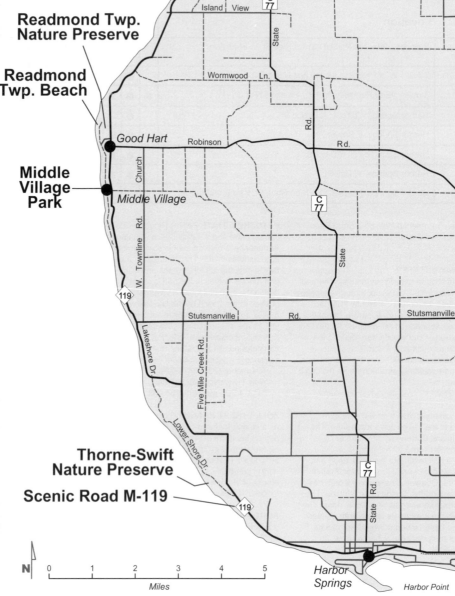

Name	Location	Entrance Fee	Parking	Modern Restrooms	Vault or Portable Toilet	Stair or Path to Shore	Swimming	Picnic Area	Drinking Water	Campground	Trailered Boat Launch	Kayak / Canoe	Marina	Fishing	Hiking	Biking	X-Country Skiing	Playground	Lighthouse	Beach Strolling	Sandy Beach	Stony or Rocky Shore	Dunes	Bluff	Wetland
M-119 Scenic Drive	Harbor Springs to Cross Village.															●								●	
Thorne-Swift Nature Preserve	3.5 miles NW of Harbor Springs. On Lower Shore Drive off M-119.	●	●	●		●		●							●						●	●	●		●
Middle Village Beach	One mile S of Good Hart on Lampkin Rd.		●			●	●														●				
Readmond Township Beach	0.8 miles N of Good Hart on N. Lampkin Rd.		●			●		●	●			●									●	●			
Readmond Township Nature Preserve	0.8 miles N of Good Hart on N. Lampkin Rd.		●												●									●	
Cross Village Township Park	Cross Village. From M-119, turn on Chippewa Drive then Waterfront Road.		●			●		●	●		●	●									●	●			

The "Tunnel of Trees," a slow drive between Harbor Springs and Cross Village, is worth getting off-the-beaten track.

M-119 SCENIC DRIVE: This Michigan scenic highway follows the shoreline for 24 miles along high bluffs. It is purposely narrow, with minimal traffic and a slow speed limit. It winds through hardwood forests, often giving the feeling of being in a leafy tunnel. It provides occasional views of the lake, but has few turnouts to pull off. It is a favorite road for bicyclists, so be careful of their presence.

THORNE-SWIFT NATURE PRESERVE: Thorne-Swift Preserve combines nature study with a short, varied shoreline. The area includes a nature center with displays about local flora, fauna and geology. There are 1.5 miles of interpretive trail, partly on a boardwalk through a coastal wetland. An observation deck provides a spectacular view of Lake Michigan and the small dunes of the preserve. The beach is rocky. Parts of the shore have restricted access. Swimming is allowed, but the amount of rock makes this unappealing for most people. Thorne-Swift is owned by the Nature Conservancy and operated by West Traverse Township. Entrance fee is $3.
   Telephone: (231) 526-6401

MIDDLE VILLAGE BEACH: Behind the old St. Ignatius Mission Church and Cemetery lies Middle Village Park Beach. A hard to find sandy beach, it is easiest to reach by turning west on Lampkin Road in Good Hart. Lampkin swings south along the lakeshore. About one-mile down, the white, wood-sided church appears with the park sign to its north. A new asphalt path and wooden stairway takes you through the vegetation from the parking area to the beach. Beaver Island lies some 20 miles from shore. This is an excellent, low-key stop.
   GPS: 45°33.116'N; 85°06.924'W

READMOND TOWNSHIP BEACH: A small park off-the-beaten path, Readmond has a great sandy beach with a few boulders accenting the shoreline. Picnic tables, charcoal grills and a small playground round-out the park. Its pretty shore has been developed in a tasteful way. From Lakeshore Drive (M-119), turn west at Good Hart onto Lampkin Drive. Travel 0.2 miles then turn north on North Lampkin Drive. Travel 0.7 miles to the park. Small signs indicate the turns.
   GPS: 45°34.441'N; 85°07.126'W

READMOND TOWNSHIP NATURE PRESERVE: Adjacent to the Readmond Township Beach, this area features short hiking paths along the hardwood-covered bluff near the beach. Its ample parking lot also serves as overflow for the beach park, a short walk away.

CROSS VILLAGE TOWNSHIP PARK: The park has a sandy beach with some stone and rock occasionally in the mix. A rickety boat ramp is adequate for launching small boats. A beach volleyball court is available as well. It is popular on summer days, but the area has ample parking.
   GPS: 45°38.709'N; 85°02.406'W

Left: Looking northeast from Sturgeon Bay Point

Below left: A wind surfer takes advantage of the steady breeze of Sturgeon Bay on a summer afternoon.

Opposite page: Miles of sandy, public beach line Sturgeon Bay.

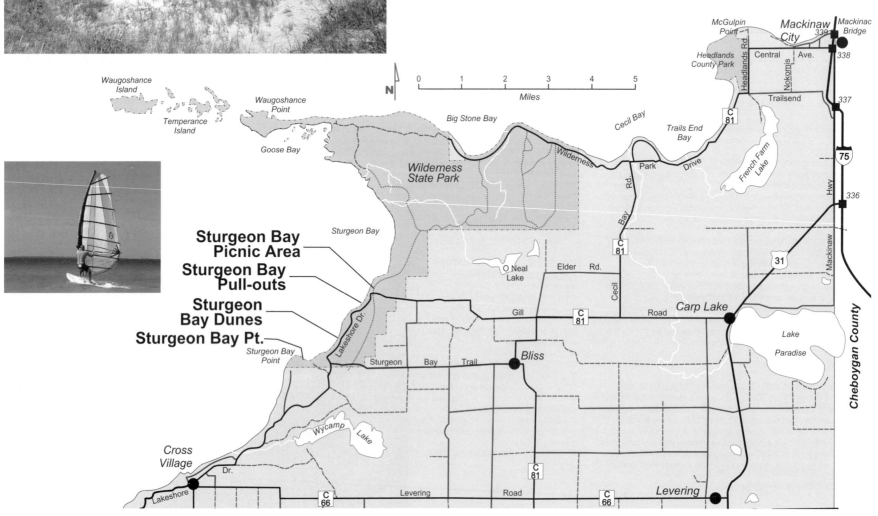

Sturgeon Bay Picnic Area

Sturgeon Bay Pull-outs

Sturgeon Bay Dunes

Sturgeon Bay Pt.

Name	Location	Entrance Fee	Parking	Modern Restrooms	Vault or Portable Toilet	Stair or Path to Shore	Swimming	Picnic Area	Drinking Water	Campground	Trailered Boat Launch	Kayak / Canoe	Marina	Fishing	Hiking	Biking	X-Country Skiing	Playground	Lighthouse	Beach Strolling	Sandy Beach	Stony or Rocky Shore	Dunes	Bluff	Wetland
Sturgeon Bay Point	4.5 miles NE of Cross Village. Take Lakeshore Dr. (see listing below)		●			●	●					●								●	●				
Wilderness State Park (south)	6 miles NE of Cross Village along Lakeshore Dr.	●	●		●	●	●	●	●			●			●					●	●		●		
Sturgeon Bay Dunes	5.5 miles NE of Cross Village along Lakeshore Dr.		●			●	●													●	●		●		
Sturgeon Bay Road Pull-offs	6 miles NE of Cross Village along Lakeshore Dr.					●	●													●	●	●	●		
Sturgeon Bay Picnic Area	6.5 miles NE of Cross Village. Lakeshore Dr. at Lakeview Rd.	●	●		●	●	●	●	●			●			●					●	●	●	●		

Sandy beach and small dunes line much of Sturgeon Bay. Excellent swimming and miles of public shoreline make this a popular destination for those who know how to find it.

STURGEON BAY POINT: Isolated just south of the Sturgeon Bay Dunes area lies the south shore of the bay. A two-track road leads through the woods to a parking turn-around. This unmarked road is approximately 0.2 miles south of Sturgeon Bay Trail Road. Though a two-track, it is hard packed and usable by automobiles. A nicely shaded parking spot in the woods has a short trail to this outstanding, sandy beach.

    GPS: 45°40.822'N; 84°59.868'W (site), 45°40.557'N; 84°58.409'W (intersection of M-119)

WILDERNESS STATE PARK: This park has miles of shoreline on Lake Michigan and several islands and bays near Waugoshance Point. The shore provides excellent swimming, great waterfowl habitat, fine fishing and camping. Away from the shore, the park has forest, wetlands and plenty of trails. The local road system separates the park into two portions. The primary park area, which includes the campground, Waugoshance Point and Cecil Bay, is found to the north (see p.166). To the south, you will find undeveloped sandy beach on Sturgeon Bay, as listed below.

    Telephone: (231) 436-5381
    Web: www.michigan.gov/dnr

STURGEON BAY DUNES: Small dunes line about 2 miles of Lakeshore Drive. Two small parking areas are found on the west side of the road. During sunny, summer days, cars will line each road shoulder as well. This is an excellent sandy beach with plenty of room to spread. Windsurfers, beach strollers, tanners and swimmers favor this spot.

    GPS: Parking sites at 45°40.965'N; 84°58.462'W and 45°41.142'N; 84°58.174'W

STURGEON BAY ROAD PULL-OFFS: North of the open dunes, the bay's bottom becomes stony and the dry shore remains sandy. Along Lakeshore Drive are a half-dozen road shoulder pull-offs. Each is

unmarked, undeveloped and has been created through years of use. Parking space is limited to one or two cars. A short path leads through the woods to the shore. This is very popular during summer sunny days.

    GPS: Pull-offs found between 45°41.704'N; 84°57.765'W and 45°41.963'N; 84°57.308'W

STURGEON BAY PICNIC AREA: This is the largest parking area along the popular Sturgeon Bay beach. It is essentially an undeveloped area with limited picnic tables and a vault toilet. Its hand-operated pump has the only drinking water available along this stretch of beach. Miles of state-owned beach lie to both the north and south along this shore. You will find both sandy and stony areas. The parking area also provides access to the multi-state North Country Trail which connects to several trails within Wilderness State Park. Michigan State Motor Vehicle Permit required.

    GPS: 45°42.148'N; 84°57.209'W,

Right: The main beach at Wilderness State Park lies on Big Stone Bay. Despite the bay's name, the naturally kept beach is mostly sand.

Opposite page: The shore on the north side of Waugoshance Point is a sand and stone mix, perfect for Piping Plover nesting.

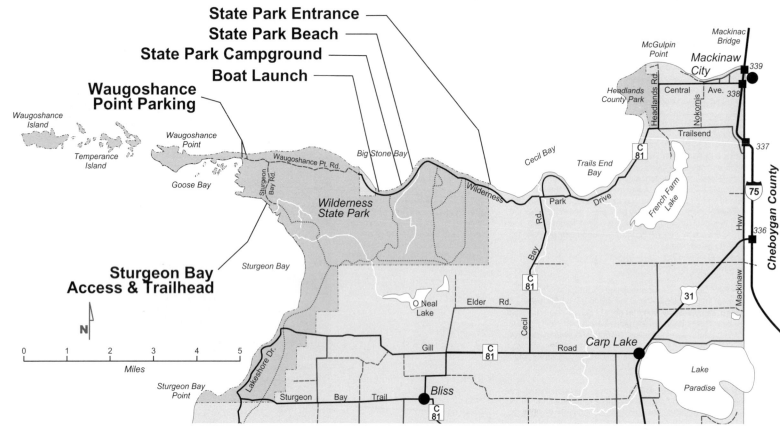

State Park Entrance
State Park Beach
State Park Campground
Boat Launch
Waugoshance Point Parking
Sturgeon Bay Access & Trailhead

Waugoshance Island

Temperance Island

Waugoshance Point

Goose Bay

Sturgeon Bay Rd.

Waugoshance Pt. Rd.

Big Stone Bay

Wilderness State Park

Sturgeon Bay

Sturgeon Bay Point

Lakeshore Dr.

Sturgeon Bay Trail

Wilderness

Cecil Bay

Park

Drive

Rd.

Bay

Cecil

O Neal Lake

Elder Rd.

Gill Road

Bliss

C 81

C 81

C 81

Carp Lake

McGulpin Point

Mackinac Bridge

Mackinaw City

Headlands County Park

Headlands Rd.

Central Ave.

Nokomis

Trailsend

Trails End Bay

French Farm Lake

C 81

Hwy

75

31

Mackinaw

Lake Paradise

Cheboygan County

339
338
337
336

N

0   1   2   3   4   5
Miles

Name	Location	Entrance Fee	Parking	Modern Restrooms	Vault or Portable Toilet	Stair or Path to Shore	Swimming	Picnic Area	Drinking Water	Campground	Trailered Boat Launch	Kayak / Canoe	Marina	Fishing	Hiking	Biking	X-Country Skiing	Playground	Lighthouse	Beach Strolling	Sandy Beach	Stony or Rocky Shore	Dunes	Bluff	Wetland
Wilderness State Park (North)	8 miles W of Mackinaw City on Wilderness Park Rd.	●	●	●	●		●	●	●	●	●	●		●	●	●	●	●		●	●	●	●		●
Wilderness State Park Entrance	8 miles W of Mackinaw City on Wilderness Park Rd.		●									●										●			
Wilderness State Park Beach	Wilderness State Park, just west park entrance.	●	●		●	●	●	●	●												●	●				
Wilderness State Park Campgrounds	Wilderness State Park, just west park beach.	●	●	●				●	●	●					●	●	●	●			●	●			
Wilderness State Park Boat Launch	Wilderness State Park, just west of campground.	●	●								●	●													
Waugoshance Point Parking	Wilderness State Park, 4 miles W of park campground.	●	●		●		●					●			●	●	●				●	●	●			
Sturgeon Bay Access & Trailhead	Wilderness State Park at end of park road.	●	●			●	●								●	●	●									

Wilderness State Park protects miles of interesting Lake Michigan shore from development. Consider it one of the top destinations on the lake.

WILDERNESS STATE PARK (CON'T): The park does not completely live up to its name, but much of it is hard to access and it is as near to pristine as its popular location allows. Good beaches, thick woods, islands and water are everywhere. The park is very popular in the summer. A number of isolated, primitive cabins on the lakeshore are available for rent. Reservations fill early in the year. Contact the park for information.
 Telephone: (231) 436-5381
 Web: www.michigan.gov/dnr
 GPS: 45°44.961'N; 84°51.512'W

WILDERNESS STATE PARK ENTRANCE: At the entrance sign to the state park lies a small parking area and a path to the west end of Cecil Bay. The area is rocky with some reeds. Swimming is not good here, but the Mackinac Bridge stands in distant view.
 GPS: 45°44.961'N; 84°51.512'W

WILDERNESS STATE PARK BEACH: A beautiful sandy beach mixed with an occasional boulder on Big Stone Bay, this is the primary day-use development of the state park. The beach is kept natural. Playground equipment, picnic tables and grills are located near the parking lot under the shade of tall pines. Short paths lead to the shore. This stop has excellent swimming, room to spread and views of lake freighters navigating the Mackinac Straits.
 GPS: 45°44.935'N; 84°53.471'W

WILDERNESS STATE PARK CAMPGROUNDS: Adjacent to the day-use beach is a popular campground with some of its 250 campsites located on the shore. The campground is usually full during the prime summer season. Reserve campsites through the Michigan Department of Natural Resources at (800) 447-2757.
 GPS: 45°44.763'N; 84°53.914'W

WILDERNESS STATE PARK BOAT LAUNCH: The boat ramp on Big Stone Bay is found a short distance past the park campground.
 GPS: 45°44.838'N; 84°54.513'W

WAUGOSHANCE POINT PARKING: Past the developed area of Wilderness State Park is the gravel Waugoshance Road. At its end are two parking areas. One accesses Lake Michigan to the north. The other views Sturgeon Bay to the southwest. There are trailheads for hiking to Waugoshance Point, about 2 miles to the west. Some of this shore is summer home for the endangered Piping Plover. This shorebird nests among the small stones mixed in the sandy beach. Portions of the shore are closed during the nesting season. Kayaking or canoeing the shore is possible. This provides access to Temperance and Waugoshance Islands, west of the point. Watch the weather as both the lake and bay can quickly become rough in high winds. Swimming is not good near the parking area but many sandy stretches can be found on the north side of the point.
 GPS: 45°45.462'N; 84°58.117'W

STURGEON BAY ACCESS: Sturgeon Bay Road provides access to Sturgeon Bay Trail and both Sturgeon and Goose Bays. The bay is shallow and rocky along the south shore of Waugoshance Point. Noted for great bass fishing, it generally requires a shallow-draft boat to maneuver around and over the rocks and shallows. Because of low water levels, the old boat ramp no longer works for trailered craft. A short carry allows launching a small boat, canoe or kayak. The shallowness of the west-facing bay means that it generates waves quickly when storm winds kick up. Be attentive to the weather.
 GPS: 45°44.574'N; 84°57.422'W

STURGEON BAY TRAILHEAD: This 2.2-mile hiking trail begins at the end of Sturgeon Bay Road and connects with the North Country Trail, Swamp Line Road Trail and South Boundary Trail within Wilderness Park. The south part of the trail ends at the picnic area by Sturgeon Bay (see p.165).
 GPS: 45°44.574'N; 84°57.422'W

Left: Headlands County Park, once a residence for the McCormick Family of farm equipment fame, now provides miles of public shore.

Opposite page: Two sandy public beaches on Trails End Bay have great swimming. The gradual drop-off makes them ideal for small children.

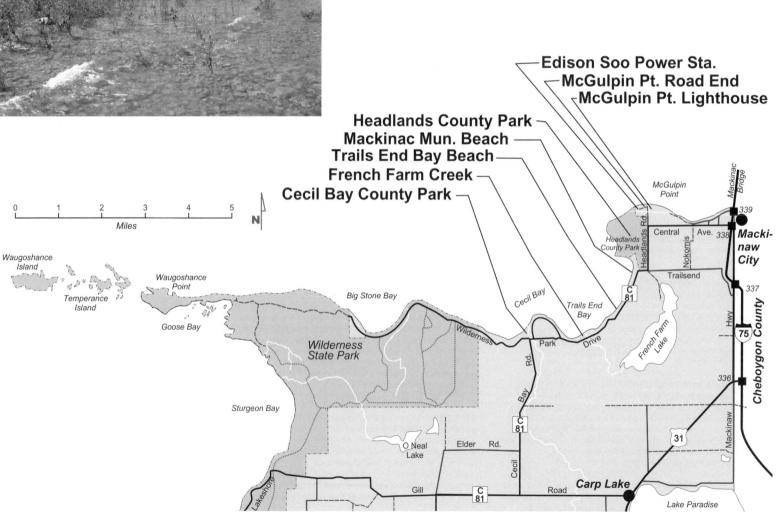

Edison Soo Power Sta.
McGulpin Pt. Road End
McGulpin Pt. Lighthouse

Headlands County Park
Mackinac Mun. Beach
Trails End Bay Beach
French Farm Creek
Cecil Bay County Park

Name	Location	Entrance Fee	Parking	Modern Restrooms	Vault or Portable Toilet	Stair or Path to Shore	Swimming	Picnic Area	Drinking Water	Campground	Trailered Boat Launch	Kayak / Canoe	Marina	Fishing	Hiking	Biking	X-Country Skiing	Playground	Lighthouse	Beach Strolling	Sandy Beach	Stony or Rocky Shore	Dunes	Bluff	Wetland
Cecil Bay County Park	Hwy C-81 at corner of Wilderness Park Dr. and Cecil Bay Rd.		●		●			●				●		●											
French Farm Creek	Hwy C-81 (Wilderness Park Drive), 5 miles SW of Mackinaw City													●											●
Trails End Bay Beach	On C-81 (Wilderness Park Rd) 4 miles SW of Mackinaw City.		●		●		●					●								●	●				
Mackinaw City Municipal Bathing Beach	W of Mackinaw City 3.5 miles on C-81, Wilderness Park Drive.		●		●		●														●				
Headlands County Park	On Hwy C-81 (Wilderness Park Drive) 2.5 miles W of Mackinaw City		●	●	●		●					●			●	●	●			●	●	●			
McGulpin Point Lighthouse	W of Mackinac City 2.5 miles. Take Central Ave. 2 miles until it ends at Wilderness Park Drive, then N 0.4 miles.																		●						
McGulpin Point Road End	W of Mackinac City 2.5 miles. Take Central Ave. 2 miles until it ends at Wilderness Park Drive, then N 0.6 miles.		●									●									●				
Edison Soo Power Station	W 0.2 miles from McGulpin Point listed above.		●																	●		●			

The Headlands look directly into the wind and weather of the Mackinac Straits. Beautiful sandy bays and rocky shore alternate along this coast. Much of it is open to the public.

CECIL BAY COUNTY PARK: This park is a large, grassy area along Carp Lake River near its mouth on Cecil Bay. A pavilion covers several picnic tables. River fishing is another activity. Kayak access to Cecil Bay is possible for the experienced. Scout for logjams before attempting.
GPS: 45°44.759'N; 84°49.866'W

FRENCH FARM CREEK: Limited, road-shoulder parking provides access near the creek's mouth. This is a reedy area with poor access, but there is a scenic, highway view of Trails End Bay.
GPS: 45°45.000'N; 84°47.553'W

TRAILS END BAY BEACH: Approximately 1 mile SW of the well-marked Mackinaw City Municipal Bathing Beach (see next listing) is a larger sandy beach with similar facilities. No sign is present but the parking area is visible from parts of the highway. It is an excellent place to swim and sunbathe.
GPS: 45°45.184'N; 84°47.206'W

MACKINAW CITY MUNICIPAL BATHING BEACH: This sandy beach on Trail's End Bay is at the end of Trail's End Road, east of Wilderness State Park. You will find great swimming; especially for those with children. The vault toilet is the modern-type, made of plastic and large enough to change in. The beach has about 300 feet of frontage on the bay. Large parking area.
GPS: 45°46.007'N; 84°46.692'W

HEADLANDS COUNTY PARK: In this mostly undeveloped area, old trail roads have become hike, bike and ski trails. The trails provide access to nearly 2 miles of shoreline most of which has a shallow, rocky bottom, making swimming less than ideal in some places. Still this is a fun area to explore with more than 600 wooded acres and solitude on the shore. Administered by the Emmet County Parks Department, it includes former private lakefront residences that may be rented.
Telephone: (231) 347-6536
Web: www.co.emmet.mi.us/parkrec/headlands.htm
GPS: 45°46.624'N; 84°46.387'W

The next three listings are reached by heading north on Headlands Road at the intersection of Wilderness Park Drive and Trailsend located at 45°46.890'N; 84°46.412'W.

McGULPIN POINT LIGHTHOUSE: The lighthouse area marks the Lower Peninsula's most northern point. The lighthouse is in private hands and is missing its dome and light. Those interested can view the old structure only from the road.
GPS: 45°47.216'N; 84°46.431'W

McGULPIN POINT ROAD END: A steep gravel road descends from the McGulpin lighthouse down to the lakehead. A circular turnaround provides adequate parking. Some houses exist along the nearby shore but there is room for a short walk.
GPS: 45°47.382'N; 84°46.450'W

EDISON SOO POWER STATION: A gravel road heads west from the McGulpin Point road end. Here Edison Soo has underwater transmission lines linking the two Michigan peninsulas. Park at the road end and walk down to the lakeshore for a nice view of the Mackinac Bridge. Rocks make swimming unpleasant. The shore to the west leads to Headlands County Park.
GPS: 45°47.286'N; 84°46.719'W

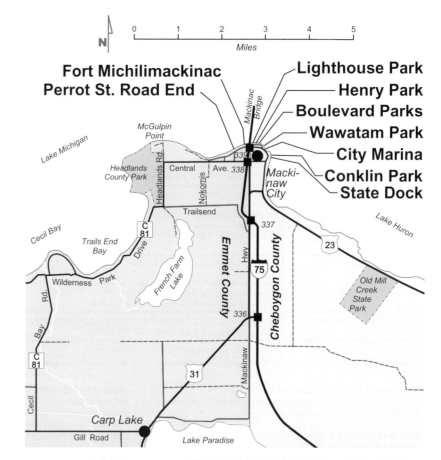

Above: The Mackinac Bridge as seen from one of the boulevard parks.

Below left: Open to the public, the castle-like Mackinac Point Light sits near the foot of the Mackinac Bridge.

Below right: Wawatum Park has sand, rock and a bridge view from the picnic area.

Emmet and Cheboygan Counties

Mackinaw City and the Straits of Mackinac

Name	Location	Entrance Fee	Parking	Modern Restrooms	Vault or Portable Toilet	Stair or Path to Shore	Swimming	Picnic Area	Drinking Water	Campground	Trailered Boat Launch	Kayak / Canoe	Marina	Fishing	Hiking	Biking	X-Country Skiing	Playground	Lighthouse	Beach Strolling	Sandy Beach	Stony or Rocky Shore	Dunes	Bluff	Wetland
		Facilities																			**Environment**				
Perrot Street Road End	Mackinaw City. Perrot St. at Lakeside Dr.																								
Colonial Michilimackinac Historic State Park	Mackinaw City at the Mackinac Bridge. I-75 at exit 339 (Jamet St.)	●	●	●		●		●	●												●	●			
Lighthouse Park	Mackinaw City. Indian Park Blvd. E of Mackinac Bridge. Exit I-75 at Jamet St. (exit 339).		●	●			●	●	●				●		●				●		●	●			
Alexander Henry Park	Mackinaw City. Indian Park Blvd. E of Mackinac Bridge.		●					●	●						●						●	●			
Boulevard Parks	Mackinaw City. Indian Park Blvd. E of Mackinac Bridge.		●					●							●						●	●			
Wawatam Park	Mackinaw City. Indian Park Blvd. E of Mackinac Bridge.		●	●			●	●	●				●					●			●	●			
Mackinaw City Marina	Mackinaw City. N Huron Ave at Central Ave.		●					●	●		●		●												
Conklin Heritage Park	Mackinaw City. N Huron Ave S of Central Ave.																								
State Dock	Mackinaw City. N Huron Ave S of Central Ave.			●	●									●											

These sites face the Straits of Mackinac, which have always been vital to the region's commerce. Today's visitors learn the history of this strategic location while enjoying enchanting views of the Mackinac Bridge and the sparkling waters. Also, passenger ferry service leaves regularly to historic and car-less Mackinac Island from several of the city's docks.

PERROT STREET ROAD END: This site sits between old cottages and has a good view of the Mackinac Bridge to the northeast.
 GPS: 45°47.188'N; 84°43.920'W

COLONIAL MICHILIMACKINAC HISTORIC STATE PARK: Fort Michilimackinac served as a fur trading base and protectorate of the Mackinac Straits during French, then British, rule. This historic fort restoration is part of the Mackinac State Historic Park system. Open May to October. Check for actual dates as well as hours and fees by phone or web. Period costuming, cooking demonstrations, musket firing, reenactments and guided tours are available. The historic parks include Fort Mackinac on Mackinac Island and Old Mill Creek, found between here and Cheboygan. A multiple site pass can be purchased at any of the parks. More details are found on page 8.
 Telephone: (231) 436-4100
 Web: www.MackinacParks.com
 GPS: 45°47.188'N; 84°43.920'W

The following listings are east of the Mackinac Bridge, a reasonable landmark for marking the divide between Lake Michigan and Lake Huron. Hence, the remaining sites are on Lake Huron. Their inclusion, plus the following chapter about Mackinac Island, helps to keep the Mackinaw City area whole and they are nice places to visit too!

LIGHTHOUSE PARK: In a grassy and shaded park just to the east of the Mackinac Bridge sits the Old Mackinac Point Lighthouse. In season, the lighthouse building is available for tours, including the Mackinac Maritime Museum and its store. The barrier-free Mackinaw City Historical Pathway follows the shore interconnecting several small parks as it meanders east and then south towards Mackinaw City. It provides one of the best shoreline opportunities for those in wheelchairs. Plaques along the trail provide interesting historic information about the Straits Area past. Modern restrooms, picnic tables and benches make it a comfortable stop. Enjoy the view of the bridge and ships passing through the narrow strait. The lake bottom is mostly stone with some sand.
 GPS: 45°47.189'N; 84°43.750'W

ALEXANDER HENRY PARK: Named for a British fur trader of the 1700's, the park is another along the historic pathway following Mackinaw City's waterfront. The park has space for about 12 cars but additional parking can be found on the boulevard. Use the telescopes to see passing freighters. Find other facilities at nearby Lighthouse Park.
 GPS: 45°47.194'N; 84°43.649'W

BOULEVARD PARKS: Three, small, lot-size parks dot the historical pathway between Henry and Wawatam Parks. They are nestled between nice homes on the waterfront. Each has limited parking. The shore is stone with some sand. A picnic table is available at each. More historical information and a view of the Straits await here.
 GPS: 45°47.152'N; 84°43.580'W, 45°47.114'N; 84°43.559'W, 45°47.081'N; 84°43.519'W

WAWATAM PARK: Chief Wawatam, an Ojibway who lived in the area during the 1700's, has been honored in many ways through the years. The railroad ferry that crossed the Mackinac Straits for seventy years bore his name. The City has dedicated this park site as well. Modern restrooms, drinking water, tables and telescopes sit under the watertower that helps mark the location. The shore is stony.
 GPS: 45°47.014'N; 84°43.378'W

MACKINAW CITY MARINA: The historical walk continues at the public marina. Parking is precious at the marina due to its location next to downtown shops and Mackinac Island ferry services. The marina has 104 slips of which 78 are available for transient use.
 Telephone: (231) 436-5269
 GPS: 45°46.917'N, 84°43.200'W

CONKLIN HERITAGE PARK: The Park's seating and bandshell are on the waterfront near the old ferry dock. The area is used for community events and festivals.
 GPS: 45°46.723'N; 84°43.546'W.

STATE DOCK: Originally built for the Mackinac Straits ferry service prior to the opening of the Mackinac Bridge, it now serves as a public fishing pier and one of many docks for the Mackinac Island ferries.

Straits of Mackinac

The Straits of Mackinac, about four miles wide at the narrow point, divide Lakes Michigan and Huron. The Mackinac Bridge, one of the world's longest suspension bridges, opened in 1957 connecting Michigan's two peninsulas across the Straits and physically drawing a line between the lakes. During the time of European exploration and colonization, the area had considerable commercial and military importance. Forts established at Mackinaw City and Mackinac Island supported the fur trade of the 18th and 19th centuries. Today, the area depends on a tourist economy that thrives on both its history and people's attraction to the coast. Hotels, restaurants, gift shops and entertainment businesses draw visitors as well.

The mainland hubs of Mackinaw City and St. Ignace have ferry service to Mackinac Island, located a few miles off the coast. Mackinac Island is best known as a place without automobiles. Since many travelers to the Mackinac area make the trip the island, the next section includes some sites worth considering on a tour of this Lake Huron treasure.

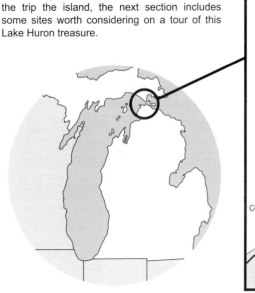

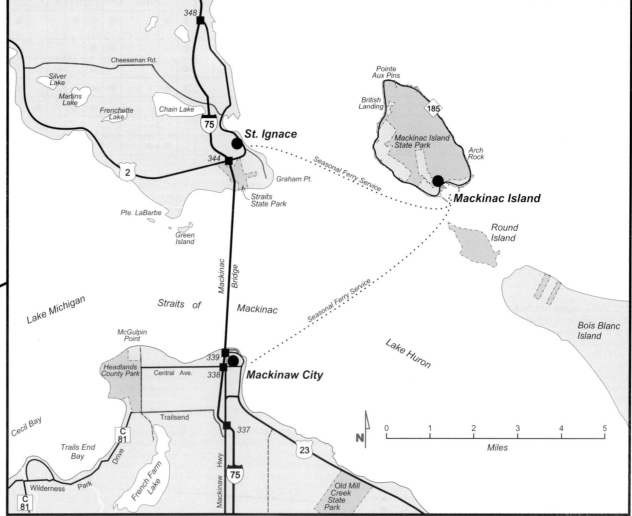

Mackinac Island

Mackinac Island might be characterized as a history theme park. The three-mile-long island, isolated in the Mackinac Straits, has no automobiles. Travel is by horse carriage, bicycle or foot. Wooden, clapboard stores and hotels line the main streets of town. Victorian-style summer mansions colorfully stand atop the isle's bluffs. The Grand Hotel, built in 1887 for the increasing tourist trade, retains the old traditions of the wealthy life-style. Fort Mackinac overlooks the town and harbor, as it has since before the American Revolution. Period dress and scheduled reenactments at the fort add to the historical flavor.

Mackinac Island's primary season runs from May through October. Three different ferry service companies operate during this period from both Mackinaw City and St. Ignace. At the height of the summer, each ferry operator departs about every half hour. In July and August the island is abuzz with tourists. Most visitors come to Mackinac Island for the day. The morning boats drop off their passengers and bring them back in the evening. The island changes character at night and in early morning as the atmosphere is less hectic without the daytime crowds. Accommodations are available in the form of hotels and boarding houses. During the winter, the island is mostly left to the permanent residents. The Straits ice over, and for a while, air travel provides the only link. When the ice freezes hard enough, snowmobilers make the trip from St. Ignace.

An 8-mile paved road circles the island. The course is flat and along the water's edge, making this an easy, scenic bicycle ride with several interesting stops on the way. Carriages, in-line skaters, walkers and runners also share the road. Think of it as a highway without cars or trucks. Many wildflowers thrive in the cool, moist environment found next to the road. The name Mackinac is derived from native words meaning "great turtle" and like a tortoise shell, the island's middle rises sharply from its edge. The steep bluffs afford lofty viewpoints. Several trails rim portions of the escarpments. The geologic formations of Arch Rock, Sugar Loaf, Skull Cave and Devil's Kitchen resulted from natural carving of the limestone during varying levels of the seas and lakes that overlaid this area in past epochs.

The island's town sits at the harbor. The business district has several blocks of restaurants, taverns, gift and fudge shops. The fudge-making tradition goes back to the late 19th century and its popularity has led to a number of candy shops where visitors watch the sweet stuff being made. This consumable souvenir has become such a staple that locals refer to tourists as "fudgies." Much of the area outside of the town is part of Mackinac Island State Park. Sprinkled in and around the park are stately summer homes. The park's *Historic Mackinac Island Visitor Guide* summarizes island history, has 7 suggested mapped tours and discusses the numerous points of interest. It is sold in the mainland cities, on the ferry boats and on the island. At $1, it is a bargain.

TRANSPORTATION TO THE ISLAND

Three ferry lines serve Mackinac Island. Each has docks in both Mackinaw City and St. Ignace. The service and price of each ferry company are essentially the same. Travel time to the island varies slightly depending on the style of boat making the run, but it generally takes about 20 minutes regardless of the point of departure. Ferries are wheelchair-accessible and have both open-air and enclosed decks.

Round-trip tickets prices in 2004
Adults (age 13 and up) - $17
Age 5-12 - $8
Under 5 – free
Bicycles - $6.50
Check for discounts such as *AAA* or group rates.

Arnold Transit Co.
(800) 542-8528
www.arnoldline.com

Shepler's Mackinac Island Ferry
(800) 828-6157
www.sheplersferry.com

Star Line
(800) 638-9892
www.mackinacferry.com

TRANSPORTATION ON THE ISLAND

Walking and Hiking
All of the City of Mackinac Island lies within a few blocks of the ferry dock and several sights listed on the following pages are an easy walk. The lack of automobiles makes every street, road and trail pedestrian-friendly. If you enjoy walking, you can visit a good portion of the island in a day of hiking.

Bicycling
A bicycle is a handy tool if you want to see more than the harbor area of the island. There are several places to rent bicycles and you will have little trouble finding them. Rates for a basic, single-speed bike are $4 per hour. Multiple-speed all-terrain-style bikes cost $6-$7 per hour (2004 prices). If you have a bike, it is worth taking it on the ferry if you plan to bike for more than an hour or two. A common bike route is the flat road around the island. With the usual tourist stops, you should plan on an hour-and-a-half to bike the 8 miles. If you are a curious visitor, or want to take a lunch break, it will be longer. Other routes require some climbing as the island interior is hilly and bikes with multiple gears will be appreciated. Virtually all the sites of interest are reachable via asphalt roads and bike paths.

Horse Carriage
Guided carriage tours travel to popular sites. The standard tour lasts just under 2 hours and costs $17 for adults and $7.50 for age 5 to 12. Horse-drawn taxi is also available. Island liveries rent drive-yourself carriages as well.

BASIC SERVICES

Public restrooms are available near the ferry docks and at the Visitor Center in the city. Arch Rock and British Landing have restrooms and drinking water. The city has many restaurants and food stands. A concession is located at British Landing.

Previous page: The sight of historic Grand Hotel, perched conspicuously on the bluff, signals ferry passengers of their impending arrival to Mackinac Island.

Lower Left: Mackinac's town and harbor from Anne's Tablet Overlook.

Lower Right: Marquette Park's grassy lawn is a place to relax. Fort Mackinac overlooks the park and town.

Opposite page: Downtown traffic is made of bicycles, pedestrians and carriages on Mackinac Island.

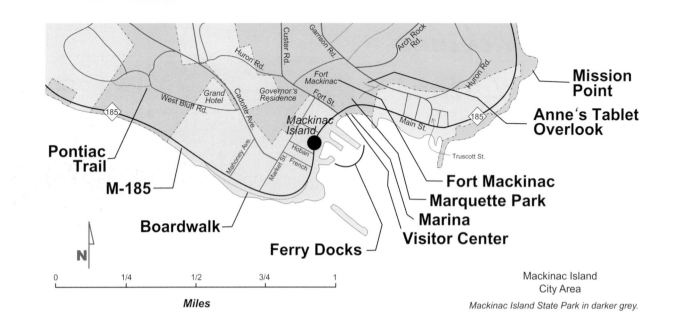

Mackinac Island
City Area

Mackinac Island State Park in darker grey.

Mackinac County

City of Mackinac Island

Name	Location	Entrance Fee	Parking	Modern Restrooms	Vault or Portable Toilet	Stair or Path to Shore	Swimming	Picnic Area	Drinking Water	Campground	Trailered Boat Launch	Kayak / Canoe	Marina	Fishing	Hiking	Biking	X-Country Skiing	Playground	Lighthouse	Beach Strolling	Sandy Beach	Stony or Rocky Shore	Dunes	Bluff	Wetland
Ferry Docks	Main Street. City of Mackinac Island.			●					●																
Mackinac SP Visitor Center	Main at Fort Street. City of Mackinac Island.			●					●																
Marquette Park	Main at Fort Street. City of Mackinac Island.																	●							
Fort Mackinac	Fort Street. City of Mackinac Island.	●																						●	
Mackinac Island State Harbor (Marina)	Main Street. City of Mackinac Island.			●				●	●				●												
Anne's Tablet Overlook	Huron Road. City of Mackinac Island.														●									●	
Mission Point	M-185, 0.5 miles E of Visitor Center.								●						●	●				●		●			
Boardwalk	W of Ferry Docks along M-185.														●					●		●			
Pontiac Trail	W end of West Bluff Rd., W of Grand Hotel.														●									●	

Most of the island's commerce is contained within the City of Mackinac Island. It includes the historic area of Market and Fort Streets along with the shops and eateries.

FERRY DOCKS: The arrival point for the island ferry services are found at three separate docks in the harbor area. All are in the heart of town. See page 173 for ferry company information.

MACKINAC ISLAND STATE PARK VISITOR CENTER: Just east of the dock area on Main Street, the Visitor Center provides a short orientation to the island and its history. An Information clerk is available to answer questions and to sell tickets to Fort Mackinac. The park includes a number of other historic buildings on Market Stree, such as John Astor's fur warehouse, a blacksmith shop and a museum dedicated to Dr. William Beaumont who discovered much about the human digestive system while on the island.
Note: purchasing combination tickets for all the Mackinac State Historic Parks will save you money if you also plan to visit Fort Michilimackinac and Old Mill Creek in Mackinaw City.
   Telephone: (906) 847-3328
   Web: www.MackinacParks.com

MARQUETTE PARK: Located across from the Visitor Center and "below" Fort Mackinac, the grassy park is a great place to relax and watch the tourist bustle about. In mid-June, the bountiful lilac trees are in bloom turning it into a green and lavender, naturally-perfumed landscape. A small playground is located on its east end.

FORT MACKINAC: British, and later, American soldiers manned this outpost from 1780 to 1895. It protected the important fur trade industry. Its most significant action occurred during the War of 1812.

In 1875, with its military significance diminished, the post became the country's second national park. In 1895, the federal government transferred it to Michigan as its first state park.

The fort's hilltop view of the straits and the outlying islands is spectacular. Add to this, historic buildings, most which go back to the mid-1800's. Staffed by period actors, fort activities include reenactments and cannon fire.

MACKINAC ISLAND STATE HARBOR (MARINA): Located at the Visitor Center, the public dock has 63 transient slips.
   Telephone: (906) 847-3561
   GPS: 45°50.667'N; 84°36.700'W

ANNE'S TABLET OVERLOOK: Heading off from Huron Street, just east of the Fort, is Anne's Tablet Trail. It can also be reached from Marquette Park by climbing the 152-step stairway of Cliff Trail which begins near the park playground. Anne's Tablet is named for the plaque commemorating a character from an island story. From various parts of this short trail, you will walk pass great views of the fort, the city, the harbor and nearby islands.

MISSION POINT: At the east end of the city, Shoreline Trail spurs from M-185 to run along Mission Point then returns to M-185. There is a little less traffic than the main street. Benches and drinking fountain are available.

BOARDWALK: A boardwalk parallels the lake and M-185 on the west side of the city. It gives walkers a break from bike and carriage traffic. Pretty Victorian homes, colorful gardens and the blue hue of Lake Huron make it a pleasant walk.

PONTIAC TRAIL: Most tourists wander up to the Grand Hotel, which sits high on the bluff overlooking the Straits of Mackinac and the Mackinac Bridge. The hotel charges a fee to enter, a move meant to control the influx of people as much as to make money. Just past the hotel on West Bluff Road are several beautiful Victorian-style homes along the bluff. At the west end of the road is Pontiac Trail, a short hiking path which skirts the bluff edge. Benches at the trailhead look back at the homes and hotel with the shimmering lake water below. Relax awhile, your time capsule has taken you back more than a century. A stairway leads down the bluff to M-185.

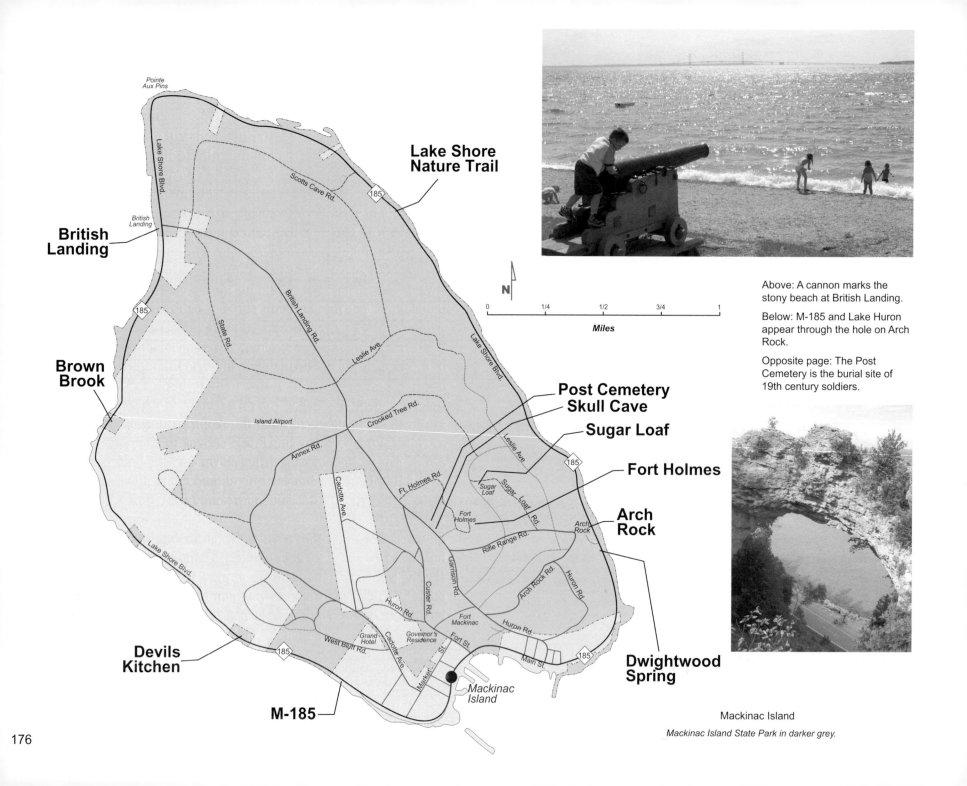

Lake Shore Nature Trail

British Landing

Brown Brook

Post Cemetery Skull Cave

Sugar Loaf

Fort Holmes

Arch Rock

Dwightwood Spring

Devils Kitchen

M-185

N

0   1/4   1/2   3/4   1

Miles

Above: A cannon marks the stony beach at British Landing.

Below: M-185 and Lake Huron appear through the hole on Arch Rock.

Opposite page: The Post Cemetery is the burial site of 19th century soldiers.

Mackinac Island

Mackinac Island State Park in darker grey.

Mackinac Island Natural Areas

Name	Location	Entrance Fee	Parking	Modern Restrooms	Vault or Portable Toilet	Stair or Path to Shore	Swimming	Picnic Area	Drinking Water	Campground	Trailered Boat Launch	Kayak / Canoe	Marina	Fishing	Hiking	Biking	X-Country Skiing	Playground	Lighthouse	Beach Strolling	Sandy Beach	Stony or Rocky Shore	Dunes	Bluff	Wetland
M-185	Circles island. Starts as Main Street in the City of Mackinac Island.		●				●	●	●						●	●				●		●			
Dwightwood Spring	M-185, near mile #1.							●							●	●				●		●			
Arch Rock	Arch Rock Rd. or use stairway from M-185 at Dwightwood Spring.			●		●			●						●									●	●
Lake Shore Nature Trail	M-185, between mile #2 and #3.						●								●					●		●			
British Landing	M-185 and British Landing Rd. at west end of island.			●			●	●	●						●	●						●			
Brown Brook	M-185, between mile #5 and #6.														●										
Devil's Kitchen	M-185.																					●			
Sugar Loaf	One mile N of city on Sugar Loaf Rd.														●										
Skull Cave	One mile N of city on Garrison Rd.														●	●									
Fort Holmes	One mile N of city on Fort Holmes Rd.														●	●								●	
Post Cemetery	One mile N of city on Garrison Rd.																								

Away from the city, the summer crowds thin some, especially in the island's center. These sites are in natural settings of forests and wildflowers. Mile-markers start at zero in the city and count up as you travel counter-clockwise.

M-185: This is the only designated state route that allows no automobiles. It is a two-lane asphalt road that circles Mackinac Island. The eight-mile road is mostly flat. Virtually all of the shore is public, especially on the east side of the isle. Mackinac beaches are stony, so great swimming spots are limited. The better places are near the Lake Shore Nature Trail and at British Landing.

DWIGHTWOOD SPRING: a small spring seeps from the limestone cliff along M-185 between mile #1 and #2. Just to the north, a long stairway leads up to Arch Rock.

ARCH ROCK: This rock formation is the most noted natural feature of the island. The island is made largely of a breccia limestone. About 4000 years ago, high lake levels dissolved a hole in the rock mass making the formation. Arch Rock rises 146 feet above M-185 and can be viewed easily from the road shoulder. As noted above, a stairway located near Dwightwood Springs will take you to the top. From the island interior, reach the formation via Arch Rock Road or Arch Rock Bicycle Trail.

LAKE SHORE NATURE TRAIL: Located near Mile #3, the short trail has self-guided plaques describing island trees and plants.

BRITISH LANDING: Found about halfway around the island, it is the spot where British troops started their successful take of Fort Mackinac during the War of 1812. Restrooms, concession and picnic area make this a popular stop for bicyclists. It is also one of the better swimming spots. British Landing Road splits the island lengthwise and from here heads into the island interior towards the city.

BROWN BROOK: Located between Mile #5 and #6 is another short nature trail where Brown Brook tumbles over rocks on its miniature journey to Lake Huron. The creek runs all year, fed by springs of stored water in Mackinac's limestone rock.

DEVIL'S KITCHEN: A small sea cave, located along M-185, was formed about 350 years ago from the action of waves on the limestone.

The following are located in the island's interior.

SUGAR LOAF: Another of Mackinac's rock formations, Sugar Loaf is a 75-foot high sea stack. Centuries ago, the stack was a small island, as water covered most of what is now Mackinac Island. The land around it eroded leaving the rock form.

SKULL CAVE: Another cave formed by ancient lakes eroding the limestone, Skull Cave was once used by the area tribe for burial.

FORT HOLMES: The British used this, the island's highest ground, to bombard and quickly capture Fort Mackinac during the War of 1812. They then established a small outpost called Fort George. During the 1814 Battle of Mackinac Island, American Major Holmes died and the fort was renamed for him following the American recapture. The current fort was reconstructed in 1936, after fire. It is not much of a structure compared to Fort Mackinac, but the view from here is fabulous. The viewpoint is 325 feet above the straits and 168 feet above Fort Mackinac. Round and Bois Blanc Islands are within easy view.

POST CEMETERY: One of three cemeteries clustered in the middle of the island, the Post Cemetery contains remains of military men and families from the 1820's until Fort Mackinac ceased in 1895.

Additional Resources

The following publications provide very useful information about Michigan and recreation activities along the Lake Michigan coast.

Fishing

Huggler, Tom, Wilson, Keith, Sutton Ed, and Barfknecht, Gary. *Let's Fish Lake Michigan*. Great Lakes Fishery Trust. 2001. Internet version available at www.glft.org. An overview of Lake Michigan fish seasons, fishing methods and descriptions of productive piers and platforms for public fishing.

Maps

Michigan Atlas & Gazetteer. DeLorme, Yarmouth, ME. 2000. Detailed mapbook featuring outdoor recreation sites and including latitude and longitude grids. *www.delorme.com*.

Michigan County Atlas. Universal Map. 1989. A detailed mapbook in county-by-county format, it is still one of the easiest to use. Universal also has folded maps by regions of the state. Each folded map includes several counties. *www.universalmap.com*.

Paddling Canoes and Kayaks

Dennis, Jerry and Date, Craig. *Canoeing Michigan Rivers*. Friede Publications, Davidson, MI. 2001. Describes and maps 45 Michigan rivers for paddlers. Includes camp sites, access and portage points. Nine of the listed rivers end at the coast depicted in this book.

Hillstrom, Kevin and Laurie. *Paddling Michigan*. Falcon, 2001. Selected rivers and coastline for canoeing or kayaking.

Newman, Bill, Ohmann, Sarah, Dimond, Don. *Guide to Sea Kayaking in Lakes Superior and Michigan: The Best Day Trips and Tours*. Globe-Pequot. 1999.

Trails for Hiking, Biking, Snowshoeing and Cross-Country Skiing

Hansen, Dennis. *Trail Atlas of Michigan*. Hansen Publishing Co., Okemos MI. 2003 Maps of virtually all Michigan trails including travel directions and trail distances.

Index

order additional copies of

Michigan's West Coast
Explore the Shore Guide

via the web at abri-LLC.com